This book is not a beginner's guide to the system of Qi Men Dun Jia. As the 18th book in the Qi Men series of books, it is assumed that the reader of this series already has substantial background and experience with using Qi Men Dun Jia in order to fully appreciate the Qi Men related contents of this book. For a complete understanding of Qi Men Dun Jia's fundamentals, beginnings, formulae, calendaring system, chart plotting and other essential concepts, please refer to Joey Yap's **Qi Men Dun Jia Compendium (Second Edition)**, *also in this series.*

Please take note that the Qi Men Dun Jia charts, designs and terminologies used in this book are the author's original literary expression and are therefore copy protected. The following are the exclusive copyrighted Qi Men terminology created by the author:

Joey Yap's Qi Men Mastery System™: Qi Men Sage Path™, Qi Men Warcraft™, Qi Men Forecasting Methods™, Qi Men Feng Shui™, Qi Men Destiny & Life Transformation™, Qi Men Strategic Execution™, Spiritual Qi Men™, Qi Men Seven Stars Steps™, Qi Men Oracle™.

Names of the Deities: *Chief Deity , Surging Snake, Great Moon, Nine Earth, Nine Heaven, Grappling Hook, Six Harmony, Red Phoenix, Black Tortoise* and *White Tiger.*

Names of the 9 Stars: *Heavenly Grass, Grain, Destructor, Assistant, Bird, Heart, Pillar, Ambassador* and *Hero.*

Names of the 8 Doors: *Rest Door, Life Door, Harm Door, Delusion Door, Scenery Door, Death Door, Fear Door* and *Open Door.*

Any reproduction of the above terminologies for the use of Qi Men Dun Jia will require permission from the author.

QI MEN DUN JIA
SUN TZU
WARCRAFT

奇門遁甲

孫子兵法篇

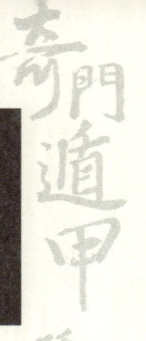

Joey Yap's Qi Men Dun Jia Sun Tzu Warcraft

All intellectual property rights including copyright in relation to this book belong to Joey Yap Research Group Sdn. Bhd.

No part of this book may be copied, used, subsumed, or exploited in fact, field of thought or general idea, by any other authors or persons, or be stored in a retrieval system, transmitted or reproduced in any way, including but not limited to digital copying and printing in any form whatsoever worldwide without the prior agreement and written permission of the copyright owner. Permission to use the content of this book or any part thereof must be obtained from the copyright owner. For more details, please contact:

Joey Yap Research Group Sdn Bhd (944330-D)
19-3, The Boulevard, Mid Valley City,
59200 Kuala Lumpur, Malaysia.
Tel   : +603-2284 8080
Fax   : +603-2284 1218
Email   : info@masteryacademy.com
Website : www.masteryacademy.com

Copyright © 2017 by Joey Yap Research Group Sdn. Bhd.
All rights reserved.
First Edition June 2014
Third Print December 2017

DISCLAIMER:

The author, copyright owner, and the publishers respectively have made their best efforts to produce this high quality, informative and helpful book. They have verified the technical accuracy of the information and contents of this book. However, the information contained in this book cannot replace or substitute for the services of trained professionals in any field, including, but not limited to, mental, financial, medical, psychological, or legal fields. They do not offer any professional, personal, medical, financial or legal advice and none of the information contained in the book should be confused as such advice. Any information pertaining to the events, occurrences, dates and other details relating to the person or persons, dead or alive, and to the companies have been verified to the best of their abilities based on information obtained or extracted from various websites, newspaper clippings and other public media. However, they make no representation or warranties of any kind with regard to the contents of this book and accept no liability of any kind for any losses or damages caused or alleged to be caused directly or indirectly from using the information contained herein.

Table of Contents

Preface	**6**
Introduction	**9**
'The Art of War' and Qi Men Dun Jia: The mightiest of weapons	10
The Five Great Chinese Military Classics	12
Who was Sun Tzu?	14
The Art of War	16
What is Qi Men Dun Jia?	18
Origins	21
Qi Men Dun Jia: The Metaphysical Tool of War	22
Qi Men Dun Jia and 'The Art of War' in actual history	23
Qi Men Dun Jia and 'The Art of War' reunited	26
孫子兵法 - The Art Of War:	
1 始計 - **Strategic Assessments**	27
2 作戰 - **Waging War**	77
3 謀攻 - **Offensive Strategy**	105
4 軍形 - **Deployment**	133
5 兵勢 - **Force**	157
6 虛實 - **The Substantial And The Insubstantial**	185
7 軍爭 - **Fighting For Military Advantage**	209
8 九變 - **The Nine Variables**	239
9 行軍 - **Maneuvering Armies**	271
10 地形 - **Terrain**	305
11 九地 - **Nine Grounds**	349
12 火攻 - **Fire Attack**	397
13 用間 - **Espionage**	417
Epilogue	**439**

Preface

Sun Tzu's 'Art of War' (孫子兵法) is possibly one of the most famous Chinese texts of all time. It's one of five texts written on the subject of military strategy throughout Chinese antiquity that is regarded as a classic and its stellar rise to fame has placed it on book shelves worldwide and seen it extend its reach from the battleground, to the boardroom and even on the football pitch. A few moments of perusal on the internet will reveal a multitude of articles and slide shows on how we can apply the works of Sun Tzu in our lives and our careers. You might go so far as to say that it's one of the oldest self-help books ever written.

In the business community 'The Art of War' and the strategies of Sun Tzu have become synonymous with winning and as such they have been translated time and time again with new commentaries and new interpretations. Its methods applied to everything from people management to marketing. I would wager that almost all enormously successful Chinese businessmen are students of Sun Tzu. It has been my privilege, throughout my career, to work with some great business leaders and over time I have been fortunate enough to call those people my friends. It has been through their eyes, their passions and their experiences that my own interest in Sun Tzu and his war treatise has been reinvigorated.

From my perspective as a practitioner of metaphysic, however, it struck me that while these great men and women were following the tactics of Sun Tzu and coming to me for my expertise, they were unaware of the fact that Qi Men Dun Jia (奇門遁甲) was designed for use in warfare and, as such, it can be used to directly guide the applications of 'The Art of War'. While Sun Tzu's war treatise is a work of philosophy, Qi Men Dun Jia is a powerful tool for gaining intelligence into the workings of the universe itself. Used correctly, Qi Men Dun Jia can give you the insight you need to help you to fine tune your strategies according to the prevailing conditions indicated by the reading. Qi Men has always been the tool of war strategists. Throughout history it has been a crucial aid to the greatest of military minds including Zhuge Liang, Liu Bowen, Zhang Liang, Jiang Ziya and Mao Zedong, and let us not forget that all these men have also been well known for their use of and respect for 'The Art of War'.

Given that Qi Men and 'The Art of War' have such obvious synchronicity, it seems surprising that so few books have been written on Sun Tzu with a Qi Men commentary or, conversely, on Qi Men with a commentary on strategic aspects taken from 'The Art of War'. But of course, most masters of Qi Men Dun Jia are not warriors and they have never lead armies into battle. They are scholars and professors, learned men and women, whose life work does not include running of multi-million dollar businesses or spearheading of organisations.

This is where I come in. I admit that I don't have experience on a battlefield; I am no soldier, and I don't claim to be an expert on Sun Tzu, but I am an entrepreneur, running a multi-million dollar organisation. I understand the real world concerns of business leaders and strategists. Through the trials and tribulations of building up my own business empire, I have spent a great deal of time reflecting on the words of Sun Tzu and the ways in which his strategies can be applied to maximum effect. But when I set myself the task of bringing Qi Men Dun Jia and 'The Art of War' together, I had very little to go on. I only found one paragraph on an exploration of Qi Men throughout Sun Tzu's philosophy in a book by Master Jiang Xun. There was no indication of further reading and Master Jiang is no longer with us for me to ask him personally.

I was forced to go for it alone. Piece by piece I brought my ideas together, untying and retying the strands of knowledge until I created a whole new tapestry of information and insight. My discoveries have astounded even myself and, after all my years of labour, building my own brand into the phenomena it is today, I can tell you for certain that business management truly is an art of war.

I present to you here the culmination of my labours: the 'Art of War' has finally been combined with the 'Tool of War.' I have designed this book to be a guide into a never before seen synthesis of the philosophy of 'The Art of War' and the practice of Qi Men Dun Jia with a specific focus on business and business philosophy. This is the eighteenth book in my Qi Men Dun Jia series and it will be used to facilitate my business centrum Qi Men program called Qi Men Warcraft and Qi Men Strategic Execution. As this book comes so late in the series, I did not deem it necessary to discuss the fundamentals, chart plotting and theories of Qi Men Dun Jia; should you have an interest in learning more, it will be necessary to refer to one of the earlier books in the series.

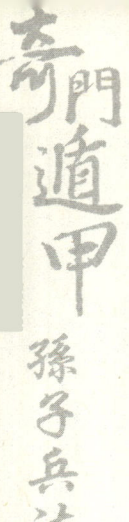

This is my first attempt at combining aspects of 'The Art of War' with metaphysical disciplines and I hope that it will be the first of many. I know that the process of compiling this book has been an eye-opener for me and it is my sincere wish that it will provide you with a fresh and exciting insight into your own philosophy on business and the ways in which you can work to further develop your strategies and make your career ambitions a reality.

Warmest regards,

Joey Yap
June 2014
Kuala Lumpur, Malaysia

PS: For the absolute beginners of Qi Men, I've prepared some introductory video clips of my Qi Men workshops for you to get acquainted with the system. Watching the videos will give you a better understanding on how Qi Men Dun Jia works. You will also get to learn some application tips so that you can immediately put the system to work for you in your daily lives. You can find the instructions to access the videos at the end of the book, after the epilogue section.

PSS: I'm on Facebook. Keep in touch

Facebook : www.facebook.com/joeyyapFB
Author's personal website : www.joeyyap.com
Academy websites : www.masteryacademy.com
www.baziprofiling.com

INTRODUCTION

INTRODUCTION

'The Art of War' and *Qi Men Dun Jia*: The mightiest of weapons.

Sun Tzu's 'The Art of War' may be one of the most famous texts in the world. It has been translated into a multitude of different languages and it has been printed and reprinted time and time again with new commentaries and new perspectives. Still a staple in the libraries of military strategists around the world and respected by many, it still offers a keen insight into modern warfare as it did in the conflicts of antiquity. 'The Art of War' has also gained a particularly strong following in the business community where it has gained a reputation as a guiding light for professionals seeking to improve their working strategies.

In our day to day lives, the marketplace and the open plan office have become our battlegrounds. We fight against our peers for recognition and advancement and we fight to raise the profile of our products and services against the competition. As managers and directors of companies, we know that we face the same problems in orchestrating and motivating our troops to work above and beyond the call of duty as does any leader of men, regardless of his or her vocation. Our art of war may not be the same as the one that Sun Tzu perfected but, somehow, I suspect that he would see the spirit of his endeavours in the actions of market leaders and senior professionals.

The modern working world is more competitive than ever. In uncertain financial times, we have to work hard to maintain our position and even harder if we want to keep moving forward. Sun Tzu would say that we need to take advantage of the prevailing circumstances in order to drive our plans forward so that they cannot fail; compelled by the mood of the moment, our strategies must lead us to victory with the same certainty that the flow of a river will lead us to the ocean. That is where *Qi Men Dun Jia* comes in.

Of all the ancient Chinese methods of divination sciences practiced in the world today, *Qi Men Dun Jia* is the most subtle and precise. *Qi Men Dun Jia* can show you the mood of the moment; it can act to support your own painstaking research and strategy development in helping you to choose the exact time and place to put your plans into motion. *Qi Men Dun Jia* is the metaphysics of war craft. Its use in developing military strategy throughout Chinese history was so prolific that it was treated as a state secret until the end of the Qing Dynasty. *Qi Men* has been used by great military minds such as Zhuge Liang 諸葛亮, Liu Bowen 劉伯溫, Zhang Liang 張良, Jiang Ziya 姜子牙 and Mao Zedong 毛澤東 and these same men were also all believed to have made use of the teachings of 'The Art of War'. It could be argued that these texts have always worked hand in glove and yet there have been lamentably few books which have used the perspective of one to enhance the other.

It is the aim of this book to correct this oversight and to bring these two mighty wisdoms of warfare together in one place. By analysing each of the concepts discussed by Sun Tzu throughout the chapters of 'The Art of War' and linking them back to the corresponding applications of *Qi Men Dun Jia,* it is my hope to offer an indispensable tool for strategic planning.

The Five Great Chinese Military Classics

China's early history, before the original unification and beyond, was marked by frequent battles between rival princes and warlords. It is not surprising, therefore, that among the lexicon of great Chinese philosophy is a significant number of works dedicated to warfare and strategy. Of all the works that discuss the art of war in detail, five military classics stand out and are considered to be the very greatest of their kind.

'Sage Jiang's Art of War' (姜太公兵法) was written by folk hero Jiang Taigong (姜太公), originally known as *Lu Shang* 吕望, who lived in the eleventh century B.C. His treatise is the oldest of the military classics and his story is one of patience. Lu Shang abandoned his post working for *King Zhouwang* 紂王 of the Shang Dynasty as he loathed the way the tyrannical ruler treated his people. He lived many years in poverty before he finally met with King Wen of Zhou 周文王 and was made his prime minister at the age of 72. As the advisor to Zhou, he was able to ultimately see the downfall of the state of Shang and the detested King Zhouwang. As well as discussing many of the same tactical approaches as Sun Tzu's Art of War, he also placed great emphasis on a wise, well-structured and compassionate government that can win the hearts and minds of the people.

'Zhuge Liang's Art of War' (諸葛亮兵法) was written by statesman and strategist Zhuge Liang during the Three Kingdoms period, famed as one of the greatest military minds in ancient China (we will hear more about Zhuge Liang later). This work is made up of two texts, '*The General's Garden*' and '*The Convenient Sixteen Strategies*' carry social and political messages as well as military approaches and continue to maintain their value in a wide range of applications.

There is some debate of who may have been the original author of 'The *Thirty-Six Stratagems*' (三十六計). The 'Book of the South Qi Dynasty' references its author as Tang Gong Dao Jin but it is possible that its words are based partly on oral history. Due to this controversy, the text is rather difficult to date. Its advice is practical and applicable; possibly its most famous piece of guidance is: '*when all else fails, retreat.*'

'Sage of Ghost Valley's Art of War' (鬼谷子兵法) is thought to have been compiled during the late Warring States Period and the early Han Dynasty. The traditional view is that Guigu Zi (鬼谷子), translated literally to mean '*The Sage of Ghost Valley*', was the master of such great military and political minds as Su Qin, Zhang Zi, Sun Bin and Pang Juan, but many modern scholars now believe it to be a corpus of writings from a variety of sources. Though this is referred to as one of the great military classics, its focus is more political in nature.

The most well known of all these great texts is, of course, the masterpiece by Sun Tzu himself. Sun Tzu's work has truly been able to withstand the test of time and its ethics and strategies, if anything, appear to have gained in relevance in the modern world.

Who was Sun Tzu?

The traditional view would have us believe that Sun Tzu was a military general and tactician who came to fame during the Spring and Autumn period of Chinese history. According to the '*Spring and Autumn Annals*' he was born in the province of Qi in around 544 BC, however the '*Records of the Grand Historian*' by Sima Qian claimed him to have been a native of the province of Wu. 'Tzu' is in fact an honorific title meaning 'Master' or 'Sage' and his true birth name is believed to have been *Sun Wu*.

Sima Qian explains that he first came to the attention of King Helu of Wu in around 512 BC and was invited to the palace to demonstrate his skills as a general by training the King's concubines to perform as a highly trained army. He first acted to divide the women into two groups and named the King's favourites as their commanding officers, he then went on to explain to the women what he expected them to do when they were given a series of instructions. His first instruction was to tell them to turn to their left. His order was not, however, met with the action he expected. All the girls could do was giggle.

When he carefully explained his instruction again and was once more met with laughter, he announced that when the general's commands are unclear, it is the general's responsibility to make sure that he is understood. However, if the general's commands are clear but ignored, it is the fault of the officers. He promptly ordered that the King's two favourite concubines be executed. In the face of the monarch's protestations, the two women were beheaded in front of the remaining women and two new officers chosen to take their place. From that moment onwards, the women performed their drills flawlessly and Sun Tzu was taken as being a man who was as good as his word.

According to Sima Qian, Sun Tzu was to go on to enjoy an illustrious career and a great number of military victories before he passed away in 496 BC. It seems that his sons and grandsons were also to follow in his footsteps as a later descendant Sun Bin, also ultimately known as Sun Tzu, wrote his own treatise on warfare which shared the same name as that of his ancestor 'The Art of War'. Though there have been questions raised over the accuracy of the accounts of the life of the historical Sun Tzu, it cannot be argued that the text he is credited to have written reveals the mind of a man who was exceptionally insightful and capable of being as just and compassionate as he was ruthless and calculating.

The Art of War

The Art of War was written across thirteen chapters, each one devoted to a different aspect of warfare: Strategic Assessment, Waging War, Offensive Strategy, Deployment, Force, The Substantial and the Insubstantial, Fighting for Military Advantage, The Nine Variables, Manoeuvring Armies, Terrain, Nine Grounds, Fire Attack and Espionage. It is one of five Chinese military classics and is by far the most famous and the most influential.

As mentioned earlier, the date of authorship for 'The Art of War' is traditionally thought to have been in the Spring and Autumn period of Chinese history, during the lifetime of Sun Tzu. However, there are some references that may appear to be anachronistic. During the Spring and Autumn period, warfare was primarily a matter for charioteers, who were a part of the elite, rather than the foot soldiers who were referred to within the text and armies were also thought to have been smaller on the whole than the figures quoted.

Many scholars now argue that 'The Art of War' was far more likely to have been written during the early part of the Warring States period. Although the Warring States period was similar in many ways to the Spring and Autumn period, as it too was characterised by widespread conflict, it was also a period of great social and political change. During the Warring States period, the emphasis in armed conflict moved away from charioteers and onto infantry. There was a drastic increase in the size of the armies and this was also the first time when the feudal landscape of China began to change and the peasant classes were regarded as having some kind of ownership or rights over the land for which they paid taxes.

Some of the ideas explored within 'The Art of War' would appear to connect more closely with political and military structures that would not have come into play until the Warring States period. It is possible that other texts were added to the original text and embellished by students and followers in the following years, resulting in a compiled work. Whatever evolution 'The Art of War' may have been through to achieve its current format, it has been proven to have existed in its current format as early as the Early Han Dynasty (206 BC – 220 AD) and, more than likely, during the early to middle Warring States period.

The fame of 'The Art of War' spread very quickly; it was credited with having helped bring an end to the Warring States period and allowed the first Emperor of China (Qin Shi Huang 秦始皇) to take his place on the throne. By AD 760, its influence had spread beyond Chinese borders and it had become a popular source among Japanese generals. The first western language translation was French in as early as 1782 by a Jesuit minister named Father Amiot and the first English language translation was published shortly after the turn of the last century in 1905.

'The Art of War' has had a tremendous influence on the development of the world as we know it. Its methods were used regularly by military commanders throughout Southeast Asia and may be responsible for a significant amount of the modern political landscape. The unification of Japan in the early modern era was inspired by Sun Tzu, as were the guerrilla tactics of Ho Chi Minh during the Vietnam War, as well as Mao Zedong during the Chinese civil war. The US military command has also now come to respect its methods following conflicts with Japan, North Korea and North Vietnam and the principles of 'The Art of War' were employed by US Generals Norman Schwarzkopf Jnr and Colin Powell during the Gulf War.

In the modern world, 'The Art of War' is no longer restricted to offering its guidance to those fighting battles with guns and bombs. It has now been used to develop political campaigns, marketing strategies, business negotiations and even football tactics. 'The Art of War' has become universally revered for its versatility and practical wisdom and is required reading for those who aspire to command.

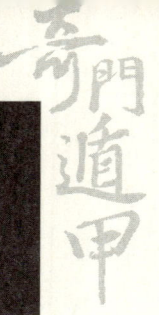

What is *Qi Men Dun Jia*?

According to *Liu Bowen* 劉伯溫, a military strategist, statesman and scholar active during the early Ming dynasty, *Qi Men Dun Jia* is a system of forecasting that belongs to the *San Yuan* 三元 school of Chinese Metaphysics. *Qi Men,* alongside *Liu Ren Shen Ke* (六壬神課) and *Tai Yi Shen Shu* (太乙神數) is one of Three Oracles that have formed a part of Chinese culture for thousands of years. *Qi Men Dun Jia* translates as '*Mystical Doors Escaping Technique*', a rather mysterious name that belies a system that relies primarily on complex mathematical equations.

Incredibly, Qi Men Dun Jia can be traced back over a few thousand years through history. It was a crucial tool for Chinese military strategists in ancient times. Here, I have broken down the translation of Qi Men Dun Jia 奇門遁甲 to provide insight into its meaning:

> '**Qi** 奇' : Qi refers to an essence with an esoteric nature, with nuances of intrigue connected to the universal rules of the cosmos. (It should be noted that this differs from the Chinese word for energy which is Qi氣)

> '**Men** 門' : Taken literally, this means 'door' or 'gate'.

> '**Dun** 遁' : This is translated as 'hide' or 'escape to remain hidden'.

> '**Jia** 甲' : This final part of the puzzle alludes to the first of the Ten Heavenly Stems. 'Jia' is also a coded reference to the General or Grand Marshal related to warfare.

When combined, Qi Men Dun Jia may be interpreted as 'Mysterious Doors Hiding Jia' a term, which is not only cumbersome but also misleading. Today, the more common translation, which is easier to grasp is *'Mysterious Doors Escaping Technique'*.

The system of *Qi Men* is based upon a historic concept of time that was shared by many of the great civilisations of antiquity, from the Mayans, to the Aztecs, to the ancient Egyptians. Where we see time as linear, a *Qi Men* strategist sees time as travelling in a perpetual cycle like the turning of the days or the changing of the seasons. *Qi Men* takes these cycles of time and seeks to connect them to the further cycles of energy at play in the universe and in the spaces around us, like a series of cogs in a great cosmic machine.

By developing an understanding of the inner workings of this machine, *Qi Men* is able to provide us with intricate knowledge of the relationships between Space, Time and the Universe and once we are able to pinpoint our own position within those relationships, we can begin to see how those forces may have an impact upon our daily lives. By arming us with this profound insight into the play of cosmic forces, *Qi Men* is able to guide our decision making so as to reap the benefits while avoiding the potential pitfalls.

At the heart of the practice of *Qi Men Dun Jia* is the plotting of a Qi Map, which anticipates the trajectory and the nature of Heaven, Earth, Man and Spirit Luck at any given moment in time. There are a thousand and eighty (1080) Qi maps in total which are divided into sectors reflecting the different kinds of luck that may influence the reading and, like any map of physical landforms, are marked with the directions of the compass. In order to use this map, and empower it to change one's fortune for the better, it is necessary to locate the position of *Jia (or the Yong Shen*用神 *(Focus Point))* within the Chart. In reflection of 'The Art of War' the *Jia* represents the leadership of your armies; you must aim to keep it safe and empower it to overcome any challenges against enemy forces.

Qi Men Dun Jia has five main applications of which **Forecasting** will be the most familiar concept to many. This facet allows a Qi Men strategist to predict the outcome of hypothetical actions in order to assist with decision making, offering a permutation of the potential outcome of any choice that might be made. This is also the primary method of application prescribed in Liu Bo Wen's classic "*The Golden Case Jade Mirror Qi Men Dun Jia*: 金函玉鏡奇門遁甲".

The next step on the journey is **Strategic Execution (Time and Activity Selection)**. After having decided upon a course of action, it is now possible for Qi Men to direct the individual to choose the exact moment to proceed with his or her plans in order to achieve the best possible outcome. For Qi Men military strategists, this would have been a truly invaluable tool, as timing would have been crucial in being able to secure a victory in battle.

At the height of Feng Shui studies during the Ming and Qing dynasties, the methods of "**Qi Men Feng Shui**" was born out of innovations to the original format of Qi Men Dun Jia. Qi Men already had the capacity to forecast and it was being used to remotely assess battlefields for military purposes. The extension of Qi Men into the assessment of properties and landforms would have seemed only natural. In the modern world Qi Men Feng Shui allows an individual to maximise his or her potential for success by harnessing the energy present at his or her new home or new office premises.

The Ming and Qing Dynasties also saw Qi Men extend its reach into the field of **Destiny Studies**. In this approach, a Qi Men strategist is able to use a person's date of birth to project the possible path that his or her life will take to gain insight into that person's inherent nature, gifts, spiritual guides, divine talents, strengths and weaknesses. Such a capacity can assist an individual to better understand their journey in life and to make choices that will enhance their happiness and allow them to live up to their full potential.

Qi Men is also one of only a few systems of metaphysics to incorporate the 'Spirit Realm' into its calculations. This may conjure images of séances and hand holding in the minds of the uninitiated; but in Qi Men, 'the spirit' refers to the subconscious mind and the effect the energy in the universe may have on an individual's thoughts, feelings and motivations. The fifth and final application of Qi Men is known as '**Spiritual *Qi Men***' and this approach allows a Qi Men strategist to understand an individual's nature and 'higher self' and the ways in which energy may influence his or her perspectives. By working with those influences and enhancing those that are beneficial and weakening those that are harmful, it may be possible to help an individual to manifest significant change in his or her life.

Origins

The exact origins of this system of metaphysics are unknown; there are those that believe that its roots can be traced back to more than five thousand years ago but legend places its genesis during the late Warring States Period. As we have already discussed, the Warring States Period was a time of great political and social upheaval and it was marked by frequent fighting. It was into this tumultuous climate that *Qi Men Dun Jia* was developed and led its first beneficiary to victory.

According to Chinese myth, a complex figure by the name of *Chi You* (蚩尤) had become the leader of the Nine Li tribe and he was held by many to have been a fierce warrior and a tyrannical leader. The mythical Yellow Emperor, or *Huang Di* 皇帝, had attempted to face Chi You in battle and nine times he walked away defeated from the battle ground. Lost and uncertain, despairing of his humiliation at the hands of the mighty Chi You, the young Huang Di fled to the mountains. It was here, when he feared that all hope was lost, the *Goddess of the Nine Heavens* (九天玄女) came to him and bestowed upon him a gift. That gift was the knowledge of *Qi Men Dun Jia,* and she assured him that he would henceforth be always victorious. Armed with the knowledge, he defeated Chi You soon after that.

In the modern world, *Qi Men Dun Jia* is still used by politicians, strategists and business magnates alike in order to enhance their decision making abilities and direct their energy and resources. Sophisticated, versatile and accessible, *Qi Men* is more than simply a system of forecasting. It has evolved over the centuries to offer support in all areas of life from finding a romantic partner to developing a career potential and even solving mysteries.

Qi Men Dun Jia: The Metaphysical Tool of War

As we have seen *Qi Men Dun Jia* was born in a time of strife and conflict and was, from the very first, used to develop military strategies that changed the face of China's destiny and then united it as the great country that we know today. It was not simply Huang Di who used *Qi Men* to develop his battle plans. Throughout the history, many great military commanders and strategists have studied the applications of *Qi Men* and used them to their advantage.

Almost every book written on the subject of *Qi Men Dun Jia* will make mention of the great Zhuge Liang. We will explore his exploits in detail later. Suffice to say, Zhuge Liang has been revered as one of the greatest military minds in Chinese history and he is also known as being one of the foremost proponents of *Qi Men Dun Jia*. Liu Bowen, who led the armies as the military strategist of the first Emperor of the Ming Dynasty Zhu Yuanzhang (朱元璋), was likewise known to have studied *Qi Men Dun Jia* as well as philosophy, magnetism, Feng Shui and astronomy.

These two men have both been connected to a series of books on the subject of *Qi Men Dun Jia* such as *The Encyclopaedia of Qi Men* [奇門遁甲統宗大全], *The Secret Handbook of Qi Men* [奇門秘籍全書] and Zhuge Liang's *Qi Men Military Encyclopaedia* [諸葛武侯奇門遁甲大全]. As is often the case with the classics of Chinese literature, philosophy and science, the exact origins of these books are unknown and many scholars are unconvinced that Zhuge Liang wrote the original versions, nevertheless it is believed that they were at least revised by Liu Bowen and they contain a wealth of information of the ways in which *Qi Men Dun Jia* would have been used to develop military strategy. *The Golden Case Jade Mirror Qi Men Dun Jia* [金函玉鏡奇門遁甲], penned by Liu Bowen, is another one of the classics of metaphysical studies, which maintains a position of authority even to this day and offers equally profound insight into the intricacies of using *Qi Men Dun Jia* on the battlefield.

Qi Men Dun Jia and 'The Art of War' in actual history

We are already starting to piece together the evidence that the methods of *Qi Men* were being used in conjunction with the teachings of Sun Tzu. From it, we now know that Qin Shi Huang partially credited his ability to end the Warring States period and unite the Chinese people through tactics described in 'The Art of War', and the assistance of *Qi Men* in developing winning strategies. We have come to understand that great military minds, well versed in 'The Art of War', have studied *Qi Men Dun Jia* throughout the centuries and used its power to their advantage. Now it is time to study the historical tales of bravery and daring that have seen both 'The Art of War' and *Qi Men Dun Jia* brought together with great effect.

Zhuge Liang was born in AD 181 in Yangdu during the Three Kingdoms Period. He was from a fairly simple farming background but he studied hard and elevated himself to the position of the Chancellor of Shu Han and distinguished himself as a great intellectual, gifted commander, war strategist and tactician before he died in AD 234. Often compared to Sun Tzu himself, Zhuge Liang, as we have mentioned, also penned some literary works of his own, including 'The General's Garden 將苑' and '*The Convenient Sixteen Strategies* 便宜十六策' which expanded on many of the methods that Sun Tzu approached in his own work.

Throughout his career, it is clear that Zhuge Liang made use of the teachings of Sun Tzu and he used them to his advantage in his lifelong battle against the Cao clan which at that time dominated the North of China. One of the key points made in 'The Art of War' is that a General should be aware of his own strengths as well as his weaknesses and compare them to the strengths of his enemy. Zhuge Liang can be proven historically to have taken heed of this advice. When faced with the might of the powerful Cao Cao in the North of the country, Zhuge Liang knew that action needed to be taken soon or Cao Cao would become an undefeatable force. He convinced his sovereign Liu Bei to ally with Sun Quan, who held a great deal of the territories in the South including those close to the Yangtze River, so that their combined forces could face the superior armies of the North. His strategy proved to be very successful but not without a little help from *Qi Men*.

Leading up to the famous '*Battle of the Red Cliffs*' *(赤壁之戰)*, according to the partially fictionalised account in 'The Romance of the Three Kingdoms', General Zhou Yu 周瑜, Zhuge Liang's counterpart who served Sun Quan, had watched anxiously while Cao Cao chained his boats together on the river and created a floating garrison. He knew that they needed to strike a blow at Cao Cao's naval might if they were to be able to secure victory in battle. They wanted to adopt a *fire attack* according to *The Art of War* (Chapter 12) in order to decimate the enemy ships ahead of the forthcoming conflict but the timing was wrong. It was Winter and the winds were blowing from the Northwest. If they were to attempt an attack, the fire would be blown back towards their own troops and they would do themselves more harm than good. In order to defeat Cao Cao, they needed the wind to blow from the East but this was unlikely to happen again until Spring.

Zhou Yu exhausted himself with worry. He saw no way to implement his plans and his anxiety grew into a sickness. Lying in his bed, deathly ill, he was convinced that all hope was lost until Zhuge Liang came to him and handed him a letter with just sixteen characters written upon it: 'If you want to defeat Cao Cao, use fire. Everything is ready, we just need the wind to blow from the East.'

"欲破曹公，宜用火攻。萬事俱備，只欠東風。"

In his weakened state Zhou Yu was shaken by his comrade's apparent ability to read his mind and he asked him, since he was so wise as to be able to ascertain the cause of his malaise, was he also able to prescribe a remedy? Zhuge Liang's prescription was the science of *Qi Men*. Zhuge Liang instructed him to build a great wall at Nan Ping Hill and to call it the Seven Star Altar. He told him that the altar should be guarded by 120 men and surrounded by banners and flags so that the enemy would see their actions and be afraid. On the twentieth day of the eleventh month, a Jia Zi 甲子 Day, Zhuge Liang would use the force of *Qi Men* to harness the energy of the universe and command would be sent up to the cosmos for the winds to change.

When the fateful day arrived, Zhuge Liang had prepared himself by fasting and bathing. He dressed in a Dao cloth and approached the mighty altar. He performed rituals and prayed. He did everything he could to make sure that the forecasted outcome would happen that day. As time ticked by, hopes for the wind to change were slowly fading. Amidst growing fears that their prayers had been ignored and that *Qi Men* had failed them, it was then that suddenly at the stroke of midnight, the banners and flags began to move. After all the tense hours of waiting, they finally saw the powerful current of an East wind coming in on full force. Zhuge Liang and Zhou Yu were able to instruct their troops to light the fires and they stood back and watched in triumph as the enemy ships were burned.

Now, of course, this dramatic retelling came from a novelisation of historical events and its portrayal of Zhuge Liang apparently commanding the winds to change is largely romanticised. In reality, the Seven Star Altar and prayers would not have been necessary in order to 'call on' the East wind. The truth is that Zhuge Liang did not conjure the East wind at all. He simply knew from the Qi Men Forecast Chart that in three days time, the winds would change direction long enough for him to go forward with his plans.

The building of the Seven Star Altar, the elaborate ceremony and prayers, the hundred and twenty guards, the flags and the banners were all meant for show. This is because aside from the use of *Qi Men Dun Jia,* Zhuge Liang was also applying strategies that he knew well from Sun Tzu's Art of War. He was using the principles of deception and distraction to divert the enemy's attention away from his real intentions. While the enemy was helplessly drawn to the spectacle on the hill, Zhuge Liang's troops were able to light their fires and make their escape in safety. He might also have predicted that Zhou Yu, being fearful of the presence of an uncertain ally at the Sun Quan camp, might turn against him once the battle with Cao Cao was over. In playing the reality of his performance close to his chest, he was also able to defend himself and his men from the actions of a nervous ally. With the aid of Qi Men Forecasting and the clever use of the art of *deception* (Sun Tzu) and the Door of Delusion (Qi Men Dun Jia), Zhuge Liang was able to turn the tide of the battle in the allies' favour and escape with his skin intact.

Qi Men Dun Jia and 'The Art of War' reunited

The lessons of history have taught us that the combination of the tactics of Sun Tzu's 'The Art of War' and the methods of *Qi Men Dun Jia* are truly a force to be reckoned with. While one guides us with insight into human behaviour, the importance of strategic thinking, the value of self-knowledge and the importance of developing a profound understanding of the challenges we face, the other offers a view of the factors that might otherwise be outside of our control. By viewing 'The Art of War' through the lens of *Qi Men Dun Jia*, we are not only able to develop practical and powerful strategies for success but we are also able to position those strategies effectively in time and space.

This book takes you through each of the thirteen chapters of 'The Art of War'. Each page of the original text is shown first in the original Chinese characters and then translated into English. This text is then followed by a commentary that brings the thoughts of Sun Tzu into focus in a modern business and life context. At the end of each chapter the Qi Men interpretation is then detailed with particular reference to Sun Tzu's own use of language and the alternative ways in which his words can be interpreted in order to guide the reader towards a complementary use of *Qi Men Dun Jia*. With two such powerful weapons in our arsenal you are already on your way to discovering the path to victory.

STRATEGIC ASSESSMENTS

始計

1

ORIGINAL TEXT:

孫子曰：兵者，國之大事，
死生之地，存亡之道，
不可不察也。

TRANSLITERATION:

Sun Tzu said: What is War? War is one of the most vital affairs of state. War is where life and death meet; it is the road to destruction or survival. It demands study.

COMMENTARY:

You may not literally be a General or Commander in charge of an army but make no mistake, you are fighting a war – a war for success in your career, business and life. Every day you fight battles in your personal life, at the workplace and within your industry. Your 'war' takes place on two levels. Externally (you must fight to stay ahead in the world) and internally (you also fight battles inside your own head). To become a better and happier human being, you have to win the war that is taking place internally. To become successful in life you have to win the war that you are fighting externally. Ideally, you must win both.

There will always be obstacles that stand between you and victory. In life, you will have many competitors. Learning how to handle both will allow you to live successfully. You only have one lifetime to succeed in – so it is imperative that you have a strategy for success. The ability to form strategy can be developed via the study of what has worked well for others. Such study reveals common strategic decisions that are conducive to victory.

Every war is comprised of many smaller battles. These individual battles – the challenges you face on a daily basis - are won or lost on the basis of your decision-making and action. If you perform poorly in these smaller battles often enough you will fail to achieve the grander designs you have for your life. Great success in life, career or business really *is* the result of doing many small things well.

Some people seem to have a knack for success; we often know these people in the form of entrepreneurs, celebrities, business magnates and athletes. These people are usually superior strategic thinkers. They make the right choices. They take action. There are countless stories that allow us to dismiss the role of mere luck in their prominence – stories where strategically minded people repeat their success in a different arena because they know how to form and execute winning plans. They "get" the rules of the game and they play to win.

Through the study of the principles of war, you can enhance your ability to think and act in a strategic way. The lessons of war can help improve your batting average, regardless of your circumstances or the size of your goals. To put it simply, understanding the rules in life allows you to formulate winning strategies.

ORIGINAL TEXT:

故經之以五事，校之以計，
而索其情，一曰道，二曰天，
三曰地，四曰將，五曰法。

道者，令民與上同意，
可與之死，可與之生，
而不畏危也。

天者，陰陽，寒暑，時制也。

地者，遠近，險易，廣狹，
死生也。

將者，智，信，仁，勇，嚴也。

法者，曲制，官道，主用也。

TRANSLITERATION:

There are five decisive factors in war, which may dictate the outcome before conflict has even begun and these must be taken into account when planning a battle strategy. It is vital to fully understand their relevance. The first is the Way (the Tao), the second is Heaven, the third is Earth, the fourth is Leadership, and the fifth is Regulation.

What is the Way? The Way (the Tao) brings the people into accord with their ruler so that they will follow him fearlessly in life and into death itself.

What is Heaven? Heaven encompasses the day and the night, the heat and the cold and the changing of the seasons.

What is Earth? This describes the location of the battleground; near or far, whether the terrain is secure or challenging and whether there are wide plains or narrow valleys. Such matters may make the difference between life and death.

What is Leadership? A wise commander should possess the five virtues of intelligence, trustworthiness, benevolence, courage and sternness.

What is Regulation? Regulation refers to the military establishment, the correct organization of troops and the control of supplies.

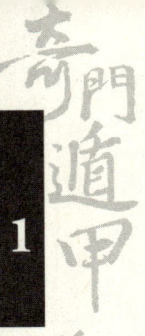

COMMENTARY:

Even before competition has begun, it's often possible to predict the outcome through comparative consideration of the five factors Sun Tzu outlined. When you want to make a strategic assessment of your own capabilities or of your rival's, think about each of these five factors in turn when making your appraisal. After this assessment, you will be able to diagnose issues in your own strategic plans and remedy them. For example, an assessment of these factors might indicate that you've chosen a poor operating location for your business or that your team is missing key personnel. Attending to these problems will improve your chances of success. The five factors allow you to predict failure or success and act accordingly.

Let's examine each of the five factors in turn.

First, the Moral Compass; The Way, *the Tao* 道. For an organization to succeed, its leader must have a *vision* which serves as a guiding compass. This vision is known as 'The Way'. A team without The Way will have no direction and no fighting spirit. Everyone will pull in different directions and very little of note will get done.

These principles also apply on a more personal level. For an individual to be successful in their own life, he too must have a *vision* or a purpose. He must find his *Tao*. A life without the *Tao* or '*purpose*' is a life without meaning. Without *Tao*, a person will pass through life like a boat adrift in the vast ocean. The *Tao* is *The Way*, the *inner moral compass*, or *the Purpose* in your life. This Purpose is what will ultimately allow you to define your vision. The *Tao* is what leads people to greatness.

From the *Tao* comes an understanding of things like abundance, success, wealth and fulfillment; these are the results of discovering and pursuing one's purpose. Without it, you will be at a loss.

Second, the Heaven 天. This means the environment and timing. In a modern context, this usually means the business market, economic circumstances, political climate and so on. Timing and positioning within the wider climate is everything – the movie business, for example, places a great deal of importance on the timing of their releases. Blockbuster movies are released in the summer months for maximum returns. Predicted bombs are relegated to the winter schedule to make room for more profitable tent pole releases. Identify the optimum timing and environment for your plans. Work within the realities of your environment.

The third factor is the Earth 地. Location, location, location. This is the mantra for success in real estate. Your choice of location can make or break your plans. In some circumstances, such as in the property investment market, your choice of location will be the critical factor. Operating in the wrong market, choosing the wrong venue or being too far from the action can all make it hard to succeed. The opposite is also true.

Fourth, Leadership 將. Leadership is critical to success and the larger the goal, the greater the need for decisive, inspirational, charismatic and courageous leadership that drives collective action. Good leaders are rare. Great leaders are even rarer. Most people in roles requiring leadership fail to provide it. To be an effective leader means that you must make decisions for the greater good of the people you are responsible for. This requires you to put their needs ahead of your own. Rising to the challenge of leadership is not easy but you must do it if you wish to win your war. People are afraid of assuming leadership roles because they require accountability. Being a leader means being vulnerable and being subjected to public scrutiny. It's impossible to lead without putting oneself, and one's point of view, out in the open for everyone else to see. This truth has led many people to shy away from leadership; they are simply unwilling to step up and put their neck on the line for their vision. You must choose to be a leader in order to win your war. Leadership arises from a number of learnable skills. Good leadership abilities can be developed. Making the commitment to become an effective leader is step one on the path to victory. If you want power, you must shoulder responsibility and be inspirational. Inspiring, rather than controlling others, creates the best results.

The fifth and final factor to consider in your evaluation is Regulation. Regulation in the context of Sun Tzu means - *Methods and Discipline* 法. This refers to the way that efforts are organized as well as any structures or conditions that you operate under. In business, this can often be described as "corporate culture". It is how you run your business. You as the leader are largely responsible for creating your own corporate culture and the 'culture' you create governs the results that you will get. For instance if a leader is constantly late for work, cuts corners and slacks off then he will find that this becomes the normal, acceptable behavior in his office for everyone. If instead a leader is meticulous and checks on work progress consistently, he will find that work is done on time and people are committed to generating a good product. Regulation in the context of Sun Tzu means what are you 'willing to tolerate.' In life, we get what we are willing to tolerate. If you tolerate mediocrity at work, you will always get mediocre work. If you tolerate excuses from your subordinates you will get more excuses. If you expect only the best from yourself and from everyone else in your team and tolerate nothing less you will set a stage for peak performance in your organization.

You will find that an in-depth, candid consideration of all five of these factors for both you and your opponent will go a long way towards helping you forecast the probable outcome of competition and improving your own strategic plans.

ORIGINAL TEXT:

凡此五者，將莫不聞，
知之者勝，不知者不勝。
故校之以計，而索其情。
曰：主孰有道，將孰有能，
天地孰得，法令孰行，
兵眾孰強，士卒孰練，
賞罰孰明，吾以此知勝負矣。

TRANSLITERATION:

Anyone who wishes to lead a group of solders into battle must appreciate the importance of the five factors. Only when he truly understands these factors will he be able to win victory for his people. Without this knowledge it is likely that he will be defeated. Therefore, in order to analyse the circumstances of war and assess your chances of victory, it is important first to ask the following questions:

Which ruler has the hearts of his people?

Which General has the greatest strength and ability?

Which side has the more favourable climate and the more advantageous terrain?

Whose discipline is more effective?

Which army is stronger?

Whose officers and men are better trained?

Who best understands the benefits of reward and punishment?

Once you have answered these questions and given careful consideration to the answers, you will be able to predict who will win and who will lose.

COMMENTARY:

In addition to thinking about the Five Factors, ask yourself which side possesses superiority in each of the matters Sun Tzu describe in this passage and to what extent. This will help you determine who is likely to emerge victorious from confrontation. If, for example, one side has a clear edge in all five then it seems likely that they will emerge on top. In other scenarios, more interpretation is required: it's up to you to determine how important each of these criteria are and to weigh them against each other as you see fit.

First, which side is more sure of its cause? Which leader has the strongest power to motivate his people? Which leader has a more 'compelling vision' that guides his people? The side which is more driven by his vision will have superiority.

Second, which side has the most effective leadership? This can be determined by comparing experience, assessing track records and gauging the support each leader enjoys in his position. There are also other factors which must be considered here. For instance, if a leader is new in his position then he will operate at a reduced level while he learns the ropes. However, a new leader can sometimes bring new, compelling ideas and tactics which give him an advantage. Think about the specifics of the situation and which side has the most gainful leadership model.

Third, think about the circumstances and which side he favours. A business with a long history of operating in a given marketplace will fare better than a newcomer wishing to enter the same niche, even if the newcomer has more capital and manpower available. In this case, the existing business will benefit from its accumulated support network, list of contacts and in-house experience. He is at an advantage over any newcomer because he is entrenched.

Fourth, look at the numbers. Compare manpower and financial capability. The more people and money that one side has, the more they can afford to throw at their objectives and the faster they can get things done, provided their spending is accompanied by a high level of organization.

Fifth, think about experience, education and training. Raw experience is more valuable pound for pound than education but training can help an organization stay abreast with new technology and thinking. More skilled people create a better service or product and for that they can charge a higher price and command superior returns. In the world of sports, the athlete who is better trained has a physical advantage. In academic pursuits, the person with the best test results will usually be chosen. Experience, education and training differentiate people and enhance the quality of their results.

When all is said and done, experience is the best teacher. Experience makes people street smart as opposed to being just book smart. People who are street smart have 'situational awareness' which means they know intuitively and understand what must be done. They are also able to see from many different perspectives. The main distinction between book smart (highly educated scholars) and street smart people is the way in which they acquire their knowledge. When you read a book, you absorb someone else's experience and knowledge. When you gain practical experience, you are required to use your own judgment to create results and so your judgment improves as you learn. Thus, experience is the best teacher. He who is more experienced will be able to exercise better judgment. This is the fifth and often most important determining factor that Sun Tzu speaks of.

Finally, you must ask which side offers the best rewards and the most effective punishments. How effective are an organization's reward and discipline mechanisms and policies and what calibre of results do they generate? Better results mean better odds.

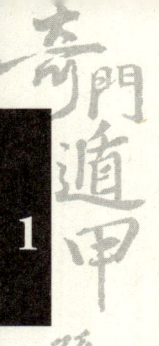

ORIGINAL TEXT:

將聽吾計，用之必勝，留之；
將不聽吾計，用之必敗，去之。

TRANSLITERATION:

The generals who heed this advice will surely be able to gain victory and maintain their position and standing, those who do not are likely to suffer defeat and as a result they may also lose their rank and station.

COMMENTARY:

Learn the value of strategic thinking if you want to achieve your goals. Know and understand the factors that contribute to success and failure. Use this knowledge to shape and guide your tactical plans. In most positions of authority or leadership, failure is not tolerated, regardless of circumstances. The higher the position, the lower the tolerance for it. If you wish to maintain your position and enjoy the power it affords you, you must actively maintain and develop your abilities as a leader. Strategic thinking and assessment will greatly improve your rate of success and help you fulfill your commitment to results.

1

ORIGINAL TEXT:

計利以聽，乃爲之勢，
以佐其外；勢者，
因利而制權也。

TRANSLITERATION:

When planning a strategy according to my counsel, it is important to act in accordance with the situation and to take tactical advantage of external factors. By taking into account the prevailing circumstances, it is possible to seize the advantage by adapting your plans.

COMMENTARY:

Think carefully about what the best approach is in the given circumstances. Circumstances change constantly and you must change your tactics as they do. Accurately identifying and using the most situation-appropriate tactics will help you win.

Here, it's important to differentiate between strategy and tactics. A leader must be a strategist first and foremost. A strategy is a long-term plan or mission. Tactics are the smaller actions that help you fulfill a grander vision. Most people think they are strategists, but actually they are merely tacticians. People today often use these terms haphazardly and interchangeably. Some don't even know the difference. For Sun Tzu, strategies are done 'above the shoulders' and tactics are performed and carried out 'below the shoulders'.

You must have a clear strategy. Then, create tactical plans that help you move towards reaching it. When doing so, you must find the winning angles that can give you an edge. What facts about the present can be exploited for your own gain? How can you subvert your position or adapt to new circumstances? Which people around you can help you reach your short-term goals and how? Think about the resources available to you – what is their optimum usage? Can you optimize your operations further? When might it be better to work in secret and when might it be better to display confidence and strength? Think about what will work best for you. Move quickly and strike out when you can, be subtle when you must. Remember that your tactics must serve your strategy. Your main obligation is to achieve long term success – to strategic victory – don't sweat the details too much. You must look to the horizon. Real leaders think about the bigger picture and the greater good and they don't get caught up over thinking their tactics or setting small goals. Identify big goals and targets that advance your interests and your organization. Then, figure out the best route as you go. Be a strategist rather than just a mere tactician. This is Sun Tzu's chief advice.

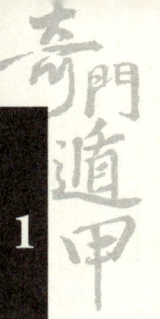

ORIGINAL TEXT:

兵者，詭道也。故能而示之不能，用而示之不用，近而示之遠，遠而示之近。利而誘之，亂而取之，實而備之，強而避之，怒而撓之，卑而驕之，佚而勞之，親而離之。攻其無備，出其不意，此兵家之勝，不可先傳也。

TRANSLITERATION:

Any successful military campaign will be steeped in deception. A commander who is competent should feign incompetence; an army that is preparing to strike should appear to delay their actions. When you are close you should appear to be far away and when you are far you should appear to be close. If an enemy seeks the advantage you should lure him further with false fortune, if he is in disorder you should capture him, if he is coordinated you should be ready, if he is strong you should avoid him, if he is angry you should goad him, if he is humble you should dominate him, if he is rested you should exhaust him and if his people are united then you should divide them. An effective leader must understand how to attack when the enemy is unprepared and how to appear when he is least expected. Deception and surprise are the key to victory and because they rely on developing circumstances, this means that it is never possible to completely formulate a fixed plan for victory in advance. You must play the game as it happens.

COMMENTARY:

Deception is an important tool and it must be used at all high levels of operation. Deception, misdirection, divergence and secrecy can all be used to create competitive opportunities from thin air. Their frequent and varied use can prevent competitors from predicting your next move and intercepting or undermining your plans. Failure to use deception when it is called for represents a serious missed opportunity. But remember, deception must *never* be used on friends, customers and teammates - only on competitors, enemies and business rivals.

Reality is a matter of perception. The price of a product or service is a matter of perceived value. The value of your offering is determined by nothing more than its perceived benefit, divided by its cost. If you can control perception, you can control your market and control other people's reactions. There are many times in business when it is strategically advantageous to present yourself or your capabilities in a deceptively unassuming way. For example, if you have plans to make a significant move in the marketplace with a new product line, service or price then it may be wise to pretend otherwise until the last possible instant. This can lure competitors into being complacent and prevent them from assembling their resources in time to compete. In this case, deception can help you secure greater market share and revenue.

Deception doesn't just let you create maneuvering room for your operations. It can help you turn the tables entirely. When properly understood and employed, it can mitigate your shortcomings and nullify the strength of your competitors. By feigning disinterest you can conceal your true intentions and sneak to your goal unchallenged. By crafting an appearance of strength or dominance you can ward off competition, secure superior contracts and minimize high-level competition. You can use deception and misinformation to plant ideas and seeds of dissent that encourage your rivals to expend energy, resources and time pursuing dead ends, freeing up the path ahead.

Knowing the power of deception, always remember that others have the power to deceive you and the greater the potential returns, the higher the incentive for them to do so. Never take anything for granted – always verify what you learn and consider the outcome if you are wrong in your assumption and thinking. Try, as far as possible, to prepare for deception.

In the modern world perspective, the art of *Deception* can be re-termed as the art of *Influencing*. In business, career or in life, your success is very much dependent on whether you can *influence* others. You win by winning their hearts and mind. Your ability to influence, persuade or convince others will determine how great a leader you are.

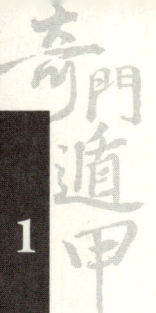

ORIGINAL TEXT:

夫未戰而廟算勝者，得算多也；
未戰而廟算不勝者，得算少也；
多算勝，少算不勝，
而況於無算乎？
吾以此觀之，勝負見矣。

TRANSLITERATION:

A military leader who considers all the potential eventualities and forecasts before the battle is far more likely to succeed than he who gives little consideration to the possibilities and takes little time to forecast. He who plans carefully will be in a far better position that he who is careless or barely plans at all; he who does not take care to consider the situation is likely to face defeat and ruin. By comparing the approaches that men take, it is possible to see who will win and who will lose.

COMMENTARY:

It is said that anything which can go wrong, will. This law of life serves to illustrate the importance of contingency planning and due caution.

All the planning in the world can't fully account for the chaos and uncertainties of life. Assume as little with certainty about the future as you can. By all means, have a fixed end goal but don't try to restrict yourself tactically. Create your tactical plans as you go so that you can account for black swan events, the unknowable irrational decisions of others and unpredictable, changing market conditions, etc. The only sensible choice is to plan for multiple outcomes – to prepare for the unexpected by remaining flexible. The more complex your strategic goals and the bigger their scope, the greater the need for risk management and backup plans.

The more outcomes you prepare for, the better your security – backup plans are a safety net that supports your efforts to grow. Ironically, over time, better security and stability allow you to take more risks and more chances.

In summary it's easy to forecast how well a person or business will fare with changing fortunes by examining how thoroughly they accept change and whether or not they plan for alternative outcomes.

QI MEN DUN JIA:

Introducing Joey Yap's Qi Men Warcraft™

Qi Men Warcraft is the name I've given to the powerful fusion of Qi Men Dun Jia and Sun Tzu's Art of War teachings. By viewing the wisdom contained within Sun Tzu's Art of War through the lens of Qi Men Dun Jia, you can become a formidable strategic player in your field.

A thorough understanding of Sun Tzu's Art of War gives you the mindset of a seasoned General – it shows you how to think, respond and act strategically. Qi Men Dun Jia can paint a portrait in space and time of the battleground that you must navigate. These two systems complement each other perfectly and together, they have wide practical utility.

In this chapter, Sun Tzu emphasizes the importance of Strategic Assessment for success. The lessons here are massively applicable in today's world. Business planning is little more than a modern form of strategic assessment, tailored to the competitive 'battlefields' of today. Because human nature has not changed since the time of Sun Tzu, his wisdom remains completely valid today in any arena where people compete for success.

We create strategies so that we can reach our identified goals. Strategic thought let you put your finger on where you'd like to be in the future. Qi Men Dun Jia is a torch you can use to illuminate the path there.

The Chinese Metaphysical art and science of Qi Men Dun Jia 奇門遁甲 reveals the hidden secrets of the present and the future. Qi Men Dun Jia, translated, means *Mysterious Doors Escaping Technique*. Qi Men Dun Jia is used to calculate the configuration of Qi 氣 (cosmic energy) at a given point in time and space. A Qi Men Chart is one way of looking at the Qi map (cosmic energy map) of the Universe. This map describes the complex interactions between Qi (cosmic energy), an individual, their actions and the Universe. Qi Men Dun Jia is a multidimensional analysis tool and we can use it to gauge the impact of different operational directions, timing, actions and interactions. In other words, it is the ultimate strategic assessment tool because it allows you to *forecast the outcome* of an action (or a decision).

Of course, the strategic power of Qi Men Dun Jia has been known and demonstrated for thousands of years. It helped shape a great deal of Chinese history. In ancient times, Generals and Commanders used Qi Men in battle. They would consult Qi Men Charts in order to determine the best time and place to carry out their attacks. If their findings indicated that an attack would fail, they would create a new plan. In this way, Generals and Commanders who used Qi Men were guaranteed victory, provided they could interpret their findings in a strategic way. Without a strategic implementation, the information you can obtain using Qi Men Dun Jia guarantees nothing. It must be acted upon properly (enter Sun Tzu!).

Qi Men itself has four basic applications, all of which I've covered individually and extensively in my other books. First, it can be used to determine an environment's **Feng Shui** characteristics. Second, for **Strategic Execution (Time and Activity Selection).** Third, to perform **Destiny Analysis** for an individual and fourth, and often most important, for **Forecasting** the outcome of an event or activity. When you combine these four applications together and filter them through the teachings of Sun Tzu, you obtain the power of **Qi Men Warcraft.** Qi Men Dun Jia is the Art of Warcraft. Qi Men Charts can be used to support strategic decision-making and expedite victory against others. When you combine Qi Men Dun Jia with Sun Tzu's philosophies then you will have an immeasurable advantage in all areas of competition.

Qi Men Chart: The Five Factors

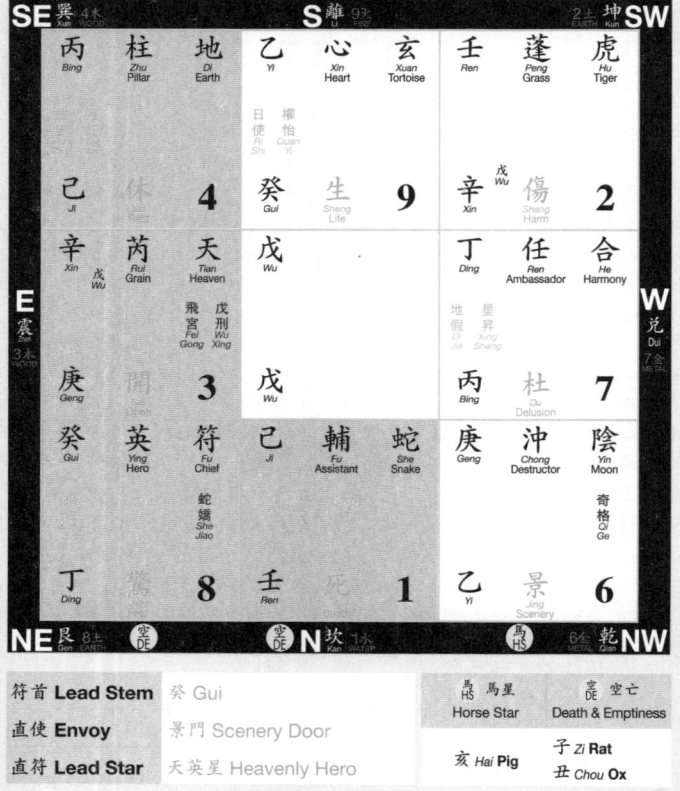

As you can see, there are 9 boxes, or sectors, in a Qi Men Chart. Each of these boxes is known as a Palace. They are named Xun (Southeast), Li (South), Kun (Southwest), Zhen (East), Center, Dui (West), Gen

(Northeast), Kan (North) and Qian (Northwest), each representing one of the compass directions. The contents of these 9 Palaces are like a snapshot of the Qi pattern for the time period that the Chart is plotted for. So, if you look at a Chart that represents a different time or time period, the 9 Palaces will have a different makeup. Qi Men Charts are dynamic and relevant.

Within each Palace lies information that we can interpret in terms of the 5 Factors. They are The Universe, Heaven, Earth, Man and Direction. These 5 Factors give depth and dimension to a Qi Men Chart; by considering each in turn and examining their interaction it is possible to predict the results of any given activity. In other words, there are 5 variables or Factors that create events and happenings in life and help shape the outcome. All five are described in a Qi Men Chart. **The 5 Factors:**

- **The Universe** 神 describes forces above our understanding and beyond your control. Divine intervention, cosmic influence. In Qi Men, these forces are represented by the 8 Deities.

- **Heaven** 天 represents the weather, and the environmental and economic conditions. In Qi Men, this variable is represented by the 9 Stars.

- **Earth** 地 denotes activity and action. In Qi Men, this variable is represented by the 8 Doors.

- **The Man** 人 factor represents the influence that humans have. In Qi Men, we analyze the 10 Stems to learn about the contribution of human perception and behavior.

- **Palace** 宮 – This refers to the 9 Directions or Sectors in the Qi Men Chart. Each Palace corresponds with one of 9 possible Directions; see how they are arranged like the points on a compass.

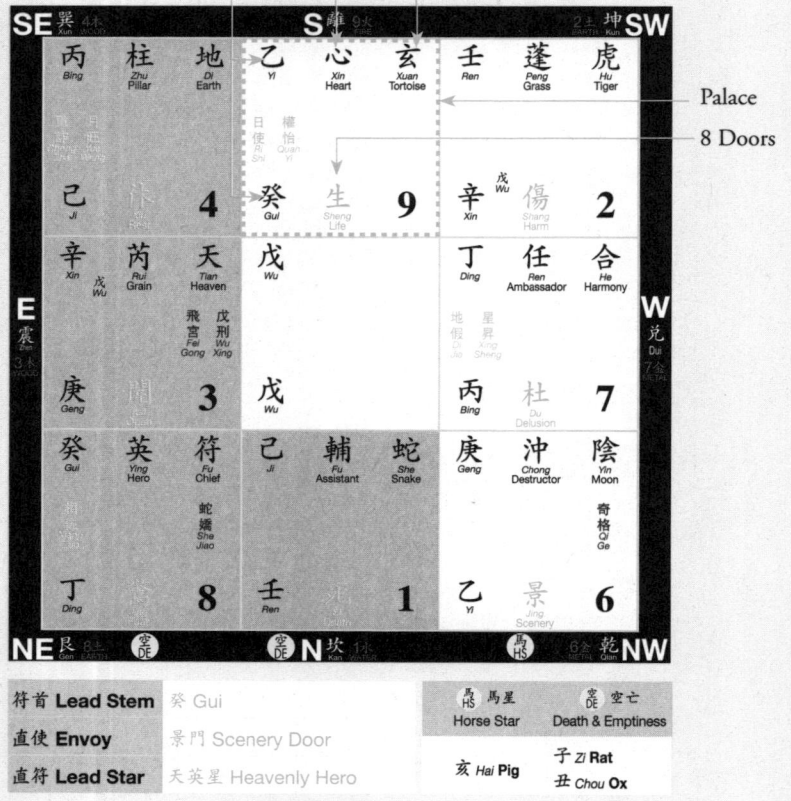

In the opening chapter of the Art of War, Sun Tzu spoke about the "5 Factors" that determine the outcome of battle. It is very easy to equate these 5 factors with the 5 factors that are considered in Qi Men Chart analysis. This is how we relate Sun Tzu's 5 Factors to the 5 Factors as they exist from a Qi Men perspective:

- To assess the role of The Way 道 or Moral Compass, we look at the 8 Deities.
- To assess the role of Heaven 天, we look at the 9 Stars.
- To assess the role of Earth 地, we look at the 8 Doors.
- To assess the role of The General 將 we look at the 10 Stems.
- To assess Method and Discipline 法, we look at Direction in the Chart, which is governed by the 9 Palaces.

In other words, the 5 Factors that Sun Tzu identified as variables in success or failure are directly tied to the 5 Factors described in every Qi Men Chart. Thus, an insightful reading of a Qi Men Chart can help us determine the outcome of any strategic proposal in accordance with Sun Tzu's time tested principles.

There are four possible timescales that can be depicted by a Qi Men Chart, each via a different Chart. You can plot Year, Month, Day and Hour Charts. Let's examine each in turn.

Year Chart 年盤
Month Chart 月盤
Day Chart 日盤
Hour Chart 時盤

The Year Chart, as the name implies, gives readings that span an entire year. The Month Chart describes outcomes on the timescale of a month or months. The Day and Hour Charts should be consulted when you are analyzing events that take place within a day or in one Chinese hour (two standard hours). Each of these four Charts is plotted in a different way and the nature of your plans and investigation will determine which you should consult. When a user plots a Year Chart, they can assess things from a long-term perspective. Month Charts and Day Charts are best suited for short-term and mid-term analysis purposes. An Hour Chart should be used when extremely timely information and guidance is required and so Hour Charts are mainly used for Qi Men Forecasting purposes. If you know what to look for and how to interpret what you see, then Qi Men can be used in conjunction with Sun Tzu's Art of War. Each Chart contains information that represents the variables of battle; terrain, topography, the forces of nature and your opponents. Learning to interpret Qi Men Charts correctly allows you to forecast the outcome of each battle you face in your life. Qi Men supports strategic planning and decision-making and allows you to forge the shortest and easiest path ahead to your goals and dreams in life and business.

Chart Plotting - Stems & Pillars

Any Qi Men analysis begins with Chart plotting. For Qi Men Forecasting purposes, an Hour Chart is usually the most appropriate. You will need to plot the Hour Chart from the hour that you conduct your analysis. *(The Chart Plotting format is already discussed extensively in my first book in the Qi Men Series – The Qi Men Dun Jia Compendium, and the readily plotted 1080 Qi Men Charts are available in the 540 Yin or Yang Hour Structure books. As such, the instructions would not be repeated here.)*

With your Chart obtained, the analysis may begin. You must first look for the *Useful God* 用神, which is the focal point of Chart analysis. (The term 'Useful God' is not a spiritual deity. It is common term in the practice of Chinese Metaphysics meaning the 'reference point' or the 'focal point'). For different analysis or assessment purposes there will be a different Useful God. These Useful Gods or representations are explained below.

A BaZi (Four Pillars Chart) of the *Date and Time* of forecast is often used in tandem with every Qi Men Chart. Hence, for every Chart, there are always four different Pillars: Hour, Day, Month and Year as shown below.

This is a Chart plotted on **7 July, 2014 at 2.30pm** and these are the Four Pillars in the Chart. These Four Pillars will be referenced in a Qi Men Chart.

時 Hour	日 Day	月 Month	年 Year	
食神 EG 辛 Xin **Yin Metal**	日元 DM 己 Ji **Yin Earth**	食神 EG 辛 Xin **Yin Metal**	正官 DO 甲 Jia **Yang Wood**	天干 Heavenly Stems
未 Wei **Goat** Yin Earth	卯 Mao **Rabbit** Yin Wood	未 Wei **Goat** Yin Earth	午 Wu **Horse** Yang Fire	地支 Earthly Branches
乙 Yi - Wood 殺 7K 己 Ji - Earth 比 F 丁 Ding - Fire 卩 IR	乙 Yi - Wood 殺 7K	乙 Yi - Wood 殺 7K 己 Ji - Earth 比 F 丁 Ding - Fire 卩 IR	丁 Ding - Fire 卩 IR 己 Ji - Earth 比 F	藏干 Hidden Stems

Each of these Pillars, particularly in regard to the location of the Heavenly Stems', carries a specific meaning and representation in a Qi Men Chart analysis. In general, the meanings that will be adopted for our purposes are as follows:

- **The Day Stem** 日干：Represents the Self 我方. You can see the Day Stem highlighted in the example below:

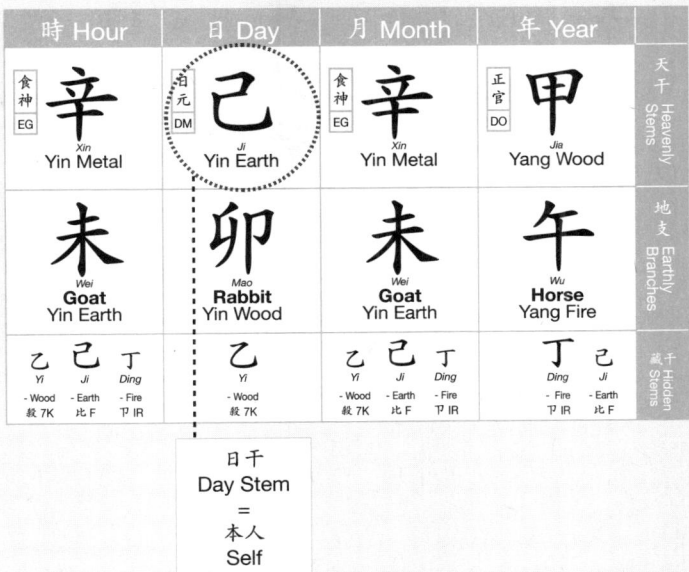

The Day Stem represents the location of the Self. In most situations, this represents you, your abilities, your current conditions and capabilities. Whether or not this Stem can be considered positive or not depends on the contents of this Palace.

- **The Month Stem** 月干：This represents the Opposition 競爭方、競爭者. In other words, it represents your competitor, your opponent or your rival and their current conditions, character and abilities. You can see the Month Stem highlighted in the example below:

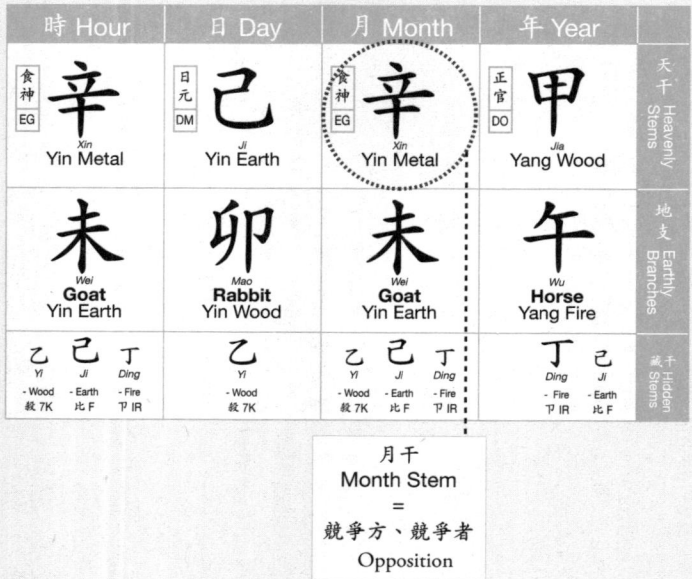

By analyzing the Month Stem Palace's contents, you can assess a competitor's strength and fortune in comparison to your own, which is described by the Day Stem Palace. Don't forget: you must consider the 5 Elements relationships and their modifying qualities when making your comparison.

- **The Hour Stem** 時干 describes the outcome of an activity or an event. In most Qi Men Forecasting analysis, the Palace where the Hour Stem resides usually represents the *subject matter*. Here's the location of the Hour Stem:

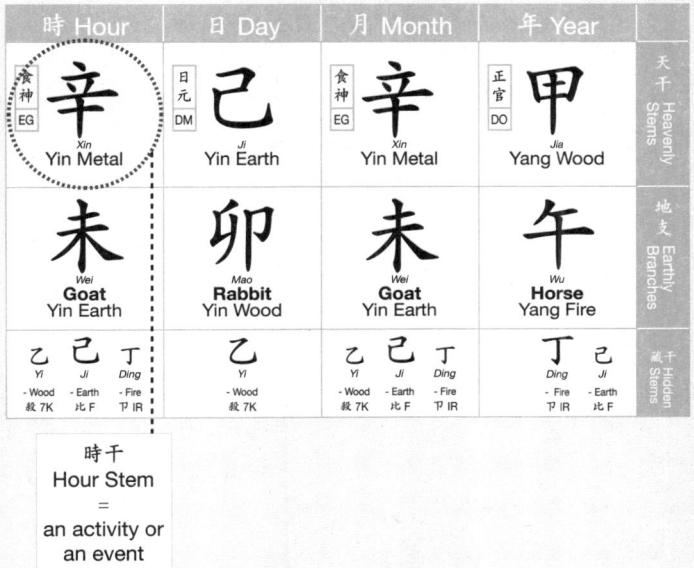

By looking at the Hour Stem Palace, we can determine whether a certain course of action will favor the side in question or their opposition. We can do this by assessing the 5 Elements relationship between the Hour Stem Palace and the Self Palace or the Hour Stem Palace and the Opposition Palace.

- **The Year Stem** 年干 is the outermost Pillar of a BaZi Chart. The Year Stem, amongst many things, represents the capabilities and prospects of the leader, or the leader of a country, the top management of a company, the corporate culture in the Forecast Chart. Here's how you find out the Year Stem for your assessment:

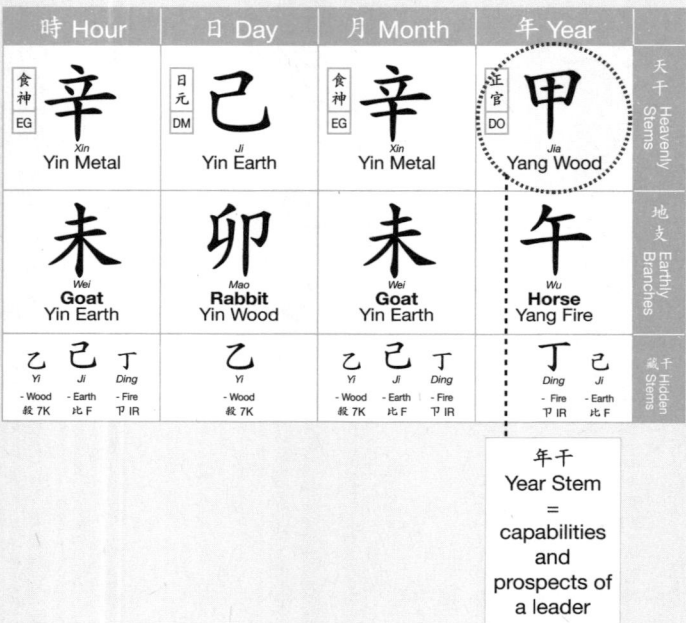

You can look at the Year Stem in order to determine a leader's vision, his *Tao* and strength in his role. Note that in the write-up above, it is assumed that the side favoured is the Host and their opposition is the Guest, although this will not always be the case. The Host and Guest Relationship will be discussed in greater depth in the next Chapter.

Now that you know what certain Palaces represent, how can you determine what their contents mean?

Each Qi Men Palace contains a combination of the **10 Stems, 9 Stars, 8 Deities and the 8 Doors.** Some of these components may be positive and some may not. Different combinations of these components lead to different outcomes and together they form unique Structures.

Here's a breakdown of each of the possible components and whether they are considered auspicious or inauspicious. You can refer back to this table as you need to.

The 8 Deities	Auspicious Deities	Chief, Great Moon, Six Harmony, Nine Earth, Nine Heaven
	Inauspicious Deities	Surging Snake, White Tiger/Grappling Hook, Red Phoenix/Black Tortoise
The 9 Stars	Auspicious Stars	Heavenly Destructor, Heavenly Assistant, Heavenly Bird, Heavenly Heart, Heavenly Ambassador
	Inauspicious Stars	Heavenly Grass, Heavenly Grain, Heavenly Pillar, Heavenly Hero
The 8 Doors	Auspicious Doors	Open Door, Rest Door, Life Door, Harm Door, Delusion Door, Scenery Door
	Inauspicious Doors	Death Door, Fear Door,
The 10 Stems	Auspicious Stems	Jia, Yi, Bing, Ding, Wu
	Inauspicious Stems	Ji, Geng, Xin, Ren, Gui

Qi Men Chart: The 7 Criteria

Aside from the 5 Factors, Sun Tzu also mentioned that there are 7 Criteria that a General or Commander needs to pay attention to in order to determine the outcome of a battle. According to Sun Tzu, after a General has considered all 7 Criteria, he or she will be able to forecast the outcome of a battle. You can do this by filtering your Qi Men findings with the same 7 Criteria as dictated by Sun Tzu.

To refresh your memory, the 7 Criteria, "七計" are represented by the following questions, all of which can be answered by a Qi Men Dun Jia Chart.

- Which of the two leaders is imbued with the better Moral compass?

- Which of the two generals has most ability?

- With whom lie the advantages derived from Heaven and Earth?

- On which side is discipline most rigorously enforced (Whose leadership is more effective)?

- Which army is stronger?

- On which side are officers and men more highly trained?

- In which army is there the greater constancy both in reward and punishment?

You can use Qi Men to address the 7 Criteria and make a strategic assessment about the likely outcome of any competitive situation between opponents, based on Sun Tzu's guidance.

Although Sun Tzu's original work was largely written from a war based perspective, his principles are still applicable in today's corporate battleground. Likewise, Qi Men - the Tool of War – still has practical use in the modern world. Although you may not draw blood when you compete in business, victory and failure still exist. Thus, these ancient systems are every bit as powerful today as they have always been as they deal in the timeless human language of competition. In a Qi Men Chart, the Day Stem can represent the Self and the Month Stem can represent a rival or someone you regard as a competitor (for instance a business rival or a competitor at the work place). In Qi Men, a forecast is performed whenever a strategic assessment of the situation or circumstances is required. In other words, we forecast in order to understand ourselves and our opponents and determine who has the most strategically advantageous position. A forecast can be extended to matters more relevant to contemporary times such as in business negotiations, sales presentations, investment decisions, money matters, relationship and even health matters.

While Qi Men can be used for a wide variety of purposes, in this book I choose to retain the original flavour of 'war' as per the Art of War. Therefore, I will use examples in the context of battle. You can, on your own with some simple adjustments and a little thought, interpret what I write metaphorically as you see fit. For instance, when I speak about two Generals, you can think of two rival CEOs instead if that brings meaning to your interpretation.

Here's how we address each one of the 7 Criteria "七計" in my Qi Men Dun Jia Warcraft System:

1) Which of the two leaders is imbued with the better Moral Compass?

There are two steps to determine this:

a) First, to determine which leader is imbued with a better Moral Compass, we need to analyze the condition of the Year Stem Palace. The Year Stem is the outermost Pillar of the forecast hour's BaZi Chart. Typically, the Year Stem is analyzed to determine vision, aspiration, beliefs and culture.

As the Year Stem represents a leader's vision and his *Tao*, its Palace can be said to represent the leader's Moral Compass. The Palace can therefore reveal whether or not a leader is passionate and whether he or she has the right moral fibre, the right guiding compass, vision or 'Tao' for the forecasted project or matter. You can see how much they believe in their cause.

b) Next we must study the Year Stem Palace's relationship with the Hour Stem Palace. In Qi Men, the Hour Stem usually represents a subject of interest. In business analysis, it can be taken to represent a project, subordinates and staff, for instance, depending on your line of inquiry.

2) Which of the two generals has the most ability? 將孰有能

a) In Qi Men Dun Jia, a Chart is plotted based on the Forecast Hour's BaZi. The Year Stem in a Qi Men Chart, or the outermost layer or Pillar, represents the highest authority and thus its contents are representative of the quality of leadership in a given organization.

In Qi Men, there are 10 Stems. The Jia Stem is the Grand Marshall, the leader of all the Heavenly Stems. It plays a very important role in the Qi Men Dun Jia system. One of the biggest threats to Jia Stem is Geng Metal because according to the Five Element relationship, Metal counters Wood. This means that Metal will harm and hurt the Jia (Grand Marshall).

To protect the Grand Marshall, other Stems need to help. The Yi, Bing and Ding Stems are known as the 3 Nobles 三奇. They have their own unique ability to protect Jia from being attacked by Geng Metal.

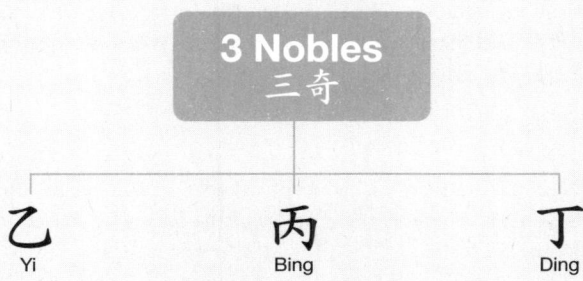

The name Qi Men Dun Jia literally means *Mystical Door, Hiding Jia*. In every Qi Men Chart, the Jia Stem is hidden in one of the 9 Palaces. The Palace or box that contains the Jia Stem is called the Lead Stem Palace. Jia can hide in one of the 6 Crescents' Palaces. The 6 Crescents are made up of Wu, Ji, Geng, Xin, Ren and Gui Stems. They are distributed around these 9 boxes.

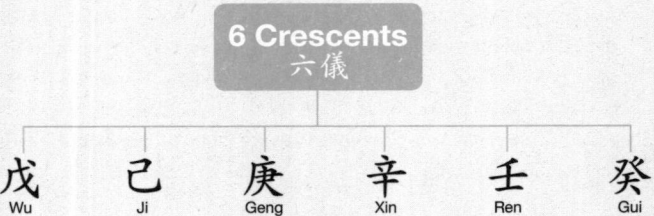

In this context, the Lead Stem represents the highest authority or leadership in an organization or in an army's camp.

Therefore, if we are looking to analyze the quality of a leader's vision in an organization (his or her ability) we must first find the location of the Lead Stem (Jia) in the Chart and then assess the quality of the Palace it is residing in.

b) Next, to compare the ability of a leader in relation to his or her opponents', compare the contents of the Day Stem Palace with the Month Stem Palace.

The Day Stem represents Self and the Month Stem represents the Opponent. The Day and Month Stem Palaces also represent middle level management.

We have to assess the Palace of Self and it's relationship with the Palace of Month Stem to determine the capabilities and competence of both leaders. We do this by assessing the 5 Elements relationship of these two Palaces.

c) To assess a leader's success in his leadership, we must also know the quality of his people. After all, a skilled leader without a skilled 'army' cannot win. In a modern context this means supporters, staff and hired help. The Hour Stem in Qi Men is usually taken to represent a leader's army.

3) With whom lie the advantages derived from Heaven and Earth? 天地孰得

In a Qi Men Chart, the Hour Stem Palace describes the current Heavenly Climate. To assess the Heavenly Climate or the conditions in which a battle will take place, we need to look at the 9 Stars that govern that Palace. As mentioned in the beginning of the book, Zhuge Liang 諸葛亮 once used the knowledge of Qi Men to forecast the direction of the wind and thus launch a successful attack against his enemy Cao Cao 曹操 in the Battle of The Red Cliffs.

Here's a breakdown of what the 9 Stars represent in terms of climate and weather conditions:

The 9 Stars	Heavenly Climate
天蓬星 The Heavenly Grass	Cloudy and rainy
天芮星 The Heavenly Grain	Misty, dew, gloomy
天沖星 The Heavenly Destructor	Lightning, storm
天輔星 The Heavenly Assistant	Rainbow, wind, pleasant and breezy
天禽星 The Heavenly Bird	Typhoon, very strong winds
天柱星 The Heavenly Pillar	Sunny
天心星 The Heavenly Heart	Frost, cold
天任星 The Heavenly Ambassador	Dust storm
天英星 The Heavenly Hero	Sunny, hot climate

4) On which side is discipline most rigorously enforced (whose leadership is more effective)? 法令執行

As mentioned earlier, the Year Stem Palace of a Qi Men Chart represents leadership. It can tell us about the capabilities and power of whoever is in charge.

To determine which side is more effective in their leadership, we must consider the Year Stem alongside the Envoy Location. The Envoy Location represents the effectiveness or ineffectiveness of an action. The Envoy is also known as the *Lead Door*.

Here's how we can locate the Envoy Door in a Qi Men Chart:

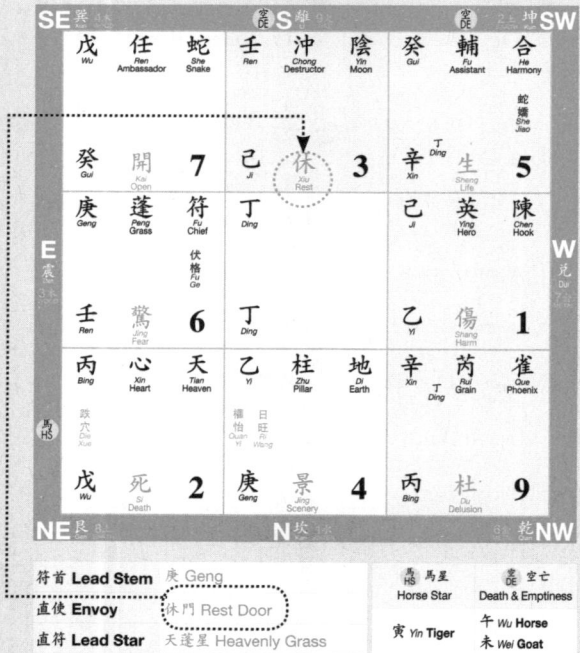

5) Which side has the stronger army? 兵眾孰強

To determine which side has the stronger "army", first recall that the Hour Stem represents action and force. In this case, we can wish to think about the force of two opposing armies. Thus, for the purpose of this question, the Hour Stem represents the manpower (ability to act) on each side.

To compare your army with an opponent, you must study the relationship between the Hour Stem Palace and other Palaces: namely the Day Stem and Month Stem Palaces. (Representing the Self and Opponent, respectively)

6) On which side are officers and men more highly trained? 士卒孰練

To find out which side has a higher standard of training, you must identify and assess the Door of Delusion in the Qi Men Chart. The Door of Delusion represents academic performance, training and education. It belongs to the Wood element. The Door of Delusion governs the transfer of information, instructions, skills and knowledge to others.

Knowing that the Hour Stem represents action and results, you must perform a comparative analysis of the relationship between the Hour Stem Palace and the Palace that contains the Door of Delusion to determine who has more highly skilled officers and men managers and staff in a modern context.

7) In which army is there the greater constancy both in reward and punishment? 賞罰孰明

Identifying which side has a better systems of punishment and reward can help you form your overall appraisal of the odds in competition.

We can answer this question by looking at the Fear Door's relationship with other Palaces. People normally act to either avoid pain or to seek pleasure. The Fear Door in Qi Men governs these two instinctive drives.

Now that we have a better understanding of Sun Tzu's 7 Criteria in relation to the Qi Men Warcraft System, let us analyse Sun Tzu's 7 Criteria based on a Qi Men forecast done on August 19, 2002 at 9.30 pm.

時 Hour	日 Day	月 Month	年 Year	
七殺 7K 乙 Yi Yin Wood	日元 DM 己 Ji Yin Earth	劫財 RW 戊 Wu Yang Earth	正財 DW 壬 Ren Yang Water	天干 Heavenly Stems
亥 Hai Pig Yin Water	未 Wei Goat Yin Earth	申 Shen Monkey Yang Metal	午 Wu Horse Yang Fire	地支 Earthly Branches
壬 Ren + Water 財 DW / 甲 Jia + Wood 官 DO	乙 Yi - Wood 殺 7K / 己 Ji - Earth 比 F / 丁 Ding - Fire 卩 IR	戊 Wu + Earth 劫 RW / 庚 Geng + Metal 傷 HO / 壬 Ren + Water 財 DW	丁 Ding - Fire 卩 IR / 己 Ji - Earth 比 F	藏干 Hidden Stems

Here is a Qi Men Chart plotted for this forecast:

Forecast Date	August 19, 2002 at 9.30 pm	
局 STRUCTURE:	日 DAY :	時 HOUR :
陰八局 YIN EIGHT	己未 Ji Wei Earth Goat	乙亥 Yi Hai Wood Pig (9pm - 10.59pm)

[Qi Men Chart diagram]

- Delusion Door
- Fear Door

符首 **Lead Stem**	己 Ji
直使 **Envoy**	驚門 Fear Door
直符 **Lead Star**	天柱星 Heavenly Pillar

馬 HS 馬星 Horse Star	空 DE 空亡 Death & Emptiness
巳 Si **Snake**	申 Shen **Monkey** 酉 You **Rooster**

In this Chart, the Day Stem for the analysis is Ji Earth and the Hour Stem is Yi Wood. The Month Stem is Wu Earth.

We must first assess the Palace in which the Day Stem resides (the Day Stem represents Self), and then analyze the Palace in which the Month Stem resides, as it represents the opponent or rival. We can make our comparisons by weighing the characteristics and contents of one against the other.

In the Li (South) Palace, where the Ji Day Stem resides, we can see a positive Structure known as the Super Assisting Structure (相佐), the Chief Deity 值符, the Heavenly Pillar 天干 (as the Lead Star) and the Earthly Stem Yi Noble 乙奇. All these are positive components. This configuration indicates a visionary leader who is reliable and determined, armed with the problem solving skills to overcome obstacles and challenges. In other words, this arrangement is indicative of good leadership abilities.

Additionally, this Li Palace (Fire element) also counters the Month Stem Palace, which is Qian (Northwest) Palace, a Metal element Palace. The Month Stem is 'Wu 戊' and it resides in the Qian (Northwest) Palace. This Palace has a negative Door (Fear Door 驚門), an inauspicious Deity (Black Tortoise 玄武) and a negative Structure. This arrangement tells us that the competitor or rival has in this case suffers from poor leadership.

Overall, the Chart indicates that the leader in question has far greater leadership abilities than his or her competitor.

The Hour Stem represents the army in the context of warfare. In the modern context of business, however, the Hour Stem can also represent the employees, manpower, supporters or people working within an organization.

In the same Chart, the Hour Stem is Yi 乙 and it is residing in the Zhen (East) Palace. We can observe that in this Palace, there are favourable Structures (Yi Noble Rising Palace 乙奇昇殿 and Real Deception 真詐) present with a positive Door (Life Door 生門) and an auspicious Deity (Great Moon 太陰). These positive components can be considered an auspicious sign as they denote a strong and well-trained army or team.

In this Chart, the Hour Stem Palace (Zhen 震 East) produces the Day Stem Palace (Li 離 South). In the Five Element Relationship, the Wood element produces the Fire element. Because productive relationships are good, this denotes that the forecaster has the stronger advantage in terms of manpower.

The Month Stem Palace counters the Hour Stem Palace. The Qian Palace (Metal) counters the Zhen Palace (Wood). This is an inauspicious sign for the opponent. His or her army may be well-trained but they are not committed to their leader or their vision. Therefore, the individual in question has an army that is well-trained and better prepared for the war effort than his or her opponent.

By considering all these indications, we can conclude that the forecaster has an edge when it comes to leadership and manpower in comparison with their rival.

Example:

Let's consider a real life example to show how Qi Men can work in conjunction with Sun Tzu's principles. A client, Mr. Yeoh, asked me to perform a forecast for a major business meeting he was about to attend. He wanted to bid on a very important project for a major client and the stakes were high – he had bet everything on the pitch and if he was not awarded the deal, his company would have to close. To make matters more serious, a competitor was also in the running for the deal.

Mr. Yeoh asked me to forecast the outcome of his pitch in order to determine whether he should proceed on the day and time in question or reschedule in some way for better odds.

He approached me on August 14, 2013 at 11.07am and I plotted a Chart based on this timing.

時 Hour	日 Day	月 Month	年 Year	
偏財 IW 丙 Bing Yang Fire	日元 DM 壬 Ren Yang Water	偏印 IR 庚 Geng Yang Metal	劫財 RW 癸 Gui Yin Water	天干 Heavenly Stems
午 Wu **Horse** Yang Fire	子 Zi **Rat** Yang Water	申 Shen **Monkey** Yang Metal	巳 Si **Snake** Yin Fire	地支 Earthly Branches
丁 己 Ding Ji - Fire - Earth 財 DW 官 DO	癸 Gui - Water 劫 RW	戊 庚 壬 Wu Geng Ren + Earth + Metal + Water 殺 7K 卩 IR 比 F	庚 丙 戊 Geng Bing Wu + Metal + Fire + Earth 卩 IR 才 IW 殺 7K	千藏 Hidden Stems

72 Joey Yap's Qi Men Dun Jia Sun Tzu Warcraft

This is the Chart I plotted for him:

Forecast Date	August 14, 2013 at 11.07am	
局 **STRUCTURE:**	日 **DAY:**	時 **HOUR:**
陰二局 **YIN TWO**	壬子 Ren Zi **Water Rat**	丙午 Bing Wu **Fire Horse** (11am - 12.59pm)

Day Stem →

SE 巽 4木	S 離 9火	SW 坤 2土
壬 Ren / 柱 Zhu Pillar / 符 Fu Chief 壬刑 Ren Xing 丙 Bing **景** **1**	癸 Gui / 心 Xin Heart / 天 Tian Heaven 庚 Geng **死 Death** **6**	己 Ji / 蓬 Peng Grass / 地 Di Earth 玉女 / 己刑 Ji Xing 戊 Wu 丁 Ding **驚 Jing Fear** **8**	馬 HS
戊 Wu / 芮 Rui Grain / 蛇 She Snake 丁 Ding 戊刑 Wu Xing 乙 Yi **杜** **9**	丁 Ding	辛 Xin / 任 Ren Ambassador / 玄 Xuan Tortoise 壬 Ren **開 Kai Open** **4**	W 兌 7金
E 震 3木 空DE	丁 Ding		
庚 Geng / 英 Ying Hero / 陰 Yin Moon 庚刑 Geng Xing 辛 Xin **傷** **5**	丙 Bing / 輔 Fu Assistant / 合 He Harmony 己 Ji **生 Sheng** **7**	乙 Yi / 沖 Chong Destructor / 虎 Hu Tiger 日使 Ri Zhi / 日墓 Ri Mu 癸 Gui **休 Xiu Rest** **3**	
NE 艮 8土	N 坎 1水	NW 乾 6金	

← Month Stem

Hour Stem →

符首 **Lead Stem**	壬 Ren
直使 **Envoy**	驚門 Fear Door
直符 **Lead Star**	天柱星 Heavenly Pillar

馬HS **Horse Star**	空DE **Death & Emptiness**
申 Shen **Monkey**	寅 Yin **Tiger** 卯 Mao **Rabbit**

Here is a rundown of how you could interpret this Chart in regard to Mr. Yeoh's query. First, check the Day Stem Palace. The Day Stem represents the Self, in his case, Mr. Yeoh. The Xun (Southeast) Palace is where the Day Stem resides. So we consider this the 'Self' Palace. Fortunately, there are positive Structures (Super Assisting Structure 相佐, Green Dragon Returns 青龍返首) in this Palace. It has both the Chief Deity 值符 and the Bing Noble 丙奇 residing within it. So far, so good.

The Month Stem, which represents the business rival who will make a competing pitch, in this case resides in Gen (Northeast) Palace. This sector falls in a Death and Emptiness position. Furthermore, it also contains a negative Structure (Six Crescent Punishment Structure 六儀擊刑), the negative Xin Crescent 辛儀 and an inauspicious Door (Harm Door 傷門). The Harm Door located in the North East Palace is known as Door Compelling Palace (門迫). From this arrangement we can deduce that in comparison to his rival; Mr. Yeoh has the advantage in terms of leadership abilities.

We also want to find out the likely outcome of Mr. Yeoh making his pitch on the date in question. To see the outcome of the activity, we must read the Hour Stem Palace. In this case the Hour Stem is Bing 丙, so we look at the Kan (North) Palace. As observed in the Kan (North) we can see many positive Structures (Bing Noble Receives Envoy 丙奇得使 and Nobility Deception 休詐). There is also the presence of an auspicious Deity (Six Harmony六合), which represents partnership, harmonious relationships, and joint ventures. These are perfect with regards to Mr. Yeoh's pitch.

There's more good news in this Chart. The positive Star (Heavenly Assistant 天輔) residing there represents that the skills and knowledge necessary for successful execution of the bid are in place within the client's organization.

The auspicious Door (Life Door 生門) in this Palace represents success. This is the most auspicious Door of all the 8 Doors. It represents wealth and profit.

All these components reside in the North sector, in the Hour Stem Palace. This (North - Water) Palace also produces the Day Stem (Southeast - Wood) Palace. This is a clear sign that Mr Yeoh can expect a positive outcome when he makes his pitch. What's more, he will be able to fulfill his promises and produce solid results for his employer after winning it, too. His competitor, represented by the Gen (Northeast - Earth) Palace, counters the Kan (North -Water) Palace, an inauspicious sign indicating that he is fighting against the tide. He may clash against the potential employer's sensibilities and he is unlikely to land the gig.

Based on the analysis of the Qi Men Dun Jia Chart outline above, I told my client that he will succeed in presenting a winning pitch. 2 weeks later after I returned from a trip to South Africa, I heard the good news that my client Mr. Yeoh, had indeed got the deal! Fantastic.

WAGING WAR

2

ORIGINAL TEXT:

孫子曰：凡用兵之法，
馳車千駟，革車千乘，
帶甲十萬；千里饋糧，
則內外之費賓客之用，
膠漆之材，車甲之奉，
日費千金，然後十萬之師舉矣。

TRANSLITERATION:

Sun Tzu said: Operations of war involve one thousand swift chariots, one thousand heavy chariots and one hundred thousand mailed troops with the transportation of provisions over a thousand li. The expenditure at home and at the front, including the entertainment of state guests and diplomatic envoys, the cost of materials such as glue and lacquer and the expenses of maintaining of chariots and armor will amount to one thousand pieces of gold a day. Such is the cost of raising an army of a thousand men.

COMMENTARY:

Run the numbers – they never lie. Projections are used in every type of business to assess how long things will take and how much they will cost. The decision to proceed often hinges entirely on whether or not such projections show a plan to be viable.

One the core benefits of creating projections is that it should determine whether or not your plans are profitable and if it would be worth proceeding. It is for this reason that a strategic budget is often a requirement in finance. If you approach a lender with a flawed business plan and meagre figures on paper then they won't approve your application. If, however, your planning indicates that there are wild returns to be made then you can of course expect their investment. Knowing the full costs before you begin allows you to allocate enough resources and time to your plan and ensure that you succeed. In addition, you may spot ways to optimize and save money while drawing up projections that would have gone overlooked. Accuracy is critical and all these benefits depend upon it. Working on the basis of an inaccurate projection can take you into troubled waters and strand you there. There are many errors of thinking that can lead to a poor appraisal of cost. Unrealistic expectations, over-optimistic deadlines and other poor assumptions can help you put together an appealing plan, but very little else. Make sure that you don't succumb to optimistic bias in your own planning and perform your own independent research to verify the facts and figures presented in the plans of others who may have been too generous in their thinking.

Finally, remember that planning is only one half of the journey. At some point you must get started and wage war! Remember that too much thinking can create problems that did not exist in the first place. Most of the problems we have in life are caused by two reasons: we act without thinking (no strategy) or we keep thinking without acting (no execution).

ORIGINAL TEXT:

其用戰也，勝久則鈍兵挫銳，攻城則力屈，久暴師則國用不足。夫鈍兵，挫銳，屈力，殫貨，則諸侯乘其弊而起，雖有智者，不能善其後矣！故兵聞拙速，未睹巧之久也；夫兵久而國利者，未之有也。故不盡知用兵之害者，則不能盡知用兵之利也。

TRANSLITERATION:

In military operations, any long and drawn out conflict will deplete your army's strength and dull your edge, even if you are winning. A protracted siege of a city will weary your troops; a lengthy campaign will be costly and test the limit of your resources. When your weapons are blunt, your ardor dampened, your strength exhausted and your treasury spent, neighboring rulers will take advantage of your weakness to rise against you. In such circumstances, even the most knowledgeable of advisers will not be able to guide you to safety. Though the pitfalls of being hasty are obvious, you should never forget to consider the difficulties of prolonged engagement, regardless of it's nature or the quality of your planning. It is never beneficial for a country to endure a lengthy war. The general who fails to understand the hazards of military operations cannot have a full comprehension of the vantage.

COMMENTARY:

Rapid execution is the best execution. Always strive to achieve your goals as quickly as possible (without compromising on the important details, of course). As the old expression goes, time is money. This is true because as time passes, the cost of completing your plans is compounded. In addition, the longer something takes, the easier it is to lose motivation, lose focus and lose track. A damaging cycle of exhaustion and mediocrity can take hold while you lose ground as others advance. In competition, standing still means failure - if you idle, your competitors may advance too far ahead, leading to your ruin. The opportunity you initially planned to seize may vanish before you're ready. A common fallacy for many is that it often seems cheaper to break a project or objective down into smaller parts and move forward at a leisurely pace. What is neglected in this way of thinking are the hidden costs of wasted time. Think about the missed opportunities, the turnover of team members who must be brought up to speed, the ever changing marketplace which must be satisfied, the rise and fall of customer tastes and needs. It goes on and on and on. As time passes, risk increases and the potential return is diminished and offset by the increased investment in realizing it. Acting quickly mitigates all of these problems.

So, to increase your effectiveness, look far beyond the short term costs and think about the bigger picture. Never lose sight of it. Break down your plan into milestones and smaller battles so that you can measure progress with ease, which increases motivation and discourages procrastination. Prioritize for maximum profit. Manage your time just like any other resource and it will serve you.

ORIGINAL TEXT:

善用兵者，役不再籍，
糧不三載，取用于國，
因糧于敵，故軍食可足也。

TRANSLITERATION:

Those adept in employing troops do not require a second levy of conscripts or more than two supplies of provisions. Having brought supplies from their own country they will then obtain provisions from the enemy state, in that way the army can be provided for without depleting state resources.

COMMENTARY:

When launching a new endeavour, aim to go from red to black as quickly as possible. The sooner you can end your reliance on the fiscal support of others and gain independence, the sooner you can move forward. This should be your top priority - get in gear and get moving towards profit as soon as possible.

One way in which you can get ahead fast is by learning to identify and capitalize on the prior investments, successes, failures and resources of others.

It takes a great deal of time and effort to build the foundations of success, much less to reach its greatest heights. The good news is that other people have done so before you and there is simply no need for you to repeat their struggles. Get close to your successful rivals and learn from their efforts. Study their history. Don't repeat their costly mistakes. Use and benefit from their experiences and precedents.

The same thinking applies to social networks, contacts and resources – virtually anything that must be built or acquired at the expense of time and money. Build and capitalize on connections with those who have already acquired what you seek.

ORIGINAL TEXT:

國之貧于師者遠輸，
遠輸則百姓貧，近于師者貴賣，
貴賣則百姓財竭，
財竭則急于丘役，力屈財殫，
中原內虛于家，百姓之費，
十去其七，公家之費，破車罷馬，
甲冑矢弩，戟楯蔽櫓，
丘牛大車，十去其六。

TRANSLITERATION:

When a country is impoverished by war it is generally because of the cost of transporting supplies to a distant place. The expense involved in transportation can leave a population near destitute. The cost of commodities will generally soar close to the battleground or near where troops are stationed; these high prices will also be place strain on common people's resources with dire repercussions. The impact of this financial depletion will mean that every household is stripped bare, seven tenths of the people's wealth will be exhausted and six tenths of the state's resources will be spent. Chariots will be broken, horses worn out and weapons lost, destroyed or blunted including armor, helmets, arrows, crossbows, halberds, bucklers, spears and shields, draught oxen will be tired and heavy wagons in need of repair.

COMMENTARY:

The damaging consequences of doing battle far from home that Sun Tzu describes are symbolic of the results of aiming too high or throwing too far in any situation. The greater the objective, the higher its cost. Sometimes that cost may be too much to bear. When faced with information that suggests your targets are unrealistic, you must either set more realistic goals or prioritize so that you can reach profit in a shorter timeframe.

When you set goals that are out of reach when you operate outside your means, there is a price to pay – the price of disappointment and possibly failure. Being realistic is extremely important. Without due caution, you can find yourself deep in quicksand, without the strength to escape! Excessive borrowing and over-spending on credit cards serve as a common cautionary tale; some people spend a great deal more than they should and then find themselves unable even to pay off their debts, owing to accumulating interest.

In the world of commerce, amateur business leaders often try to run before they can walk. This tendency is commonly observed in start-ups who spend massive amounts of their capital on things that should come later. Trendy office space in a prime location, fancy furniture and equipment, too many employees, etc. When profits fail to materialize at the rate predicted, desperate damage control begins. Unfortunately, the very lack of operating funds required for damage control also means that the business in question lacks the means to turn things around. They are trapped and slide into bankruptcy, unable to invest in anything that could create the real growth they desperately need. The typical result? The business is forced to close its doors because it did not operate within its means.

Growth must happen at a sustainable pace. The leader must keep a low or better yet - zero overhead growth. Most people are busy fighting the external battle and they overlook the internal battle. The external battles are sales growth, career growth and increasing market share. The internal battles are cost control and proper financial management. This is the same for whether you are running your own business or running your own life. Prioritize and manage your time so that you begin generating results in the shortest timeframe, allowing new goals to be set. Figure out your limits before you are ruined by them. Even if you crawl to victory, what is the point in achieving something if it leaves you destitute? How will you fight the next battle?

ORIGINAL TEXT:

故智將務食于敵，食敵一鍾，
當吾二十鍾，萁稈一石，
當我二十石。

TRANSLITERATION:

A wise commander should strive to gain food and provisions from the enemy state. Each zhong of food taken from the enemy is equivalent to twenty zhong transported from home, one dan of enemy supplies is worth twenty dan supplied by the state.

COMMENTARY:

Learn to take what you can directly from your competitor. You must think in abstraction about how to do this – it does not mean you should literally rob them. Instead, build upon their effort, learn from their expertise and use their infrastructure. There is no need to spend your own money when you can benefit from their existing investments.

For instance, if they have a proven model for success that is more effective than your own, adopt it and immediately gain from their improved level of experience, without going through the process of acquiring it through trial and error. Patterns of excellence are meant to be duplicated and improvised. Recognizing and then building upon their proven successes will save you time and resources immensely. This approach will allow you to leapfrog them entirely in due course.

ORIGINAL TEXT:

故殺敵者怒也，取敵之利者貨也。
故車戰，得車十乘以上，
賞其先得者，而更其旌旗，
車雜而乘之，卒善而養之，
是謂勝敵而益強。

TRANSLITERATION:

If you want to slay the enemy, you must first rouse your troops to anger. If you want to plunder the enemy you must offer your troops material reward. To this end, following a chariot battle in which ten chariots have been captured, those who captured the first chariot should be rewarded, the enemy's flags replaced with our own, the captured chariots combined with yours and mounted by your men. Captured soldiers should be treated well and taken care of. In this way, you are able to gain in strength while defeating your enemy.

COMMENTARY:

Get your team fired up about your targets and create a sense of urgency. Huge morale creates huge results. Unify them with team building exercises, group work and fair, demonstrative leadership. Communicate the importance of the shared cause to them. Articulate your vision in absolute clarity. Make your team own this vision. Make it their vision. Reward effort just as much as achievement to help ensure that everyone brings their A-game to the table, every time. To motivate in other ways, offer rewards both material and social in nature– recognition, fame, awards, promotions, bonuses and simple acknowledgements are all good ways to not only create loyalty but also encourage friendly competition within your team.

Keep an eye out for talent and newly available people who hail from the other side of the fence. You never know what they might bring to the table and what insight they can bring from their past experiences.

Remember, it is more profitable to subjugate your enemy than to ruin them. Let this wisdom permeate all of your competitive plans.

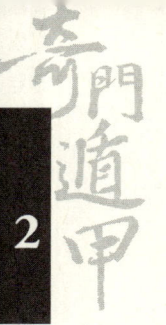

ORIGINAL TEXT:

故兵貴勝，不貴久；
故知兵之將，民之司命，
國家安危之主也。

TRANSLITERATION:

In military operations it is vital to aim for a speedy victory and to avoid a prolonged campaign. The commander of the armed forces has it in his power to determine the fate of the people and the security of the nation.

COMMENTARY:

Every leadership position confers a burden of responsibility because everyone you lead relies upon your vision and your decision making. Take this responsibility seriously and never forget it. Prioritize your targets, create your strategy and act decisively so that you can reach your goals as rapidly as possible.

Don't hesitate, move forward and grow as quickly as the circumstances allow you to. Constantly be on the lookout for new ways to speed up the journey to your goals. As a leader, it's ultimately up to you to make it happen! Leave no stone unturned and work hard.

QI MEN DUN JIA:

A Qi Men Dun Jia Chart can help you allocate resources in keeping with Sun Tzu's time proven principles.

This chapter focuses on the cost of waging war and the need to allocate resources intelligently and in sufficient quantities for success. It's no good having a brilliant plan if you don't have or can't assign sufficient funding to see it through to completion! Equally similar, you can throw a great deal of money at a terrible plan and you still won't get results. The resources you have available and how you use them determine your results; Qi Men Dun Jia can be of assistance in this area.

In Qi Men, resources are usually governed by the Wu 戊 Stem. Specifically, the Wu Stem represents capital and cash. Therefore, when seeking information about any kind of resources, your focus should be on the Wu Stem. In modern times, Wu Stem represents capital while the Life Door 生門 represents profits. This explains why any modern investment and wealth orientated Qi Men forecast deals with the Wu Stem and the Life Door.

Here's how to locate the Wu Stem and the Life Door in a Chart. In this example, the Chart was plotted on 27 April, 2013 at 11.15am.

作戰 2

Forecast Date: 27 April, 2013 at 11.15am

局 STRUCTURE:	日 DAY:	時 HOUR:
陽八局 YANG EIGHT	癸亥 Gui Hai — Water Pig	戊午 Wu Wu — Earth Horse (11am - 12.59pm)

SE 巽 4木		S 離 9火		SW 坤 2土	
辛 Xin / 芮 Rui Grain / 陰 Yin Moon (丁 Ding) 權怡星旺鬼假星使 朱投 Zhu Tou		乙 Yi / 柱 Zhu Pillar / 合 He Harmony 日使 Ri Shi		丙 Bing / 心 Xin Heart / 陳 Chen Hook 月使 Yue Shi	馬 HS
癸 Gui / 死 Si Death	**7**	己 Ji / 驚 Jing Fear	**3**	辛 Xin (丁 Ding) / 開 Kai Open	**5**
己 Ji / 英 Ying Hero / 蛇 She Snake		丁 Ding		庚 Geng / 蓬 Peng Grass / 雀 Que Phoenix 奇格 Qi Ge	
E 震 3木 壬 Ren / 景 Jing Scenery	**6**	丁 Ding		乙 Yi / 休 Xiu Rest	**1** W 兌 7金
癸 Gui / 輔 Fu Assistant / 符 Fu Chief		壬 Ren / 沖 Chong Destructor / 天 Tian Heaven		戊 Wu / 任 Ren Ambassador / 地 Di Earth 龍返 Long Fan	
戊 Wu / 杜 Du Delusion	**2**	庚 Geng / 傷 Shang Harm	**4**	丙 Bing / 生 Sheng Life	**9**
NE 艮 8土 空 DE		N 坎 1水			NW 乾 6金

符首 **Lead Stem**	癸 Gui		馬 HS 馬星 Horse Star	空 DE 空亡 Death & Emptiness
直使 **Envoy**	杜門 Delusion Door		申 Shen **Monkey**	子 Zi **Rat**
直符 **Lead Star**	天輔星 Heavenly Assistant			丑 Chou **Ox**

The task here is to analyze the condition of the Palace where the Wu Stem resides. In the above Chart, the Wu Heavenly Stem is residing in the Qian (Northwest) Palace. Together in this Qian Palace we can also see the auspicious Life Door 生門, Heavenly Ambassador Star 天任星 and Nine Earth Deity 九地. All these are auspicious components.

The Life Door itself governs profits. This indicates that there are abundant and healthy levels of financial resources available.

A Qi Men strategist can forecast the condition or availability of capital resources by analyzing the condition of the Wu Heavenly Stem. This means looking at the set-up of the Charts: the Stars, Deities, Doors and the Earthly Stem which the Wu Stem shares a sector with. If the components are auspicious, this means the capital resources are sufficient. If the components are negative, this means the resources are insufficient or are at an unhealthy level. The auspicious and inauspicious components are discussed in the previous Chapter.

A sector may not be directional alone; it may also describe Internal or External conditions as well. Every Qi Men Chart has Internal and External Palaces. This is explained in the following Qi Men Chart which was plotted on 6 March, 2011 at 5.30am:

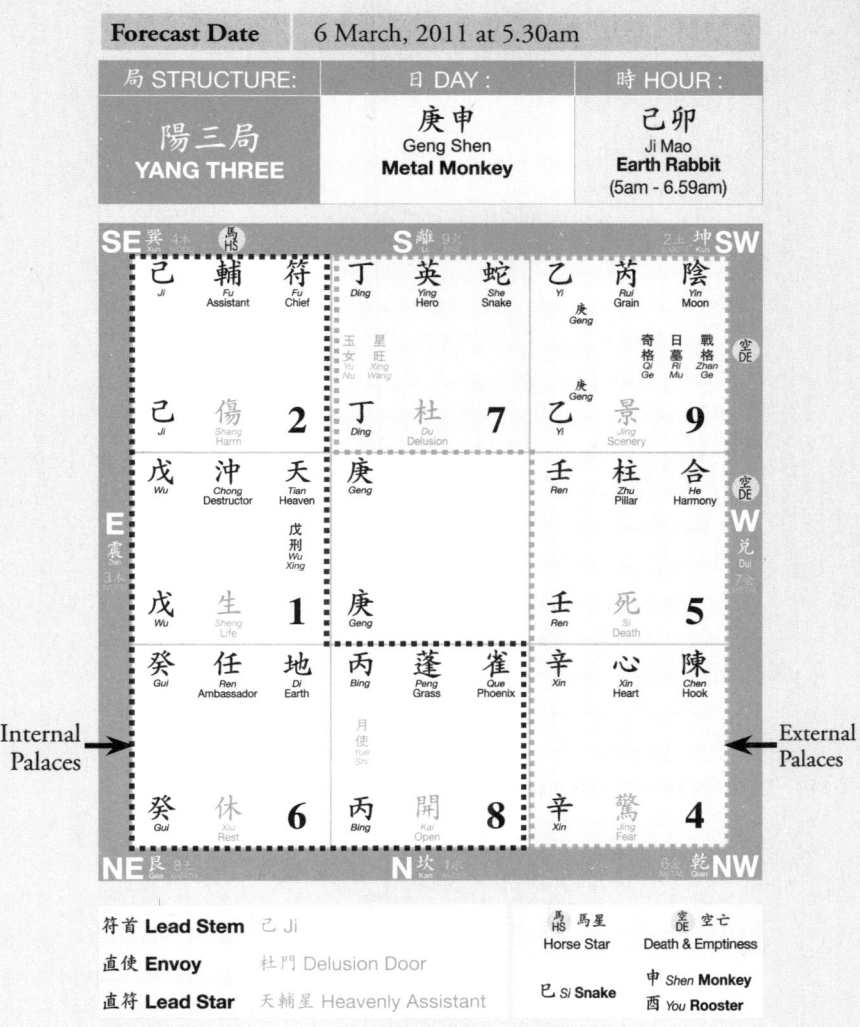

Internal Palaces represent resources that are close as well as short-term goals, actions or events. In war or competition, Internal Palaces represent resources or supplies that are available and which fall within the grasp of this individual. That is to say, they may be used by the individual in question. Think about liquid assets and set-aside operating cash as being examples of "close" resources.

Just as the Internal Palaces show us what is close at hand, the External Palaces represent what is distant in time and availability. In a war, for example, they represent resources that are distant in time, location or availability which are difficult to acquire. The cost of doing so may be so high that it would not be profitable to do so.

By looking at the position of the Useful God 用神 (the Qi Men Focal Point) - the Wu Stem in this case – we can determine the availability of desirable resources to this individual. By understanding this, we can say whether or not they are in a position to act upon their ideas. In addition, the connection between the Day Stem Palace's position and the Hour Stem Palace's position reveals the time factor and chances the person's strategy (for which they seek resources) will be a successful one.

We need to check the relationship between the Wu Stem Palace and Self Palace to determine the amount of resources (if Wu Stem Palace produces the Self Palace) available.

If the Wu Stem is in the External Palace and the Day Stem which represents Self - is in Internal Palace, the resources are distant in time, place or availability.

Example:

In this analysis, the Chart was plotted for 2 January, 2009 at 11.49pm. The Day Stem is Ding 丁 Fire and it is residing in the Northeast Palace. The Wu 戊 Stem Palace is the South Palace.

時 Hour	日 Day	月 Month	年 Year	
正官 DO 壬 Ren Yang Water	日元 DM 丁 Ding Yin Fire	正印 DR 甲 Jia Yang Wood	傷官 HO 戊 Wu Yang Earth	天干 Heavenly Stems
絕 Extinction 子 Zi Rat Yang Water	冠 Youth 未 Wei Goat Yin Earth	絕 Extinction 子 Zi Rat Yang Water	絕 Extinction 子 Zi Rat Yang Water	地支 Earthly Branches
癸 Gui - Water 殺 7K	乙 Yi - Wood 卩 IR / 己 Ji - Earth 食 EG / 丁 Ding - Fire 比 F	癸 Gui - Water 殺 7K	癸 Gui - Water 殺 7K	藏干 Hidden Stems

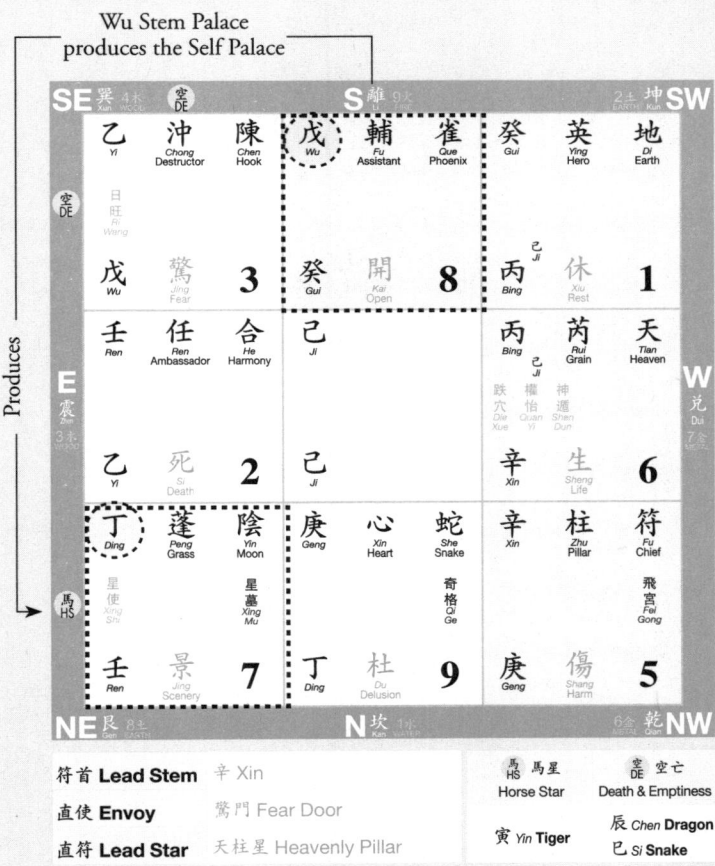

Forecast Date	2 January, 2009 at 11.49pm	
局 STRUCTURE:	日 DAY :	時 HOUR :
陽四局 YANG FOUR	丁未 Ding Wei **Fire Goat**	庚子 Geng Zi **Metal Rat** (11pm - 12.59am)

符首 **Lead Stem**	辛 Xin	馬 HS 馬星 Horse Star	空 DE 空亡 Death & Emptiness
直使 **Envoy**	驚門 Fear Door		
直符 **Lead Star**	天柱星 Heavenly Pillar	寅 Yin **Tiger**	辰 Chen **Dragon** 巳 Si **Snake**

In this Chart, the Wu Stem Palace produces the Self Palace which indicates that a great deal of resources and capital are readily available. This is because the Fire (Palace) produces Earth (Palace) element in the 5 Elements relationship.

Although this is prosperous, we must also consider the External and Internal conditions of the Chart to see the complete picture. We can see that the Wu Stem Palace is in External portion of the Chart, while Self Palace is residing in the Internal section. Since the Wu Stem is in External Plate and the Day Stem is in Internal Plate, this means that the capital or resources described are distant and hard to reach. It may be hard to acquire them and the benefits of doing so must be calculated and considered before a decision to do so is made.

In modern day Qi Men usage, this analysis technique has massive utility in regard to investments or business growth planning. You can use a Qi Men Forecast to determine whether or not an investment is a wise one and when – if ever you can expect a return on it.

The following example illustrates how Qi Men can be used to help support investment related decision making. Granted, this example may go over your head if you are just beginning your studies of Qi Men but nevertheless, it demonstrates the power of Qi Men in financial planning. If you are entirely new to the subject of Qi Men, it may be worthwhile referring to some of the previous Qi Men books in this reference series before returning to this example.

In the interest of catering to readers with a wide range of skill levels, I will simplify things as much as possible in this story.

On June 1, 2012, I had a Feng Shui consultation scheduled. I plotted a Qi Men Chart for my Feng Shui sessions because I knew that my Feng Shui clients typically had questions which could be best answered using Qi Men analysis techniques. I always use the hour that I meet my client as the basis for plotting a Qi Men Chart.

This particular client stayed in a penthouse in The Binjai, a luxurious condominium in the heart of Kuala Lumpur. He had contacted me to perform an annual Feng Shui check up and to answer a specific question. He wanted to purchase his friend's business at a cost of RM90 million. The business seemed to have good growth potential and his friend simply wanted to cash out and retire. Obviously, given the money involved, this was not a trivial investment decision and so he sought a Qi Men Forecast in order to determine whether or not he should proceed with the acquisition.

I plotted a Qi Men Chart based on the hour of the meeting, which is shown below:

時 Hour	日 Day	月 Month	年 Year	
正官 DO / 戊 Wu / Yang Earth	日元 DM / 癸 Gui / Yin Water	食神 EG / 乙 Yi / Yin Wood	劫財 RW / 壬 Ren / Yang Water	天干 Heavenly Stems
絕 Extinction / 午 Wu / Horse / Yang Fire	胎 Conceived / 巳 Si / Snake / Yin Fire	胎 Conceived / 巳 Si / Snake / Yin Fire	養 Nourishing / 辰 Chen / Dragon / Yang Earth	地支 Earthly Branches
丁 Ding - Fire 才 IW / 己 Ji - Earth 殺 7K	庚 Geng + Metal 印 DR / 丙 Bing + Fire 財 DW / 戊 Wu + Earth 官 DO	庚 Geng + Metal 印 DR / 丙 Bing + Fire 財 DW / 戊 Wu + Earth 官 DO	癸 Gui - Water 比 F / 戊 Wu + Earth 官 DO / 乙 Yi - Wood 食 EG	藏干 Hidden Stems

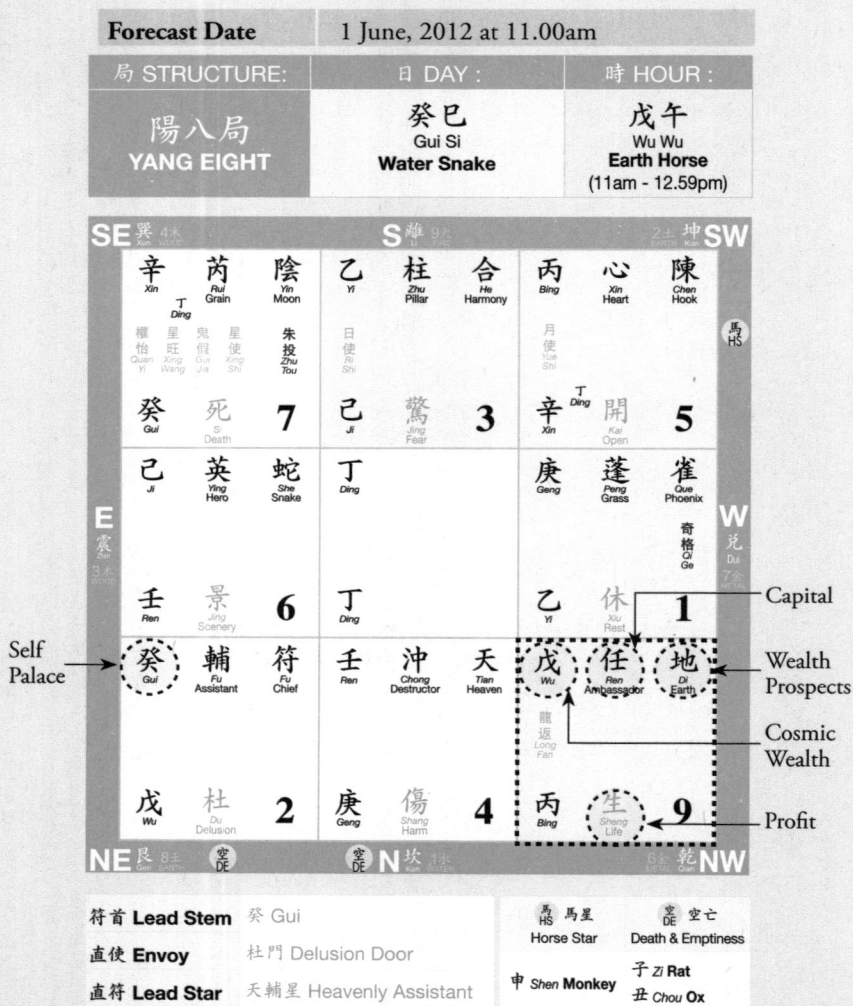

符首 **Lead Stem**	癸 Gui
直使 **Envoy**	杜門 Delusion Door
直符 **Lead Star**	天輔星 Heavenly Assistant

| 馬 馬星 Horse Star | 空 空亡 Death & Emptiness |
| 申 Shen Monkey | 子 Zi Rat / 丑 Chou Ox |

In this Chart, the Day Stem is Gui 癸 and it is located in the Gen (Northeast) sector. The Hour Stem is Wu 戊 and it is located alongside in the Qian (Northwest) sector.

For any investment related forecast, it is necessary to focus on the condition of the Wu Heavenly Stem and the Life Door 生門. To this end, the Useful God 用神 (Focal Point) for the purpose of this analysis is the Wu Heavenly Stem and the Life Door.

As usual, the Day Stem represents the Self, in this case, my client, as I was working on his behalf. The subject of the Forecast - the acquisition - is represented by the Hour Stem which is located in the Qian (Northwest) Palace.

For matters of finance or investment, we must pay attention to the Wu Stem which represents capital or cash. This Chart shows that the Hour Stem which represents the acquisition and the Useful God (focal point) lie in the same Palace. This makes our analysis more convenient. Next we must analyze the condition of the Wu Heavenly Stem in the Qian (Northwest) Palace.

In this Chart, The Wu Stem resides within a Palace along with the auspicious Life Door. In Qi Men, the Life Door represents profit. This means the acquisition is likely to be profitable. Additionally, the Life Door in the Qian (Northwest) Palace is in a favorable location. Furthermore, the quality of the Wu Stem benefits from the presence of the Heavenly Ambassador Star 天任星. This Star is also known as the Wealth Star. Its influence leads to good financial prospects. The Deity in charge of this Palace is the Nine Earth 九地. This is yet another good sign, as the Nine Earth is in charge of cosmic wealth matters. This means that the universe will bring a positive force to bear on the acquisition my client was considering.

Moving forward in our analysis, we must analyze the "relationship" between the subject matter of the forecast – the acquisition - and the Self – my client. In other words, we must assess the relationship between the Qian (Northwest) Palace (subject matter) and the Self (Northeast) Palace.

The Qian (Northwest) Palace is of the Metal element while the Gen (Northeast) Palace belongs to the Earth element. In this case, the Self Palace produces the Qian Palace, indicating an outflow of energy.

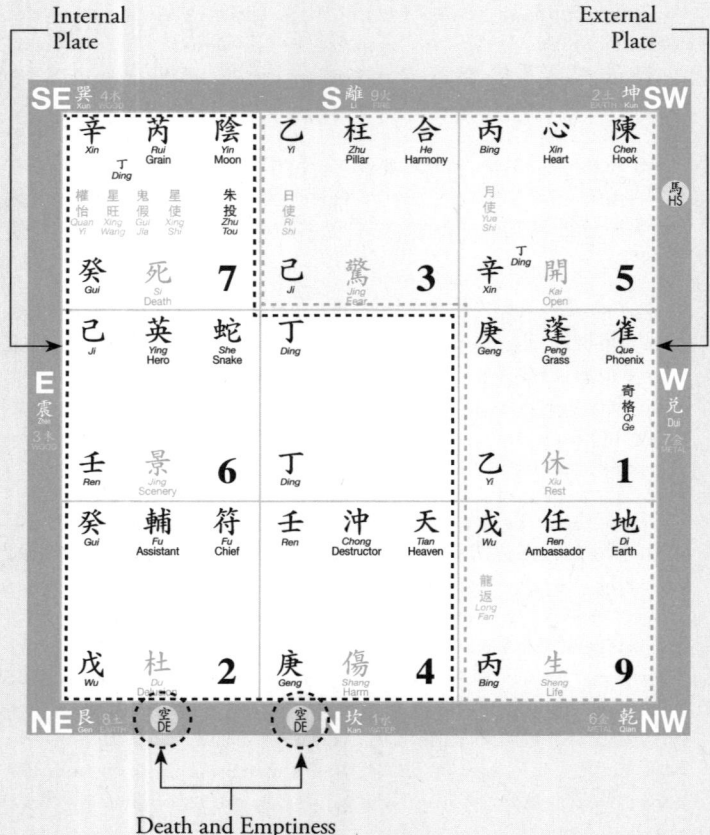

Death and Emptiness

Secondly, we can see that the Gen (Northeast) Palace contains Death and Emptiness 空亡 (DE). This indicates a 'void' Palace. Thirdly, the Self Palace (Gen - Northeast) is in the Internal Plate while the Subject Matter (Qian - Northwest) is at the External Plate. The final word is that it will be profitable for the client to buy the business, due to the quality of the Qian Palace but that it will take a long time before the client sees a return on this investment, in light of the reasons above.

Hearing this news, my client asked when exactly he could expect to see a return on his investment. I told him that he will see profits by year 2015. I knew this because the *Death and Emptiness* is in the Chou 丑 (Ox) sector of the Northeast palace. 2015 is a Goat 未 (Wei) Year and Goat clashes with the Ox (according to the theory of the 6 Clashes), thereby removing the Emptiness, and filling up the void in the Chart.

My client went ahead and bought the new business from his friend. At the time of writing, he has already turned a profit and it is now his intention to sell the business in 2015. As indicated in the Qi Men analysis in 2012, he has done well from this business venture.

OFFENSIVE STRATEGY 謀攻

3

ORIGINAL TEXT:

孫子曰：凡用兵之法，
全國爲上，破國次之；
全旅爲上，破旅次之；
全卒爲上，破卒次之；
全伍爲上，破伍次之。
是故百戰百勝，非善之善者也；
不戰而屈人之兵，善之善者也。

TRANSLITERATION:

Sun Tzu said: The principle of war is that it is far better for the enemy state to surrender than it is for it to be destroyed; subjugating an enemy's army is preferable to crushing them; making a battalion, company or squad kneel is better than slaughtering them.

Therefore, winning one hundred victories in one hundred battles is no proof of a commander's skill but winning one victory by subduing the enemy without shedding blood is the mark of true greatness.

COMMENTARY:

Your objective should never be to destroy or ruin your competitors – it is wasteful and small-minded. Instead, subdue them and convert them to your cause. With this strategy, you can gain twice as much. First, you remove your opponent from competition and second, you can directly increase your own power and accumulate resources as you take theirs. This can be done without direct conflict of any kind, provided that you conceal your intentions and that you are skilled in negotiation.

In the business world, the benefits of strategic alliance over rivalry and competition are well understood. Intelligent companies often seek to merge with or acquire their rivals as a means of growth. They know that it is better to subjugate your rivals than it is to duke it out in the marketplace at great, protracted expense. One difficulty in all of this is that you must make sure that any transition or rebalance of power is a profitable one for you. The incorporation of new assets, people, skills and existing customer relationships into your own operation must be worthwhile. The idea is to acquire your rival's strength but not their liabilities and problems.

To summarise; alliances, partnerships and co-operative arrangements are all preferential to direct competition. Look for genuine win-win solutions. Convince your rivals to work for you. In this way, you can 'beat' them without a fight!

ORIGINAL TEXT:

故上兵伐謀，其次伐交，
其次伐兵，其下攻城。
攻城之法，為不得已；
修櫓轒輼，具器械，三月而後成；
距闉，又三月而後已；
將不勝其忿，而蟻附之，
殺士卒三分之一，而城不拔者，
此攻之災也。

故善用兵者，屈人之兵，
而非戰也；拔人之城，而非攻
也；毀人之國，而非久也。
必以全爭于天下，故兵不頓，
利可全，此謀攻之法也。

TRANSLITERATION:

The best approach in any military operation is to gain victory by means of strategy, the next best approach is to disintegrate the enemy's alliances by means of diplomacy and the inferior method is to launch a direct attack on the enemy, storming cities and seizing territory.

The siege of cities should always be a last resort. It may take as many as three months to make mantles, get shielded vehicles ready and to prepare the necessary arms and equipment. It can take a further three months to pile up mounds of earth against the city walls. If the commanding officer becomes impatient and orders his men to swarm up the city walls like ants, the likely outcome is that he will lose a third of their number and make no dent in the city at all. Such is the potential calamity of attacking cities.

A commander, who is well-versed in military operations, should aim to secure surrender without excessive bloodshed, capture cites and strongholds without storming them and bring the enemy state to heel without engaging in protracted military operations. He must strive to gain complete victory all-under-heaven. Strategy is used in order to triumph over one's enemies with minimal struggle.

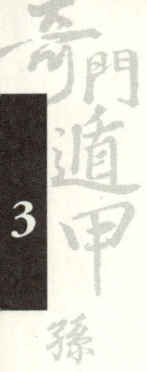

COMMENTARY:

The key here is to be creative with your growth strategies. Direct confrontation is often the most difficult way of getting what you want. Strategy, negotiation and diplomacy can create far more cost-effective opportunities for growth.

Identifying profitable ways of working with your rivals requires more finesse but the benefits are clear. You can forego any kind of protracted, expensive and difficult competition and skip straight to a profitable new paradigm.

Present your profitable collaborative plans in a way that highlights the benefits of playing ball with your competitor. Demonstrate the true beneficial value of working together. Be genuine in your win-win strategy. Many businesses, competitors or even work colleagues are happy to let you take the lead if there is security and support or if it spares them the cost of further competition. Many start-ups in Silicon Valley begin with the explicit goal of being bought out by larger corporations such as Google or Microsoft. They are content to trade dominance and autonomy for security and other benefits. In turn, larger corporations owe much of their success to the acquisition of these start-ups. Many of your competitors, rivals or colleagues will happily choose the safety of playing second fiddle if you present it to them in the right way.

In conclusion, whenever negotiation can take the place of confrontation, choose negotiation. Every "enemy" is a potential ally who has something valuable he or she can offer you. So don't burn bridges, cross the bridge and profit instead!

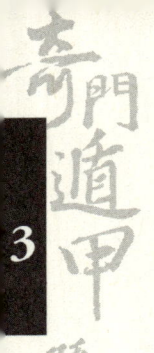

ORIGINAL TEXT:

故用兵之法，十則圍之，
五則攻之，倍則分之，
敵則能戰之，少則能守之，
不若則能避之。故小敵之堅，
大敵之擒也。

TRANSLITERATION:

Toward this end, the rule of thumb in deploying troops is to surround the enemy when your strength is ten times his, storm the enemy when your strength is five times his, to attack in a pincer motion when your strength is twice his, to resist him when you are equal, to know the way of retreat when he is stronger and to avoid him altogether when you are at your weakest.

If a weak army battles on, stubbornly refusing to take its disadvantage into account, it will surely be conquered by more powerful forces.

COMMENTARY:

You must know when you are in a position of superiority and when you have the bargaining power. If not, save your strength for another day. Look at the facts and figures and see if they support your ideas. If not, it is foolish to proceed. Skilled leaders understand that they should only act once they are already in an absolute desirable position. If you aren't in a good bargaining position, you will not be able to subjugate your competitors or make them a worthwhile offer. If you aren't in a position of strength then your top priority is to achieve it via creative maneuvering and by leveraging your unique competitive advantages. You must know your place. If you are at a disadvantage to your competitor, it pays to be aware of the fact. Consider an example where an over-ambitious person decides to challenge a superior for power without first examining if he has the proper leverage or advantage to do so. Obviously in this situation, the said person will be at a severe disadvantage and will likely be at the losing end of the deal.

Don't be afraid to bide your time and grow in capability quietly. When you are a in winning position, then it is imperative that you take the action necessary to consolidate it and secure your goal. Knowing when and when to act not to act is the key.

ORIGINAL TEXT:

夫將者，國之輔也，
輔周則國必強，輔隙則國必弱。

TRANSLITERATION:

The most senior military commander supports the ruler in governing a nation. If he performs his task well, the nation will be great; if he does not perform his task well, the nation will surely suffer.

COMMENTARY:

Choose the people who make up your inner circle wisely. You become the sum total of the group of close friends you commonly meet. You mix with a group of winners - your thoughts, mindset and behavior will be shaped like a winner. You surround yourself with dramatic, sensitive, pessimistic rumour-mongers and inadvertently, you become one of them. Always remember that a life filled with social drama and gossip indicates that you are disconnected from your Tao or your purpose. This means your life lacks meaningful goals. Therefore, it is imperative that you choose your inner circle wisely.

Make sure that your team of capable friends, staff and colleagues are loyal to you and your vision. If they aren't, you'll find yourself in a constant power struggle to assert your dominance. Everything you do may be second guessed and serious betrayals may even occur if your top people harbour ill-intent. Problems close to a leader can trickle down through an entire organization, poisoning everyone and everything if left unchecked. Choose your key staff and close friends with great patience, clarity and care. They can either extend your productivity and growth or impede them.

ORIGINAL TEXT:

故君之所以患於軍者三：
不知軍之不可以進，而謂之進，
不知軍之不可以退，而謂之退，
是爲縻軍；不知三軍之事，
而同三軍之政，則軍士惑矣；
不知三軍之權，而同三軍之任，
則軍士疑矣。三軍既惑且疑，
則諸侯之難至矣，
是謂亂軍引勝。

TRANSLITERATION:

A ruler can bring misfortune upon himself and his army in three different ways. Firstly, if he orders an advance without being aware that his army cannot go forward or if he orders a retreat while being ignorant of the fact that they cannot fall back, he may leave his troops trapped and unable to maneuver. Secondly, if he interferes with the administration of the army without understanding its internal affairs, he will create confusion and misunderstanding. Thirdly, if he becomes involved in directing the army without understanding the principles of military strategy he will create anxiety and apprehension in the minds of his men which will inevitably lead to suspicion and unrest. The princes will take advantage of this disorder and lack of cohesion to rise in revolt. This is what it meant when people say that a ruler threw his army into confusion and paved the way for the enemy's victory.

COMMENTARY:

As a leader, there are three primary ways that you can create failure.

The first is to act upon insufficient information and create a losing situation. Run the numbers, do your research and stay informed so that this cannot happen. Don't ignore the details. Seek feedback in order to stress test your plans to this end. A leader can also create a losing situation if they are too confident and have an ego that outsizes their capabilities. So know your limits.

The second is especially common – it is through micro-management. Micro-management is tantamount to self-sabotage; your staff will be unable to do their best work when they are subjected to constant interference. Sometimes leaders can throw a spanner in the works when they attempt to exert control in areas where they lack expertise or if they reach too far below their own level of authority and contradict middle management. A real leader creates inspiring conditions for their people and then guides only as and when it is necessary to do so. They trust people and they filter their instructions and wishes through the appropriate channels in their organization so everyone is on the same page.

The third way in which leaders create the conditions for failure is via a poor understanding of strategic thought itself and an inability to lead in a way that supports their vision. Poor tactical decision making can create strategic failure and the people on the ground will understand this long before this failure manifest itself. For example, a leader who does not understand strategy might be too conservative when the conditions call for confident action.

Poor leadership creates the conditions for chaos, confusion and poor results. If you fail to appreciate and avoid these three pitfalls, your people will become disenchanted with you and you will fail to hit your targets and fulfill your objectives, paving the way for your competition to get ahead.

ORIGINAL TEXT:

故知勝者有五：
知可以戰與不可以戰者勝，
識眾寡之用者勝，上下同欲者勝，
以虞待不虞者勝，
將能而君不御者勝；
此五者，知勝之道也。

TRANSLITERATION:

There are five qualities and abilities that are commonly found in a commander who can lead to victory. First, he will know when to tilt and when to yield. Second, he understands the military arts and knows how to respond according to the number of his own troops and the attitude of his enemy. Third, he leads a group of soldiers and generals who fight with one heart and think with one mind. Fourth, he is always well prepared while his enemy is unprepared. Fifth, he is wise and capable and his sovereign trusts him too well to interfere in his plans. These five qualities and skills are the hallmarks of military success.

COMMENTARY:

There are a number of common abilities and traits that are found in capable leaders. These are habits and facts that produce success. Firstly, they know when they are in a winning position and when they aren't. When they know exactly where they stand in competition, they know when to fight and when to lie low.

Second, they understand that the most strategic approach is to focus their strengths against the identified weaknesses of their competitors. They gather the necessary facts, figures and information to identify where exactly these strengths and weaknesses are for maximum results, at the minimum cost.

Third, effectual leaders have a vision that they use to inspire and unite. They create a sense of purpose and direction, bringing many different people with different areas of expertise together to operate as one stronger force.

Fourth, leaders identify opportunities before others and act before their competitors do. They are prepared for multiple outcomes and so they are never caught short when they could have avoided it.

Fifth, leaders enjoy success when they operate under conditions of freedom and support – from above and below them.

ORIGINAL TEXT:

故曰：知彼知己，百戰不殆；
不知彼而知己，一勝一負；
不知彼，不知己，每戰必敗。

TRANSLITERATION:

It is said that if you know both your enemy and yourself, you will be able to win a hundred battles and never see defeat. If you are ignorant of the enemy and are only able to know yourself, your chances of winning and losing are equal. If you know neither your enemy nor yourself, you will certainly be defeated in battle.

COMMENTARY:

Successful leaders recognize that they can't excel in every area and so they seek to identify and appreciate their own strengths and weaknesses. They know that they need to focus on their core competence in order to achieve success.

Having this kind of awareness allows you to put your best foot forward and delegate when you are out of your element. People who don't know their own shortcomings can become their own biggest obstacle – so find out what yours are if you want to work at your peak capacity. After all, if you don't know what your strengths are, how will you be able to use them? Try to make a similar assessments of others. Know what your rivals excel at and don't compete against them in that discipline. The most effectual strategies are those which pit strength against weakness, not strength against strength or weakness against weakness. Find out where these line in yourself and others so that you can create an unfair advantage and make competitive breakthroughs. This is offensive strategy in its purest form.

QI MEN DUN JIA:

In this chapter, Sun Tzu described principles that can guide successful offensive strategy. He highlights the need to know yourself, your competitor and the circumstances so that you can anticipate the results of your actions, before taking action. He also illustrates the need for strong, vision driven leadership. You can use Qi Men Dun Jia to support your offensive strategy policy making. When you combine the information you obtain from Qi Men with the principles of Sun Tzu, excellence can be achieved in all types of competition. You can use Qi Men to accurately determine whether or not you are in a strategically advantageous position and, thus, act only when it is profitable to do so. Qi Men also reveals opportunities to craft strategic alliances with your "enemies", without the need for any conflict whatsoever.

How To Win Without Fighting

It is possible to predict who will win in direct competition by finding out which side occupies the best strategic starting position. If the favored side launches their attack from an advantageous position, then they can win with a bare minimum of effort – in other words, they can win without fighting. The arrangement and characteristics of the Qi Men Chart allow us to determine when and how this may be possible. To assess strategic viability, we must look at something known as the Host & Guest relationship in a Qi Men Chart. Comparing the Host and Guest's Palaces can indicate which side is in the superior starting position.

First thing first: what is a Guest and what is a Host in a Qi Men Chart and what are their characteristics? Whoever arrives at the 'battleground' first is considered the Host. They are followed by the Guest. The Host is typically passive and defensive in nature, they favor the internal environment and taking action at close proximity. The Guest is always on the move; they take initiative and attack. They favor action from a distance and the external environment. The trick here is to determine which is the Host Palace and which is the Guest Palace in the Qi Men Chart.

There are many ways to determine where the Host and Guest Palace lie. It depends on what the 'Useful God' or *Yong Shen* is in the Qi Men Forecast. However, generally speaking, the Earthly Stem is normally assumed as the Host. The Heavenly Stem in each box (Palace) of the Qi Men Chart is regarded as the Guest.

Here's how you can quickly identify the Heavenly Stem and the Earthly Stem in a Qi Men Chart:

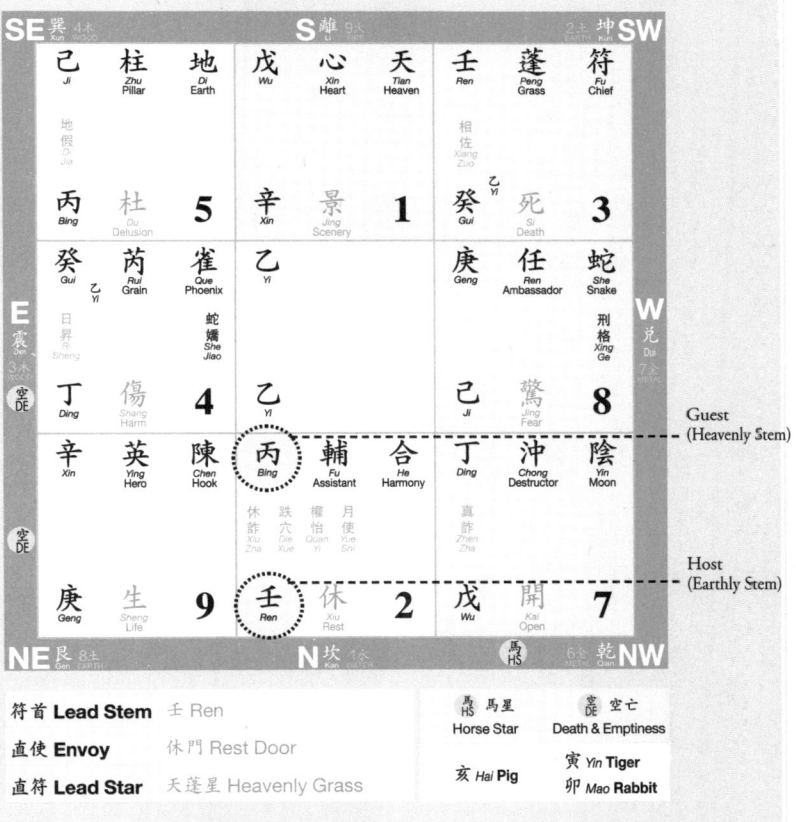

Once you've identified the Host and Guest relationship in a Qi Men Chart, the next step is to assess their Palace relationship. Look at the position and strength of the Host and Guest Palaces in relation to one another. If the Guest Palace produces the Host, this indicates that the battle between the Host and Guest is tilted in favor of the Host. Let's consider an example.

Example:

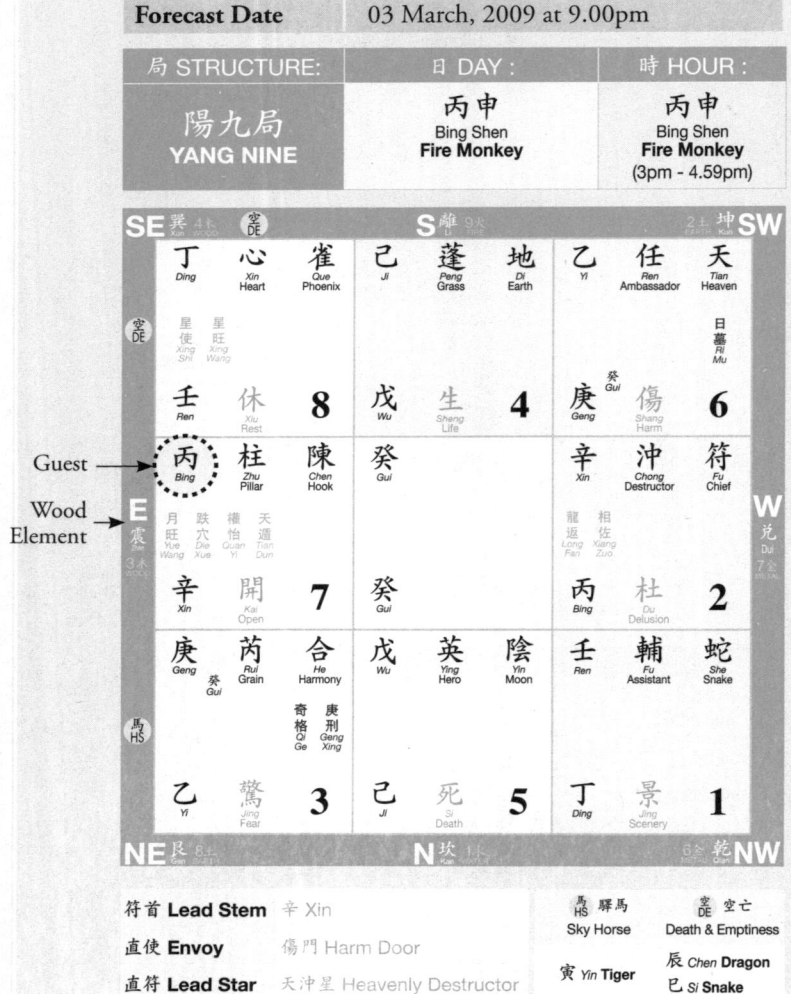

In the Zhen (East) Palace, the Earthly Stem Xin is the Host and the Heavenly Stem Bing is the Guest. The East Palace belongs to the Wood element. In this Palace, the Guest is favored. This is because the Wood element produces the Fire element, according to the relationships of the 5 Elements. This Palace also weakens the Host according to the 5 Elements relationship. The conclusion here is that the Guest has the strategic advantage in this situation and the odds are therefore with them.

Certain setups will produce an unfavorable relationship between the two Palaces (i.e.: Counter 剋, Compel 迫 or Restrict 制 relationships). This indicates that the odds are not in favor of the Host and that the Host will require more resources to win.

The harsher and more marked the relationship between the two Palaces in the Qi Men Chart means the greater the struggle for victory will be. In such cases, it is worth considering whether or not it would be wise to proceed at all. Of course, the battle will come to an end eventually if the Palace of the Host contains favorable Qi Men Structures, but the victory may come at a great cost.

Let's consider an example that illustrates how you might subvert the information you obtain using these techniques and make the situation work in your favour.

In the modern world, you might consider the negotiating table as a kind of 'battleground'. You can use Qi Men to determine whether it would be more advantageous to assume the role of a Host (of the negotiation meeting) or that of the Guest. With this knowledge, you can strategically place yourself to come out on top by either holding negotiations at your own office or holding them elsewhere.

Awareness Of One's Own Strengths & Weaknesses

Sun Tzu famously said: 知彼知己，百戰不殆, meaning that "If you know the enemy and you know yourself then you need not fear the results of a hundred battles."

This means that understanding your own strengths and weaknesses is the key to positioning yourself strategically for success. You can use a Qi Men Chart to identify your own capabilities, unique advantages and shortcomings, relative to your opponents'.

As explained in the preceding section, analyzing the 9 Palaces and determining the Host and Guest in each allows you to assess your strength. (The Host and Guest relationships are explained in the previous section). Comparing the Host and Guest Palace in a Qi Men setup will allow you to assess your strength in comparison to your competitor.

We begin by looking at the Day Stem, which represents yourself. The Month Stem denotes your opponent. A comparison of these two Palaces will give you the outlook of the competition.

Once you've established a reference point, examine the specific Palace and analyze its setup based on the Stars, Doors, Deities and Stems. The combination of these components forms a Structure. Each Palace has one. Structures can be either positive or negative. An auspicious Structure indicates strength. A negative Structure indicates weakness. For instance, the Palace containing the Wu Stem may be taken to represent a person's current cash flow. If this Palace produces the Host Palace, then this indicates that their cash flow is strong. Conversely, if the Wu Stem Palace enters Emptiness, then that's an indicator that the person in question may be experiencing financial difficulty.

Example:

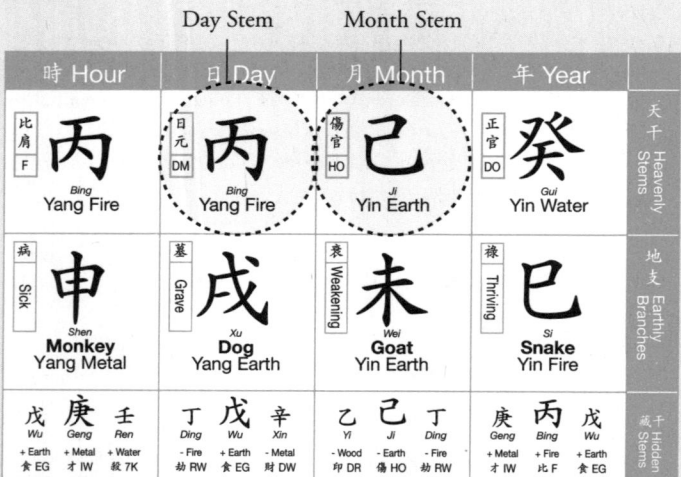

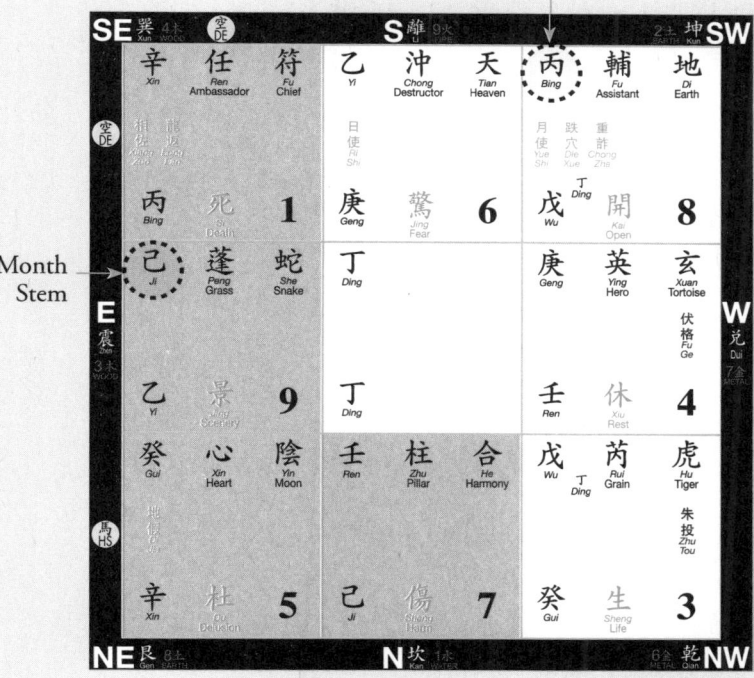

The Day Stem, Bing Fire, denotes you and your position. The Month Stem in the Chart is Ji Earth. It represents your opponent.

The Bing Stem resides in the Kun (Southwest) Palace. It resides within positive Structures (Bing Noble Receives Envoy 月使, Flying Bird Fall into Cave 飛鳥跌穴, Double Deception 重詐), with a positive Deity (Nine Earth 九地) and a good Star (Heavenly Assistant Star 天輔星). This is a desirable configuration. It is also timely in the Southwest Palace. The Bing Stem with Open Door indicates good fortune and a strong outlook for the foreseeable future.

The Month Stem, by comparison, is in the Zhen Palace and resides within an inauspicious Structure. This setup indicates weakness and problems for the enemy. By comparison, it is obvious that this arrangement favors the Day Stem – you – in competition. The Ji Stem with Scenery Door indicates that the future holds legal issues.

Leadership

In Qi Men, there are 10 Stems. The Jia Stem is the leader of all the Heavenly Stems and it represents the Grand Marshall or the Commander. In other words, it represents whoever is in charge – the leader of an organization. By studying the Lead Stem's Palace and its relationship with the remaining 8 Doors, we can determine the quality of leadership. An auspicious Structure indicates excellence, an inauspicious one indicates incompetence. In many cases, the location of the Jia Stem also determines whether a Qi Men chart can be considered favorable or unfavorable.

The name Qi Men Dun Jia literally means *Mystical Door, Hiding Jia*. This is because the Jia Stem is hidden in one of the 9 Palaces. The box that contains the Jia Stem is called the Lead Stem Palace. The Jia Stem can hide in one of the 6 Crescents' Palaces. The 6 Crescents are made up of Wu, Ji, Geng, Xin, Ren, Gui Stems. They are distributed within these 9 boxes.

Note that the biggest threats to the integrity of the Jia Stem is the Geng Metal. According to the relationship of the Five Elements, Metal counters Wood. This means that Metal will harm and hurt the Jia (Grand Marshall) in situations where it has influence over the Jia.

Example:

Forecast Date	15 February, 2011, 5.49pm	
局 STRUCTURE:	日 DAY:	時 HOUR:
陽五局 YANG FIVE	辛丑 Xin Chou **Metal Ox**	丁酉 Ding You **Fire Rooster** (5pm - 6.59pm)

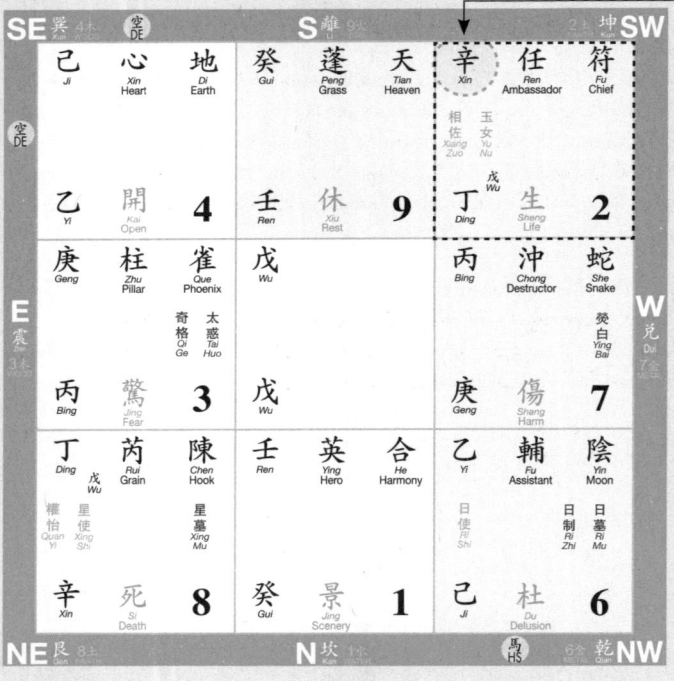

The Jia Stem is hiding here in this Chart as Xin Stem is the Lead Stem.

符首 Lead Stem	辛 Xin
直使 Envoy	生門 Life Door
直符 Lead Star	天任星 Heavenly Ambassador

馬星 Horse Star	空亡 Death & Emptiness
亥 Hai **Pig**	辰 Chen **Dragon** / 巳 Si **Snake**

The Lead Stem is Xin. It is where the Jia Stem is hiding in this Chart.

The Day Stem in this example is Xin Metal. The Lead Stem of this Chart is also Xin Metal. This means the Jia is *hiding* with the Xin Stem in this Chart. We must examine the Xin Stem Palace in the Chart.

In the Xin Stem Palace, there are positive Structures (相佐 Super Assisting Structure), Chief Deity and also a good Door (Life Door) and Star (Heavenly Ambassador Star). This configuration means that this Palace is an auspicious one.

The conclusion we must reach is that the leader in question has a clear vision and that he is inspiring and effective in power. He can be expected to lead his organization to victory.

DEPLOYMENT

4

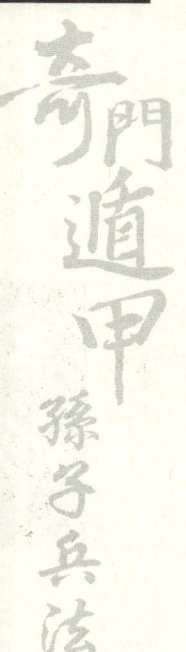

ORIGINAL TEXT:

孫子曰：昔之善戰者，
先爲不可勝，以待敵之可勝，
不可勝在己，可勝在敵。
故善戰者，能爲不可勝，
不能使敵必可勝。故曰：
勝可知，而不可爲。

TRANSLITERATION:

Sun Tzu said: In the past, the greatest warriors would first free themselves from the risk of defeat and then await the opportunity to destroy the enemy. To become invincible in battle, it is necessary to bide your time and then take the initiative in order to exploit the enemy's errors as they unfold.

Not even those skilled in war will be able to drive the defeat of the enemy with full control. That is why it is said that you may foretell a victory but you cannot be sure of obtaining that victory in exactly the way that you wish, since it often comes as a result of seizing opportunity.

COMMENTARY:

In business and in the workplace, dominance is achieved through a combination of defensive and offensive action. That is to say, in both making your own position unassailable and in finding ways to exploit the circumstances, mistakes and flaws in others may unfold to your benefit.

First, you must do what you can to minimize your liabilities. The first step in doing this is to identify what your shortcomings are. Employ risk analysis and seek independent and constructive feedback. Look to your past failures and identify their root cause. It's hard to identify your own vulnerabilities since people rarely volunteer their insight on the matter so you must enquire for it. If you are willing to actively seek out and acknowledge such information then you immediately put yourself at an advantage over others. Once you know the ways in which you might gain an upperhand, protect against the downside in any way you can.

The second requirement for victory is readiness. You must be able to strike when the most opportune moment arrives. For example, when there is a change in the market, there may be a brief window in which you can easily reposition yourself or capture new market share, if you act quickly. The trick to obtaining victory with ease is to look for the gaps and stepping stones ahead. Awareness is the key. If you are not in tune with your industry, your market or your workplace, you will lose out on opportunities. Your competitors will constantly create areas of opportunity for you through omission, oversight or error. Look for them, act upon them and you can gain the upper hand without any direct confrontation. Patience is necessary since many opportunities are transient, but they will come.

You can't choose the circumstances you operate in but you can choose how you work within them. Success is what happens when preparation meets opportunity; so be prepared to act.

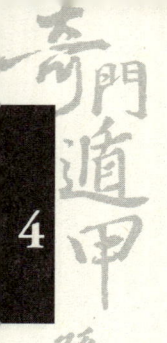

ORIGINAL TEXT:

不可勝者，守也；
可勝者，攻也。
守則不足，攻則有餘。
善守者，藏于九地之下；
善攻者，動于九天之上，
故能自保而全勝也。

TRANSLITERATION:

When there is no chance of winning, assume a defensive position; when there is a possibility of victory, launch an attack. If your weaknesses are exposed, you should protect them, if the occasion calls for your strengths then rise to it. Those who are skilled in defense will be able to disappear as if hidden in the depths of the earth and those skilled in the attack will strike at the enemy as if they are armed with the glory of the heavens themselves. Therefore those who are knowledgeable in the ways of war will have the ability both to protect themselves and to forge their way to victory.

COMMENTARY:

Seize opportunities as they come – when they aren't forthcoming, prepare for them instead and consolidate your existing position. In this way, you can act when you see a profitable chance to do so and you will be able to launch your efforts from a base of security with full, rapid force. With quick action you can secure many advantages, such as the first mover's advantage. If you are the first to operate in a newly created market niche, for example, then you will be in position to set the rules that others must play by.

Defend your interests and practice readiness. Observe market trends, current events and the competitors' movements to identify the stepping stones to your goals as they appear. When they do, act with fierce intensity for fierce results!

ORIGINAL TEXT:

見勝，不過眾人之所知，
非善之善者也。
戰勝，而天下曰善，
非善之善者也。
故舉秋毫，不爲多力；見日月，
不爲明目；聞雷霆，不爲聰耳。
古之善戰者，勝于易勝者；
故善戰者之勝也，無智名，無勇功。
故其戰勝不忒，不忒者，其措必勝，
勝已敗者也。故善戰者，
立于不敗之地，而不失敵之敗也。
是故勝兵先勝，而後求戰；
敗兵先戰，而後求勝。善用兵者，
修道而保法，故能爲勝敗之政。

TRANSLITERATION:

The capacity to foresee a victory is not beyond the common sense of any man. It is not the pinnacle of excellence, nor is a victory that is won through fierce fighting, even though it may be universally praised. He who can lift a shaft of hair does not have unusual strength, he who sees the sunset and the moonrise does not have especially keen sight and he who can hear a thunderclap does not have especially acute hearing.

It was said in ancient times that those who are skilled in war always defeat the enemy who is easily conquered. Those who are truly skilled in battle and win their victories cleanly with minimal bloodshed will not be reputed for their wisdom , nor praised for their valor. Nevertheless, because they have planned for their victory, they will always find themselves in an invincible position and will miss no opportunity to defeat their enemy. They are bound to win, as surely as their enemy is destined to be defeated.

A truly great army is one that will not fight until it is assured of victory, while a poor army is one that will plough into battle recklessly and expect to claw their way to victory in the thick of the fray. He who is adept in the principles of war knows that victory is entirely in his hands and will adopt the approach required to achieve that goal.

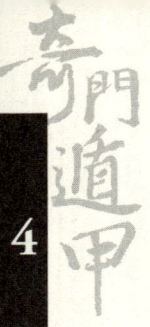

COMMENTARY:

Sometimes successful people seem to get what they want, effortlessly, again and again. To those who fail, they see 'success' as simply a matter of luck. It is tempting to dismiss their victories and achievements as the result of uncanny luck. However, in these cases, what you probably don't see – and what accounts for their 'luck' - is that they choose their battles wisely. Their visible power and success is the predictable result of having done this over and over again. They have mastered the principle of sustainable growth.

Successful leaders know that they need only reach for the prizes that are already within their ever widening grasp. They move from achievement to achievement at a sure, steady pace and use their returns to create and develop on new and bigger possibilities. They only fight the battles they can win quickly and easily. There is nothing magical about the process and it is completely repeatable and sustainable. They walk, then, they run.

If you seek growth then your first order of business should be to identify the competitive avenues that you are able to dominate. This process requires a serious and honest self-evaluation. If you do not know your value, you will have nothing to offer anyone. Look at the numbers, search deep within yourself, look at what is possible and ask yourself what you haven't tried or where you might expand without resistance. Life becomes better as 'you' become better. Identify areas of emerging and untapped opportunity and make your move. Consolidate your returns and power and set your sights higher. Rinse, repeat!

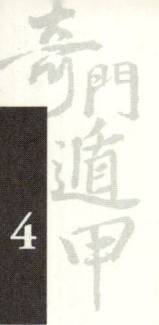

ORIGINAL TEXT:

兵法：「一曰度，二曰量，三曰數，四曰稱，五曰勝；地生度，度生量，量生數，數生稱，稱生勝。」

TRANSLITERATION:

There are five important factors that need to be accounted for before it will be possible to develop a military strategy. The first is a survey of the land and topographical analysis, the second is the calculation of manpower and material resources, the third is an estimation of military strength, the fourth is a comparison between the strength of one's own army and the strength of the enemies and the fifth is an assessment of the chances of victory or defeat.

A truly great general should know how to assess the terrain and the physical features of the battlefield, how to calculate the manpower and resources of both sides and how to identify any advantage afforded to them by the topography of the land, as well as how to analyze the way in which these things benefit or hinder himself and his enemy. Considering all of these things, he will be able to predict the likely outcome of battle.

COMMENTARY:

Understanding these five factors will allow you to develop winning strategic plans.

First, consider the nature of your chosen market and any developing trends within it. Understanding what customers within your market want and what they may want in the future shows you exactly what you must provide for profit. Identifying trends will allow you to predict and profit from them. The formula for success here is very simple – find out what they want, go get it, and give it to them.

Second, think about your own resources and your competitor's resources. Run the numbers and do your financial homework. If you cannot do this, you must find someone who can and knows how to do this for you. It is imperative that you have sound financial data. Many budding entrepreneurs make the fatal mistake of making 'assumptions' based on their gut 'feeling' of the market. Often this feeling is biased and not based on real facts. Solid figures make for solid conclusions. Do you have enough capital to give your ideas or plans the necessary support, production and marketing? Resources can be plentiful or scarce. If your rival is hard up then there might be an opportunity for you to grow in their stead.

Third, consider strength. Who has the greatest power and influence? Who has a greater support network? If you do not have the latter then do you know who you can rely on for it? Find measurable metrics that allow for comparison. Strength takes many forms but it can generally be described as one's capability to use force or take action. It can wax and wane in relation to other factors.

Fourth, compare numbers. Think about your financial situation and manpower comparatively. Who has better, more experienced leadership? Who has more highly trained staff and in what number? In this regard, more is usually better.

Fifth, make sure that you size up the situation accurately. Determine the outcomes before you commit to action, based on everything you know. Be honest. It can be just as ruinous to underestimate other people as to overestimate yourself. Double check, verify and question your insights – anticipate trouble and create contingency plans.

ORIGINAL TEXT:

故勝兵若以鎰稱銖，
敗兵若以銖稱鎰。
勝者之戰民也，
若決積水于千仞之谿，形也。

TRANSLITERATION:

A victorious army in comparison to a defeated army is like one yi in comparison to one zhu. The former has an obvious advantage over the latter. The general who is certain to win will command his troops to fight with a force akin to the torrent of mighty rivers tumbling from heights of ten thousand feet. This is the nature and the spirit of true military might.

COMMENTARY:

Victorious leaders create a position of advantage and act from it so that a successful outcome is assured. When you operate from a strong position, there is very little risk of failure and this allows you to act with great force and with huge momentum. In human terms, fighting from the high ground gives people confidence. Knowing that they are on the winning side, your staff will be highly motivated and productive. Conversely, people who know they are on the losing side will feel defeated and dejected from the moment conflict commences, putting up the bare minimum of resistance.

QI MEN DUN JIA:

Before a General or Commander chooses to deploy his troops in battle, he can seek extra guidance from the Universe itself. The 'divine force' that he can tap into and map out can be described using Qi Men terminology.

In the second paragraph of this chapter, Sun Tzu spoke about the terms *Nine Earth* (九地) and *Nine Heaven* (九天). Don't be confused by the "number" nine: in many of today's translations of the original Art of War, the number nine is taken as a number of extremes. Thus, the term Nine Earth refers to something deep in the ground and the term Nine Heaven refers to something high up in the sky, if we think literally.

In relation to Qi Men, Sun Tzu's mentions of the *Nine Earth* and the *Nine Heavens* actually refer to the Spirit Realm (8 Deities 八神) in a Qi Men Dun Jia Chart. In other words, they refer to the universe's influence in battle: the Cosmic influence that the Universe (or some would say, divine intervention) has on the outcome.

When I speak about a 'Deity' in this context, I'm not referring to any kind of religious entity per say. Instead, I am referring to the cosmic influence of the Universe. In Chinese Metaphysics, 'Deity' is the name given to an influence which is present in all activities at all times. The question we must pose is: which side will benefit from this influence in a given battle? We can use a Qi Men Chart to determine this.

In a Qi Men Chart, the Nine Earth and Nine Heaven are associated with different charactersitics:

九地 **Nine Earth**	<ul><li>Traditionally known as the *God of Persistence and Perseverance*.</li><li>Represents traits such as humbleness, respect, steadiness, kindness, and gentleness.</li><li>Denotes things that are hidden or buried under the earth.</li><li>Indicative of all that is subtle and concealed.</li><li>Represents problems happening on the ground, at a grass root level.</li><li>In terms of natural disasters, it represents the possibility of an earthquake.</li></ul>
九天 **Nine Heaven**	<ul><li>Traditionally known as the *God of Valiance*.</li><li>It represents the cosmic influence of the universe. It grants foresight, clarity and courage.</li><li>Represents beauty, fame, dynamic people and movement, marching/war, the execution of plans and intelligence.</li><li>Denotes long term activity and events.</li><li>Also denotes problems or issues happening up in the sky or above the ground.</li></ul>

One of the key factors that shapes the outcome of any battle is the choice of battleground.

In Qi Men, there are 8 Deities. Each governs a different type of environment where conflict or battle can take place. You've just read about two: *Nine Earth* represents battles that take place underground or under the ocean waves. *Nine Heaven* represents any battle that takes place in the sky. As an example, think of the 9/11 bombing of the World Trade Center where an attack took place from a position in the sky itself.

Now, although Sun Tzu only mentioned 2 of the 8 Deities from Qi Men, we can safely assume that the other 6 Deities in the Spirit Plate of a Qi Men Dun Jia Chart are also taken into consideration when we perform an analysis.

The 8 Deities and their domains are described in the following table:

The 8 Deities	Natural Environment
Chief 直符	Meadow, barren wasteland, city.
Surging Snake 螣蛇	Graveyard, wilderness, coastline, river, mountain vein.
Great Moon 太陰	Cliff, cave, marsh.
Six Harmony 六合	Grassland, garden, forest, pond.
White Tiger 白虎/ Grappling Hook 勾陳	Forest, hunting ground, cliff, volcano ground.
Red Phoenix 朱雀/ Black Tortoise 玄武	Market, seashore (Black Tortoise), pond, lake.
Nine Earth 九地	Deep ocean, caves, underground, roads, tunnels, lowland.
Nine Heaven 九天	Skies, space, airspace, above ground, large city, main street.

In this chapter, Sun Tzu spoke about attaining 'invincibility' by choosing to fight only battles that you are sure to win. You can do this by aligning your choices with 'divine intervention'. In more scientific terms, this means you have to tap into the power of your subconscious mind and 'win' the battle mentally first. This will lead to a manifestation of the desired reality. By positioning one's mind and programming one's thoughts, imagined success will become reality. In other words, you can use Qi Men to identify the battles you can fight and win, in accordance with the 8 Deities in the Chart.

By developing a clear goal and using Qi Men Dun Jia, we can control the power of the subconscious mind to position ourselves for success. Developing our ability to consciously control our subconscious mind's function with deliberate and focused intention through Qi Men Dun Jia is a crucial aspect of becoming enabled and empowered. This is to begin willfully, purposefully and intentionally create more of what we want and less of what we don't want in life. Each of the 8 Deities represent a different latent power in our subconscious mind.

Here is the basic list of subscioncious mind qualities of each of the 8 Deities:

The 8 Deities	Attributes
Chief 直符	This Deity is also known as the Great Spirit. It denotes helpfulness and healing – the usual traits found in teachers, advisors etc. With this Deity, the presence of a Nobleman is likely.
Great Moon 太陰	This Deity represents Wisdom. It denotes someone who is knowledgeable. This Deity will play the role of an advisor and for others to ask insights from.
Six Harmony 六合	This Deity represents Love. There will be the presence of cupid, matchmakers and Noble people, helping the individual along the way. Matters revolving relationships will progress smoothly with the help of this Deity.
Nine Earth 九地	This Deity represents Wealth. It denotes someone who has the keenness and perception for business or someone with remarkable business instincts. Matters involving money and God are related to this Deity.

The 8 Deities	Attributes
Nine Heaven 九天	This Deity represents Foresight. The Nine Heaven Deity is likened to having the presence of an angel which could aid in foretelling what will happen in the near future. The power of premonition allows warnings to be noted as well.
Surging Snake 騰蛇	This Deity is also known as the Master of Occult. An exemplary role/character would be like Gandalf from The Lord Of The Rings series. He or she will have the focus and the drive to concentrate on all matters
Black Tortoise 玄武	This Deity represents Courage. It could also lead to luck in wealth. It denotes someone who's interested in dark arts – much like a warrior.
Grappling Hook 勾陳	This Deity is represented by Land or Earth. It is influenced by ancestors. It involves issues of land, field, property, home, houses, agricultural and plantation.
Red Phoenix 朱雀	This Deity represents Connection and Communication. It denotes speaking and engaging with others to cultivate moments of breakthrough. It is likened to a phoenix rising from ashes countering life challenges, rebirth or renewal matters.
White Tiger 白虎	This Deity represents Infinite Energy. It denotes someone who has the necessary stamina, vitality and strength to succeed and move forward.

You can use what is known as the Chief Deity in Qi Men to attain 'invincibility' in your battle plans.

This is how you can find the Chief Deity in the Chart:

Forecast Date	28 July, 2013 at 11.30pm	
局 STRUCTURE:	日 DAY:	時 HOUR:
陰七局 YIN SEVEN	乙未 Yi Wei **Wood Goat**	丙子 Bing Zi **Fire Rat** (11pm - 12.59am)

SE 巽 4木		S 離 1火		SW 坤 2土	
戊 Wu / 柱 Zhu Pillar / 蛇 She Snake		己 Ji / 心 Xin Heart / 符 Fu Chief		丁 Ding / 蓬 Peng Grass / 天 Tian Heaven	
辛 Xin / 開 Open	**6**	丙 Bing / 休 Xiu Rest	**2**	癸 Gui / 生 Sheng Life	**4**
癸 Gui / 芮 Rui Grain / 陰 Yin Moon		庚 Geng		乙 Yi / 任 Ren Ambassador / 地 Di Earth	
壬 Ren / 驚	**5**	庚 Geng		戊 Wu / 傷 Shang Harm	**9**
丙 Bing / 英 Ying Hero / 合 He Harmony		辛 Xin / 輔 Fu Assistant / 虎 Hu Tiger		壬 Ren / 沖 Chong Destructor / 玄 Xuan Tortoise	
乙 Yi / 死	**1**	丁 Ding / 景	**3**	己 Ji / 杜 Du Delusion	**8**
NE 艮 8土		N 坎 1水		NW 乾 6金	

符首 **Lead Stem**	己 Ji	馬 HS 馬星 Horse Star	空 DE 空亡 Death & Emptiness
直使 **Envoy**	開門 Open Door	寅 Yin Tiger	申 Shen Monkey
直符 **Lead Star**	天心星 Heavenly Heart		酉 You Rooster

符首 **Chief Deity**	• Traditionally known as the *Heavenly Yi God*. • Bestows protection, healing and safety. • Represents fame, wealth, success, bliss, protection, leadership, high rank, Noblemen. • It is auspicious for those seeking healing, success and an increase in wealth. • Denotes help and assistance from someone with natural leadership ability; someone with integrity, elegance and charisma. • The Chief exerts most of its positive influence under a good formation.

The use of Deities for the purpose of 'invincibility' in battle is highlighted in a line of an ancient Qi Men text: 急則從神緩從門 (For quick results, look for the Deities. For permanent results, seek the Door).

If you seek to fight a quick battle, look for the 8 Deity Directions in a Qi Men Forecast Chart and walk towards one. Alternatively, if you are familiar with meditation and visualization, you can sit with your back towards this direction and enter your 'alpha' state. In Qi Men I call this entering your 'Sage Mode'. This can be done by meditating and consciously lowering your brain waves to the alpha level. In this state, you can seek the assistance of one of the 8 Deities' energy in the chart to achieve your goals.

If you'd rather engage in a longer and steadier battle, seek out the Direction of the auspicious Door instead. Both Doors and Deities reside in every Palace in a Qi Men Chart. By analyzing the Chart, and determining which Direction (Palace) is most favourable, you will know where to stage your competitive efforts and which direction to take your business in next.

With this in mind, re-study this chapter with the 8 Deities of Qi Men in mind. Use a combination of the principles in this chapter and Qi Men to guide your decisions. You can also use Qi Men as described above to program your subconscious mind into manifesting the reality that you desire. Let's look at an example.

Example:

The Day Stem is Geng Metal and the Jia Stem is hiding with the Ji Stem in the Qian (Northwest) Palace. See the following Chart plotted on 28 July, 2012 at 11.30pm.

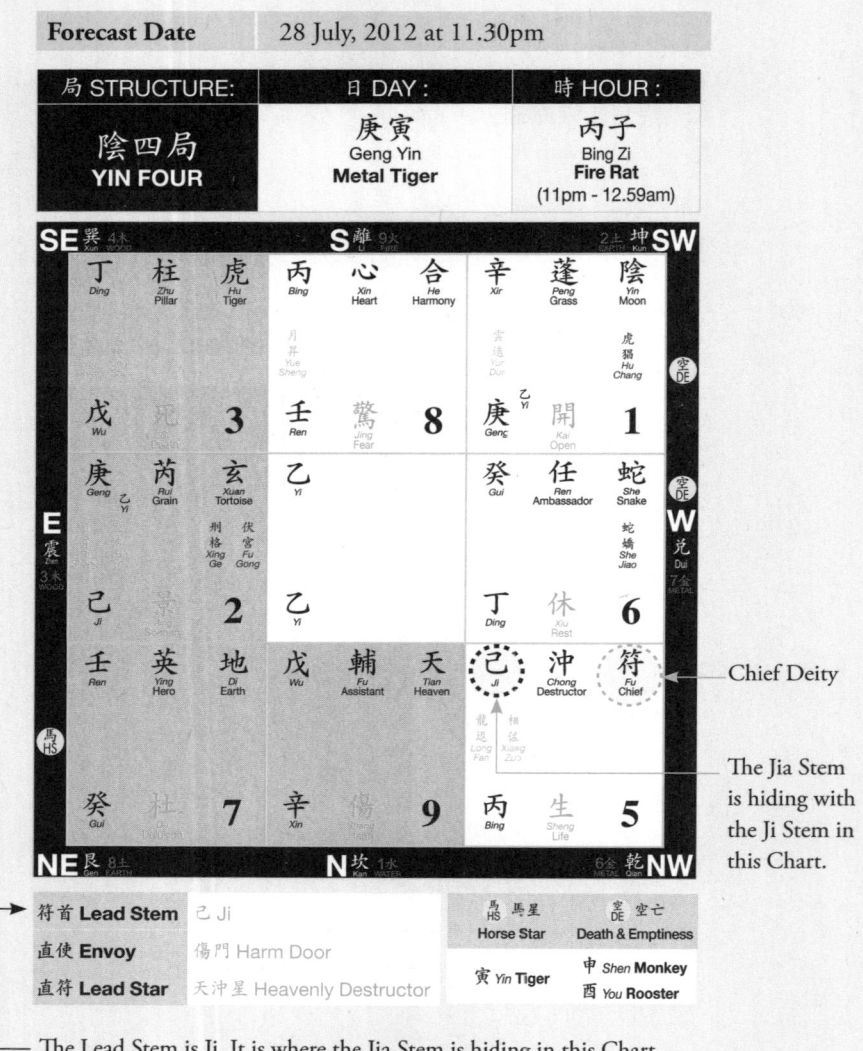

In the Qian (Northwest) Palace, the highly auspicious Chief Deity can be found there. There is also a very auspicious Door called the Life Door. This Palace also contains an extremely powerful Qi Men formation known as "The Green Dragon Returns 青龍返首". This is a favourable direction to either deploy troops or launch a campaign if you are in siege mode. Since this formation is highly auspicious, we can use this in negotiations to overcome our competitors or in meetings to dominate the discussion.

If no external battle is required then this formation can also be used to help us win the battle in our own mind. It can successfully help us tap into our subconscious mind. We can then program our mind for success and manifest love, happiness and wealth into our lives.

FORCE 兵勢

5

ORIGINAL TEXT:

孫子曰：凡治眾如治寡，
分數是也。鬥眾如鬥寡，
形名是也。三軍之眾，
可使必受敵而無敗者，
奇正是也。兵之所加，
如以碫投卵者，虛實是也。

TRANSLITERATION:

Sun Tzu said: Managing a big army is, in principle, the same as managing a small army: it is all about organization and co-ordination. Whether you lead a large or small group, leadership calls for the same degree of strict and impartial command. What leads an army to victory is a matter of adopting a combination of orthodox and unorthodox tactics. In order for the troops to crush the opponent as easily as a grindstone crushes eggs, they must steer clear of the core of the enemy's forces and strike at its weak points.

COMMENTARY:

Regardless of the size of your team or the scale of the project, good organization and results go hand in hand. Without good organization, measurement and tracking, you can expect haphazard results at best. The need for structure grows with your ambitions and responsibilities. The more complex your operation and the greater your goals, the more crucial a strong organization and a clear command structure become.

Through a tiered management structure, you can manage even the largest teams and projects. A superior level of organization can, indeed, put men on the moon! A clear vision, with measurable goals, intelligent delegation and a measurement system that recognizes effort can all drive a collective human performance and in a collective effort, the individual weaknesses of people become irrelevant. If you put the right people in the right positions and unite them for a common purpose then you will be in charge of a power greater than the sum of its parts.

One danger you must face when you manage a large operation is that you can easily lose your ability to maneuver and react as quickly as smaller, more agile opponents. Bigger businesses often fail to seize opportunities for growth in a timely manner. This common weakness is the cumulative manifestation of interests and ties within larger organizations. Unfortunately, this is often the fatal flaw that brings large, successful businesses to their knees.

To this end, try to keep bureaucracy at a minimum within your organization.

Make sure that your organization or team is structured in a way that allows it to respond rapidly and adapt promptly to changes. Create a clear chain of command so that information can flow rapidly and take active steps to retain your authority above all else as your responsibilities grow. Your organization or team needs a leader with a clear vision.

ORIGINAL TEXT:

凡戰者，以正合，以奇勝。
故善出奇者，無窮如天地，
不竭如江河，終而復始，
日月是也；死而復生，
四時是也。聲不過五，
五聲之變，不可勝聽也。
色不過五，五色之變，
不可勝觀也。味不過五，
五味之變，不可勝嘗也。
戰勢不過奇正，奇正之變，
不可勝窮也。奇正相生，
如循環之無端，孰能窮之哉！

TRANSLITERATION:

During warfare, an able general should use a combination of orthodox and unorthodox tactics, both confronting the enemy directly and taking them by surprise. He who is adept in these methods can apply them in any number of ways; the approaches he may adopt are as infinite as heaven and earth and as inexhaustible as the great rivers. These may come to their natural end but they are born again, like the sun and moon in motion, they die back and are renewed with the same inevitability as the turning of the seasons. These endless combinations may be compared to music where just five notes can be structured into countless beautiful melodies so many that we will never be able to listen to them all, or to the five primary colors which may be blended to create such a multitude of wondrous shades and hues that a lifetime is not long enough to appreciate them all, or, indeed, to the five tastes that can be combined to present such an array of delicacies that we shall never have the opportunity to taste them all. In this very same way, military strategy is about far more than just orthodox and unorthodox approaches, it is about the myriad combinations of these tactics that create the maneuvers of war. Orthodox and unorthodox tactics are interdependent and mutually reproductive; each one will give rise to the other in a cycle with no beginning and no end. Who has the power to exhaust them?

COMMENTARY:

If you want to stay one step ahead of your competitors, don't allow yourself to become predictable. Dazzle, confuse, distract and surprise. Make others chase you. Become better than you were yesterday. Be unpredictable, change things up and try new things and ways of thinking constantly (learn to quickly discern whether new ideas are effective or not). Being varied prevents your rivals from overtaking, intercepting or undermining you. If they can't guess your next move, they won't be able to prepare against it.

Outstandingly creative and powerful strategies produce outstanding results.

Different situations call for different tactics. You must be flexible and adaptive. You must continue to evolve and change. It stands to reason that for almost any approach, there are superior approaches that you either have not tried or have not thought of trying. By opening yourself up to this possibility you give yourself the chance to hit gold.

Stadium pitches, intelligent pricing, irresistible offers, surprising promotions, new product ranges, moonshot research projects and so on are amongst the tactics a business can deploy to stay ahead and turn heads. Masterfully mix things up, encourage black swan benefits and subtly undermine your competitor's bottom line. The biggest brands employ this kind of thinking to keep sales fresh and smaller brands use it to tilt the odds. In the case of soft drinks, for example, companies occasionally try out new and exotic drink ideas. They can be fairly certain that these new drinks won't create massive additional revenue per say, but they help customers become excited once again about the brand. Customers discover it anew, boosting the companies long term outlook and making their competitors look unimaginative and dull.

Creatively blending tactics to form new strategies is obviously a great idea in business, but what about on a more personal level? It's easy to overlook the human benefits, but they surely exist. Variety not only prevents burnout – it encourages creativity, innovation, excitement and passion, all of which spill over into the final product – a better version of yourself. Try new tactics and re-evaluate your game plan based on new information and you'll be amazed at what happens. If you want extraordinary results you have to try out an extraordinary approach or two.

So remember this - when you are willing to step into the realm of uncertainty and ambiguity, you open yourself up to infinite possibilities.

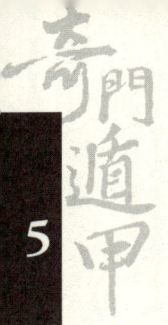

ORIGINAL TEXT:

激水之疾，至于漂石者，勢也。鷙鳥之擊，至于毀折者，節也。是故善戰者，其勢險，其節短，勢如張弩，節如機發。

TRANSLITERATION:

A fast flowing torrent of water can be powerful enough to move heavy boulders, carried along by the momentum. A hawk that flies rapidly and strikes with accuracy will catch its prey due to the precision and speed of its movements. The same is true of a mighty warrior who can exploit his vantage point to launch a swift and sharp attack. His force is like the power in the taut string of a bow and his swiftness is like that of an arrow.

COMMENTARY:

Speed is everything; it brings you to your goals in a shorter time. Sustained and unbroken speed is the best of all. It allows you to build up what is known as momentum. Momentum is like a kind of potential energy, which you can accumulate and then release at a moment of your choosing for the winners' profit.

Doing something with great momentum, passion and force always leads to a good end result.

What's more, the faster you complete a task, the lesser the cost incurred. Speed plus timing equals exceptional success. You must act quickly and decisively in order to build up the force of momentum and then, when the timing is right, release it with your full power.

Conversely anything that is done in a slow and time consuming way often loses momentum. In projects involving a group of people, the longer the task is delayed, the harder it is for the team to keep morale and spirits up – leading to a higher chance of failure or quitting.

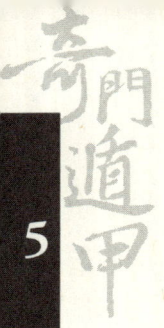

ORIGINAL TEXT:

紛紛紜紜，鬥亂，而不可亂也。
渾渾沌沌，形圓，而不可敗也。

TRANSLITERATION:

In the tumult of battle an army should remain calm. In the chaos of war they should be organized and directed. At all times they should remain invulnerable.

COMMENTARY:

You can't always choose your struggles but you can always choose to keep a cool head. When you panic, fret or lose your temper, you lose the ability to think clearly and make decisions that will help you address the source of your frustration in the first place. You must learn to control your emotions. When you can control your emotions, you control your life.

Your team takes its cue from your attitude, not just your words. This is especially true when the stakes are high. When you are brave, confident, calm and assertive, your staff will adopt a 'can do' attitude, too. Corporate culture is created by the leader of the company. Corporate culture is nothing more than a set of unwritten 'rules of the game' in an organization. Every organization, big or small, has them. The leader of the organization sets these rules – most of the time, unknowingly. His attitude, beliefs and behavior set these rules. Why does a company have a high attrition rate? Why do employees keep leaving? Why does everyone feel gloomy, tense and unhappy in the office? Usually there's a corporate culture problem. The leader has to take responsibility in order to rectify this and they must change corporate culture by example.

In any crisis situation, you can either show strength and competency or show weakness and indecision. The greater the challenge, the greater the chances to prove yourself. If you can keep your head in a competitive situation when others cannot then you will find yourself at an advantage.

Many of the world's best leaders made their name during a trial by fire and you can too.

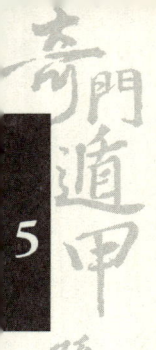

ORIGINAL TEXT:

亂生于治，怯生于勇，
弱生于強。治亂，數也。
勇怯，勢也。強弱，形也。

TRANSLITERATION:

Disorder can emerge from order, cowardice can be born of courage and weakness may be the offspring of strength. Order or disorder is a matter of organization. Courage instead of cowardice is a matter of momentum. Strength, rather than weakness, is a matter of formation.

COMMENTARY:

Organization and momentum make any competitive goal possible.

Good organization in its many forms will create order, security and a sense of direction that helps you focus all of your action towards your goal with laser-accurate-precision, creating breakthrough success.

Moving forward quickly creates unstoppable confidence. Momentum will confer bravery to even the most reserved people in your organization. With momentum behind them, people can accomplish anything. This 'invisible force' drives everyone forward. It does so by drumming out courage from everyone. With courage people can take action. This is because action always cures fear. Without action, fear grows and it only becomes more difficult to act. Begin immediately with your actionable plans, don't look back and don't break your momentum once you have built it.

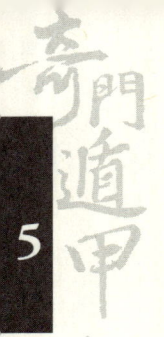

5

ORIGINAL TEXT:

故善動敵者，形之，敵必從之；予之，敵必取之；以利動之，以實待之。

TRANSLITERATION:

He who is adept at the use of artifice can create an appearance that will draw the enemy into action. He will be able to tempt the enemy with that which they are sure to take. He will draw the enemy out with the promise of gain and wait in strength to ambush them.

COMMENTARY:

By actively cultivating your appearance and image, you can create false impressions that convince your competitors into taking action that benefits you. For example, you can create the illusion that you are unprepared and weak when in reality nothing could be further from the truth. Seeing this, your competitors will become lax or come to you with a complacent mindset, creating a window for you to act with massive force and take what you want easily. This is the art of concealing your strength.

ORIGINAL TEXT:

故善戰者，求之于勢，
不責于人，故能擇人任勢；
任勢者，其戰人也，如轉木石，
木石之性，安則靜，危則動，
方則止，圓則行。故善戰人之
勢，如轉圓石于千仞之山者，
勢也。

TRANSLITERATION:

A capable general will capitalize on the circumstances he faces to create force without making excessive demands of his subordinates. He will employ the right men for the job and will work to fully exploit the prevailing conditions to drive his plans forward in the same way that one might roll a rock or log. If the surface is flat, a log or rock will not roll but if the ground is sloping then the log will roll effortlessly. If the log or rock is square it will stop as soon as it is pushed but if it is round it will soon develop momentum. In this way, when a strategy is correctly employed, the force of the army may be compared to the descent of a rock down a mountain of ten thousand feet. This is the meaning of potential.

COMMENTARY:

Insightful leaders create the conditions for results and then allow them to happen. You shouldn't have to force your people to produce results. Instead, you should create an environment and a culture conducive for results and place the right people within it.

Choose highly skilled and motivated people. A great deal of thought and effort must go into your hiring process and for good reason, because without good people you can't get good results. Most people would just hire people they like or worse, hire their friends. They often confuse competency with compatibility. Just because someone is likeable or seemingly 'compatible' with you does not mean they are necessarily competent to get things done.

There are all kinds of methods and systems which can help you select an A-Team. Consider BaZi personality profiling, Qi Men Destiny Analysis, Human Resource departments, recruitment agencies and so on. It's no coincidence that the best companies have the best people. As a leader, you cannot be afraid of choosing people who are smarter or more skilled than you – your job is to find the best people for the mission, not to protect your own ego. In fact, if you can find people more capable than you, brilliant! All you have to do is direct their talent in accordance with your vision. That's the job of the leader, nothing more nothing less.

Once you've brought the right people and resources together, make the importance of your goals well known to everyone. Have a vision and communicate it clearly. You must effectively enroll your teammates into your mission. You must get a wholehearted buy-in from every member. Then, set challenges with deadlines which are conducive to your larger goal. Let your staff work: delegate fitting tasks and empower them with the responsibility and autonomy they require to achieve them. Teach, train, motivate and then trust them. Intervene only when necessary; give people the freedom to solve problems on their own and assign them sufficiently challenging objectives to bring out their best. Micro-management should be about helping people who are not performing as well as they could rather than constantly interfering without cause. Reward effort at all times and you will further perpetuate success by creating an environment where everyone is keen to give their best effort.

By harnessing the power of perpetual momentum through effective leadership, you need not fight to control or dominate people. You will have a group of raving teammates inspired by you. When you win their trust, you have access to their strength. You get better results because you laid solid foundations. This is how you can unleash potential.

QI MEN DUN JIA :

Qi Men Dun Jia relates to Chapter 5 of Sun Tzu's Art of War because it deals directly with the concept of force, albeit in a unique way.

Sun Tzu names two types of force in this chapter. He use the terms *Zheng* 正 and *Qi* 奇 to describe them. Many translations in English refer to these as 'Ordinary' and 'Extraordinary' forces. The Zheng 正 force is usually explained as the mundane, ordinary, direct force – the kind which creates average results and outcomes. The second kind of force called Qi 奇, which governs the extraordinary, unconventional, uncommon and mysterious actions. These are actions that create extraordinary results. Sun Tzu said that if you can master these two forces, especially the Qi 奇 force, you can overcome any enemy and win any battle.

Qi Men Dun Jia has a more direct take on these two terms. As you may already know by now, the Chinese word "Qi 奇"(from 奇門遁甲 Qi Men Dun Jia) is the exact same Chinese character.

Qi 奇 in the Qi Men system is represented by the ***3 Nobles*** (consisting of the 3 Heavenly Stems, Yi 乙, Bing 丙 and Ding 丁). In Chinese, they are known as the San Qi 三奇 – meaning 3 Nobles. It is these 3 Nobles which can give rise to the so-called Qi 奇 force that Sun Tzu talks about in this chapter. Whenever these 3 Nobles appear in a Qi Men Chart, they require your special attention. To understand why, you must first understand the 10 Stems.

On the other hand, the term **Zheng** 正 in Qi Men is represented by the *Liu Yi* 六儀 or 6 Crescents (consisting of the Heavenly Stems, Wu 戊 (Yang Earth), Ji 己 (Yin Earth), Geng 庚 (Yang Metal), Xin 辛 (Yin Metal), Ren 壬 (Yang Water) and Gui 癸 (Yin Water).

Qi Men Dun Jia is the study of the configurations of the 10 Stems and how they are allocated in the 9 boxes (or Palaces) of a Qi Men Chart. The 10 Stems are Jia, Yi, Bing, Ding, Wu, Ji, Geng, Xin, Ren and Gui.

Here is a simple breakdown of the 10 Stems in Qi Men:

甲 *Jia* **Yang Wood**	Jia is known as the *Heavenly Bless Star* 天福 and it is associated with many good things including leadership, strength, courage, authority, kindness, helping others, exerting a positive influence and rewarding good deeds. Also known as the *Green Dragon* 青龍.
乙 *Yi* **Yin Wood**	Yi is known as the *Heavenly Virtue Star* 天德. It governs affinity, connection, influence, persuasiveness, enchantment and encouragement. It also embodies sympathy and understanding. Also known as the *Yi Noble* 乙奇.
丙 *Bing* **Yang Fire**	Bing is known as the *Heavenly Power Star* 天威. It helps one exude charisma, personal magnetism, charm, power and grandeur. Also known as the **Bing Noble** 丙奇 or **Moon Noble** 月奇.
丁 *Ding* **Yin Fire**	Ding is known as the *Jade Maiden* 玉女. It is good for scholarly pursuits, outsmarting enemies, thinking, enlightening, teaching, forming strategy and analyzing. It is known as the **Ding Noble** 丁奇
戊 *Wu* **Yang Earth**	Wu is known as the *Heavenly Force Star* 天武, a star that is good for commanding others and executing plans effectively and efficiently. It is good for managing resources like finances and time. In some literature, Wu is also known as the *Heavenly Gate* 天門.

己 *Ji* **Yin Earth**	Ji is also known as the *Ming Tang Star* 明堂 and it is good for matters of invention and creation. Ji is resourceful in nature. In some literature, it is also known as the *Earth Gate* 地戶.
庚 *Geng* **Yang Metal**	Geng is known as the *Heavenly Penalty* 天獄, a Star for legal ballets, legal challenges, pain, suffering and the determination of punishment. In some literature, Geng is also known as the *Great White* 太白.
辛 *Xin* **Yin Metal**	Xin is known as the *Heavenly Court* 天庭, a Star that is associated with scheming, conniving, manipulating and punishing wrong deeds. In some literature it is also called the *Deity of Mishaps* 厄神.
壬 *Ren* **Yang Water**	Ren is known as the *Heavenly Prison* 天牢, a Star that governs dispute, arguments, disagreement, distrust, misunderstandings and protracted debates. Its appearance usually invokes long disputes, miscommunication and disagreement. In some literature it is known as *The Small Snake* 小蛇.
癸 *Gui* **Yin Water**	Gui is known as the *Heavenly Conceal* 天藏 is a Star related unpleasant emotions, anxiety, fear, depression, gloominess and jealousy. It is also known as the *Heavenly Net* 天網.

The Jia Wood is the Grand Marshall, or leader, of the 10 Stems. It plays an important role and dominates all the Stems. In every Qi Men Chart, the Jia is hidden in one of the Palaces. It will reside with one of the other 9 Stems. Hence the name of the system – Mystical Doors 'Hiding' Jia – Qi Men Dun Jia.

Geng Metal is considered the natural enemy of Jia due to their relationship in the Five Elements Cycle. Geng (Yang Metal) counters Jia (Yang Wood) just as Metal can harm Wood according to the Five Elements Cycle. Thus, any interaction between Jia Wood and Geng Metal will weaken the Jia Wood and mitigate its positive effects.

Desirable configurations protect Jia Wood and its positive effects. This protection comes about when other Stems bring a helpful influence into play. The 3 Nobles - Yi Wood, Bing Fire and Ding Fire all protect Jia Wood.

Yi (Yin Wood) can form a combination with Geng Metal to negate the latter's effects (it is part of a formation known as the Heavenly Ten Stem Combination which will be explained further in Chapter 13). This combination will convert the enemy (which is Geng in this case), into an ally. The relationship between Jia and Yi can be likened to that of "brother" and "sister".

Bing (Yang Fire) and Ding (Yin Fire) can counter Geng. This is because Fire counters Metal in the Five Elements Cycle. The relationship of Jia with Bing and Ding can be likened to that of "father" and "child". Jia can "use" both Bing and Ding Fire since Wood produces Fire.

You should understand by now that each Palace in a Qi Men Chart corresponds to a potential outcome or strategy. Sun Tzu teaches that direct efforts (Zheng 正 force) are never as effective as extraordinary ones (Qi force). Because of their protective powers, Yi Wood, Bing Fire and Ding Fire are known as the **San Qi** 三奇 or 3 Nobles. These Heavenly Stems protect the Jia and allow it to exert a positive effect on your life, as indicated by the Qi Men Chart. Their combined presence in an analysis indicates that extraordinary results are possible for you.

The opposite line of reasoning is true, too. For example, if Ren and Xin appear in a particular Palace of a Qi Men Chart, then this Palace indicates a less favored strategy since both Ren and Xin are among the 6 Crescents which represent direct, mundane results, which are of course not as desirable as extraordinary ones. Furthermore, as both Ren and Xin are considered negative Stems, their presence indicates a negative outcome if you pursue your intended plan of action.

Example:

In this example Chart plotted on 26 June, 2009 at 1.30pm, the Day Stem is Ren Water and the Hour Stem is Ding Fire.

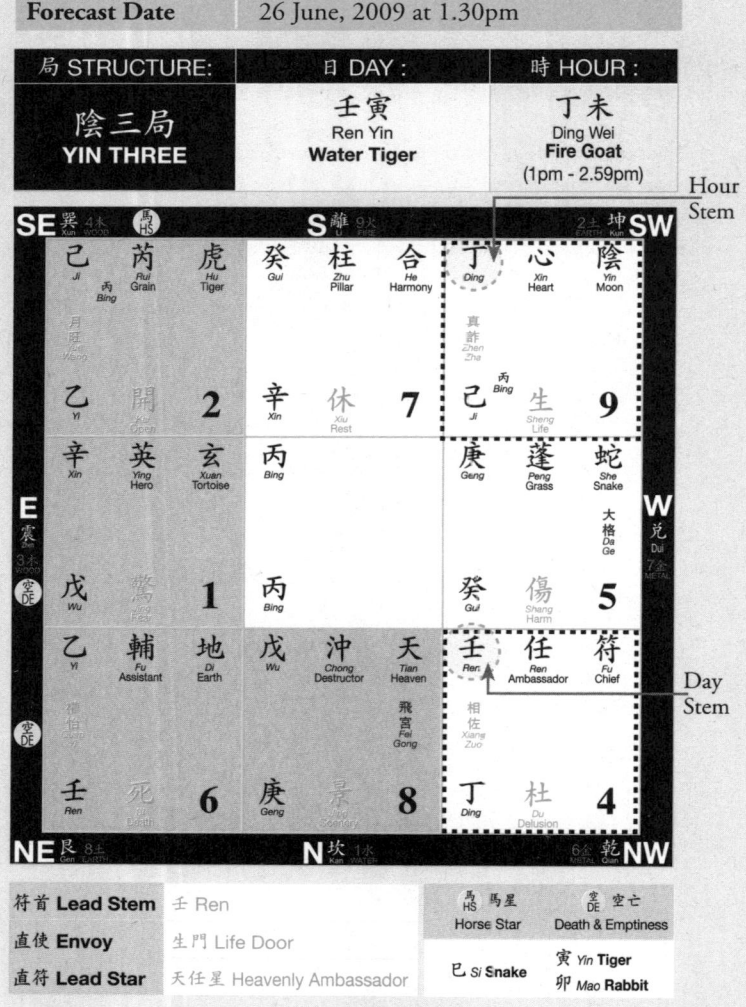

The Ding Stem resides in the Kun (Southwest) Palace which belongs to the Earth element. Both the Ding and Bing Stems appear together in this Palace. This combination will create extraordinary results because both are considered positive Stems and they also belong to the 3 Nobles.

The Ren Day Stem is residing in the Qian (Northwest) Palace which belongs to the Metal element. The Hour Stem Palace produces the Day Stem Palace, which is ideal.

In Qi Men Dun Jia, the Day Stem Palace represents the Self or the person seeking Qi Men advice. The Hour Stem Palace represents the outcome of the forecast. In this case, if the main focus of the forecast was to determine the outcome of a business venture, then this configuration of the Chart would denote that the outcome is highly favorable. This is because the Hour Stem Palace has such auspicious configurations.

Let us get a better understanding by analysing another example. You are scheduled for a very important sales presentation and your desire is to ensure a successful delivery of the presentation. The end result is to close the deal. You can plot a Qi Men Chart for *Qi Men Strategic Execution* to achieve this goal.

We will assume the presentation is set on June 1, 2014 at 9.30am. This is the Chart plotted for that mentioned time and date:

時 Hour	日 Day	月 Month	年 Year	
偏財 IW 丁 Ding Yin Fire	日元 DM 癸 Gui Yin Water	七殺 7K 己 Ji Yin Earth	傷官 HO 甲 Jia Yang Wood	天干 Heavenly Stems
巳 Si Snake Yin Fire	卯 Mao Rabbit Yin Wood	巳 Si Snake Yin Fire	午 Wu Horse Yang Fire	地支 Earthly Branches
庚 丙 戊 Geng Bing Wu +Metal +Fire +Earth 印 DR 財 DW 官 DO	乙 Yi -Wood 食 EG	庚 丙 戊 Geng Bing Wu +Metal +Fire +Earth 印 DR 財 DW 官 DO	丁 己 Ding Ji -Fire -Earth 才 IW 殺 7K	藏干 Hidden Stems

182　Joey Yap's Qi Men Dun Jia Sun Tzu Warcraft

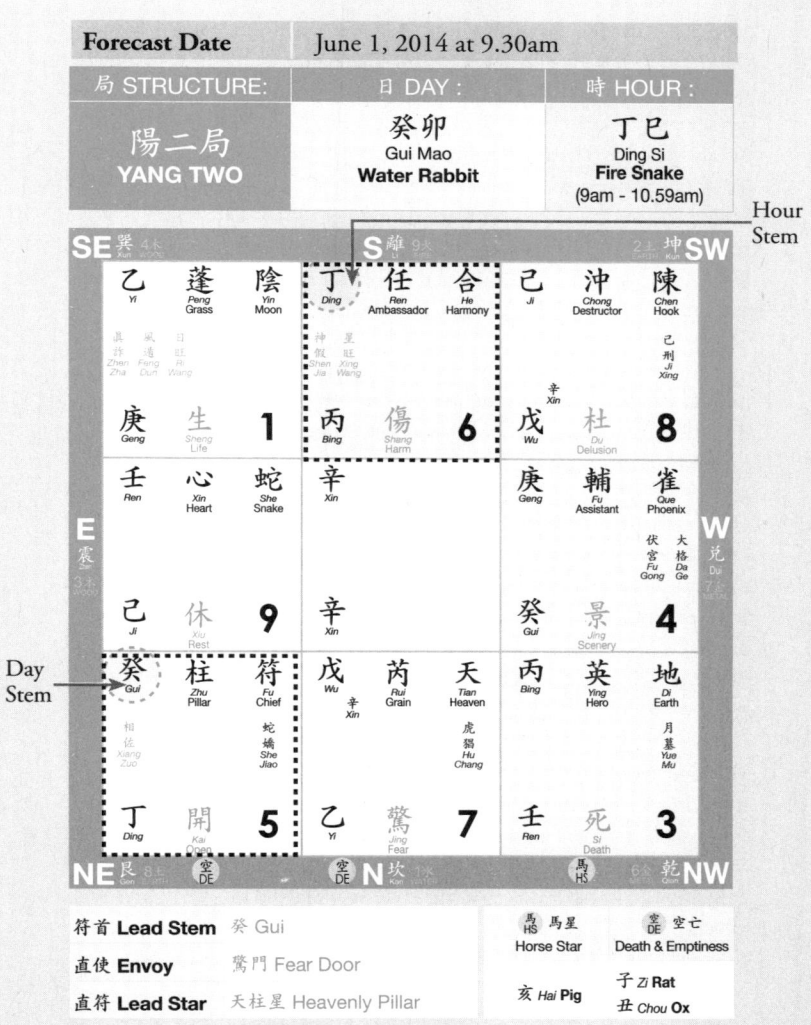

In this Chart, the Day Stem is Gui Water and it resides in the Gen (Northeast) Palace. The Hour Stem, Ding Fire is residing in the Li (South) Palace. This Palace (which belongs to the Fire Element) is producing the Day Stem Palace (which belongs to the Earth Element). The Li (South) Palace also contains the highly favorable Ding and Bing Nobles formation. Along with the auspicious Star (Heavenly Ambassador Star) and positive Deity (Six Harmony Deity), this Palace contains very positive energy. More importantly, it contains the Door of Harm which is generally regarded as one of the best Doors for sales related activity. Since conditions are extremely favorable in the Chart, extraordinary results can be expected.

During the presentation time, stand with your back towards the South direction. Physically positioning yourself in the most powerful Qi Men formation will give your sales presentation the unfair advantage.

The above are two simple examples of Qi Men application. Each Qi Men Dun Jia Chart contains combinations of the Zheng and Qi forces in each of the sectors. In a Qi Men Forecast Chart, the Day Stem always represents the "Self" and in most general cases, the Hour Stem represents the "Subject Matter". Sometimes, in advanced forecasting, the *Yong Shen* 用神 (also known as the Useful God which represents the subject matter's focus point) needs to be specifically determined.

The location of the Hour Stem or the *Yong Shen* in a Qi Men Chart will allow you to forecast the outcome of an event or an action. Such is the power of a Qi Men Dun Jia Forecast. War strategists use this to ascertain what is the best action or route to take to subdue an enemy. How can we do this? It is simple – by analysing the *Zheng* and *Qi* forces in these two Palaces. If the Palace is primarily made up of *Qi* forces, you know the outcome will be favorable. This is especially true if the Hour Stem or the *Yong Shen's* Palace produces the Day Stem Palace.

THE SUBSTANTIAL AND THE INSUBSTANTIAL 虛實

ORIGINAL TEXT:

孫子曰：凡先處戰地而待敵者佚，
後處戰地而趨戰者勞。
故善戰者，致人而不致于人。
能使敵人自至者，利之也；
能使敵不得至者，害之也。
故敵佚能勞之，飽能飢之，
安能動之。

TRANSLITERATION:

Sun Tzu said: He who arrives at the battlefield early and awaits his enemy will be rested and at ease; he who arrives late will be tired and will wage war in haste. Those who are skilled in war will always have the upper hand over their enemies and they will never be manipulated.

If you provide the enemy with the right incentive, it will not be hard to lead them into a trap. Equally, threaten them with danger and they will halt their advance. A skillful commander will exhaust the enemy while he remains invigorated, starve the enemy while he is replete and force the enemy into action while he awaits his opportunity.

COMMENTARY:

A skilled leader only places himself in situations that gives him the advantage. He also knows how to manipulate and tire his opponents in order to tilt the odds further in his favor. Fairness is not a requirement in competition – all that matters are the results. For easy victory, give yourself an 'unfair advantage'. Find the angles that you can exploit.

Being proactive is one way of placing yourself in a substantial – or advantageous – position over your competitor. In this passage, Sun Tzu explains the importance of making the first move. By choosing the time and place of battle and arriving first, the intelligent commander ensures that his competitor has no choice but to pursue him and arrive exhausted. Which side do you guess is more likely to win in the ensuing battle?

Create situations and competition that are rigged in your favor. Use diplomacy and manipulation to lure your rivals into a weaker spot so that you can overcome them. When you make others chase you, they must compete on your terms or not at all. If they choose to compete, you will have a great advantage over them because you get to set the house rules.

ORIGINAL TEXT:

出其所不趨，趨其所不意；
行千里而不勞者，行于無人之地也；
攻而必取者，攻其所不守也；
守而必固者，守其所不攻也。
故善攻者，敵不知其所守；善守者，
敵不知其所攻。微乎微乎！
至于無形；神乎神乎！
至于無聲，故能爲敵之司命。

TRANSLITERATION:

Make your appearance at a time and place where you are least expected and where the enemy has not yet set up camp. The only way that you can march your men a thousand li without exhausting them is if you march through territory where the enemy has not yet set up a perimeter. In this way, you can be sure to retain that which you defend, as the enemy will not be there to attack it and you are certain to take that which you pursue, as it will be far too late for the enemy to fortify it.

Those who are skilled in the attack achieve their victories because the enemy does not know where, how, or what to defend. Those who are adept in defense are secure because the enemy does not know who or what to attack. Be silent and enigmatic so that no soul will ever hear your secrets and be covert and elusive so that nobody will ever find a trace of you. If you can do this, you will hold the enemy's very fate in your hands.

COMMENTARY:

Be unpredictable and covert. Defy your opponents' expectations. Act first, fast.

By varying your competitive tactics, you gain the element of surprise. This will force your opponent to defend against all possibilities equally and so they will spread themselves thin, which creates opportunity. When you launch a strong attack against an undefended, unprepared opponent then this usually results in success for you. Strike out against your opponent in creative ways and keep them guessing. Their attempts to defend against all possible outcomes will exhaust them and deplete their morale. This is known and understood in the sporting world where athletes use false movement and deceptive plays to wear down defending opponents. Clever and unpredictable maneuvering allows you to take what you want without resistance.

Speak rarely of your plans and only to the people you need to help make them a reality. Within your organization or team, keep important information on a need to know basis. From time to time, release incorrect or conflicting information to your competition. Pursue multiple lines of inquiry and make this known so that your rivals cannot be sure of your next action. Secrecy and misdirection go a long way towards awarding you the element of surprise but at the end of the day, your actions speak volumes, so varied posturing must be backed up by varied action. Even if you find a winning strategy, use another one the next time. In short, make your opponents work hard to keep up.

ORIGINAL TEXT:

進而不可禦者,衝其虛也;
退而不可追者,速而不可及也。
故我欲戰,敵雖高壘深溝,
不得不與我戰者,攻其所必救也;
我不欲戰,雖劃地而守之,
敵不得與我戰者,乖其所之也。

TRANSLITERATION:

Very often, a general's offensive is powerful simply because he attacks where his enemy is weak and at a loss to mount a defense. Equally, he may be able to retreat without being overtaken because he moves so swiftly that the enemy has no hope to pursue. Though the enemy may be entrenched and firm in their position with high ramparts and deep trenches, we may yet compel him to fight, and abandon his stronghold, if we attack in such a place where he has no option but to make haste to defend it. If we wish to be secure, even though we may put up few defenses, we may yet be safe from attack if we divert the enemy's attention away from our encampment, making him go where we want him to and not where he had planned.

COMMENTARY:

Focus on the right targets. Your effective strength is decided primarily by the way you use what you have – money, manpower, skill, time - rather than by how much of these resources you have. A team of five who lead a well-directed effort can accomplish more than a team of twenty who lack focus. Look for the gaps that your competitor hasn't got covered – that's where you can make your competitive breakthroughs, even if you are outgunned.

Small businesses come to topple larger ones by constantly looking for the edge; the chance to focus their substantial power against their competitor's insubstantial fronts. Nobody can be strong everywhere, after all.

In order to identify such gaps, ask yourself what you can do better. What can set you apart? Price? Quality? Find out what specialized services or skills your opponent offers at a poor standard and then outclass them. In doing so, you are guaranteed to win their market share in the niche. By concentrating their force on the right targets, a small businesses can achieve superiority in a successive series of small, niche markets. Eventually, they can grow in size and strength and become a real contender, all under their opponent's nose. This is strategy.

To defend your own interests, use diversion. You can coax more viable rivals into competing against you in unfamiliar territory or outside their comfort zone so that their advantages are nullified. Set the bait and direct your opponent down wasteful avenues. It is easier and cheaper to mislead than it is to duke it out head on in order to protect your interests.

ORIGINAL TEXT:

故形人而我無形，
則我專而敵分，我專爲一，
敵分爲十，
是以十攻其一也。
則我眾而敵寡，能以眾擊寡，
則我之所與戰者，約矣。

TRANSLITERATION:

If we are able to uncover the location of the enemy's troops and their exact disposition while maintaining the security of our own, we may be able to work to further divide the enemy troops while ours remain concentrated. If the enemy forces are dispersed into ten groups while we remain combined, we will outnumber them ten to one in any single location. In using the many to strike at the few, we will be able to take victory with ease.

The location we intend to attack must remain a mystery to the enemy. If they do not know our intentions, they will be forced to defend several key places at once in order to cover every eventuality. The more areas that they are forced to defend, the fewer troops they can deploy to each location.

COMMENTARY:

Even the largest competitor can be overthrown via a series of well chosen smaller attacks. By hitting them where they are vulnerable and in an unpredictable pattern, you can take their market share and profit away, little by little. The trick is to compete on smaller fronts where you are more specialized and capable and to do so with overwhelming force, assuring dominance.

To win in this way, you must first learn about your competitor and their market. Knowledge is power. Find out what areas they operate in and find out where they are under performing. In other words, find out what you can do better and do it. By achieving domination in a series of smaller niches you can grow in strength overall. If you combine focused force with explosive speed against an opponent's mediocre operations then you can relegate them to second place.

Note that you must keep your attack strategies and tactics secret. If your competitor sees you coming, they will be able to block your efforts. As you impede more and more upon their territory, they will become more keen to stop you. Mix it up and throw them off balance. In their efforts to cover all eventualities they'll spread themselves thin, weakening their entire defense.

ORIGINAL TEXT:

吾所與戰之地不可知，不可知，則敵所備者多，敵所備者多，則我所與戰者寡矣。故備前則後寡，備後則前寡，備左則右寡，備右則左寡，無所不備，則無所不寡。寡者，備人者也；眾者，使人備己者也。

TRANSLITERATION:

If the enemy takes great pains to defend his forward position then his rear is likely to be undefended. If he has deployed his troops to fortify the rear, his forward position may be left open. If he has taken measures to strengthen his presence to the right, his left position may be weakened and likewise if his left flank is covered, his right may be exposed. If he has taken pains to defend all areas equally, his forces may be spread too thin and all areas will be equally undefended. Those who are weak must prepare to defend against every eventuality as those who are strong will demand it.

COMMENTARY:

Victory is the inevitable result of bringing great strength to bear against weakness; of pitting the substantial against the insubstantial. You must identify areas of weakness in regard to your competitors and focus your efforts there to make breakthroughs.

You can often determine your opponents' weaknesses and shortcomings by looking at their strengths, which can be determined with ease. Everyone advertises their strengths with great confidence and at a high volume but nobody ever advertises or broadcasts their shortcomings. By looking at the way others present themselves and what isn't said you can make an educated guess about where their weaknesses may lie.

If you notice that a rival has many lines of business and interests then they may be too diversified. This is a weakness. With a little force, you should be able to surpass them in any specialty of your choosing.

If you are small and weak, you must be prepared to defend yourself rigorously. Budget and plan accordingly.

ORIGINAL TEXT:

故知戰之地，知戰之日，
則可千里而會戰。不知戰地，
不知戰日，則左不能救右，
右不能救左，前不能救後，
後不能救前，而況遠者數十里，
近者數里乎？以吾度之，
越人之兵雖多，亦奚益于勝哉？
故曰：勝可爲也，敵雖眾，
可使無鬥。

TRANSLITERATION:

If a general knows the exact time and place of a battle, he may march his entire army a thousand li and still expect a decisive victory if his troops are strong. However, if he does not know the time and place of the battle, his men will be dispersed; his left wing will not be able to assist his right wing and his right wing will have no hope of supporting his left wing, his forward troops will not be able to turn back in time to help those at the rear and those at the rear will not be able to catch up in time to back up the troops at the front, all this without even investigating distant outposts which may be a few li away or even tens of li away.

My opinion is that the army of the state of Yue is very powerful and they have a great many men, but taking into account the above principle, does this make them any more certain of victory than a smaller army? Victory can be made. Even if the enemy's troops are many, we can find a way to weaken them and render them defenseless.

COMMENTARY:

Get organized. Study your opponents, know your customers and research the market thoroughly. Put yourself in your customer's shoes so you can truly understand where you stand as a service provider and how you might be able to excel.

If you are well organized, you can tackle even the largest objective with minimum confusion, fatigue or difficulty. The prerequisite is that you must have a crystal clear understanding of what you want to achieve. For having clarity itself is power. If you are disorganized or you lack vision, then you will be unable to create and execute tactics that support your strategic ideas.

In a team environment, good organization can create amazing results – with organization comes unity and productivity. The pitfalls of having a disorganized, unclear or dysfunctional team environment are obvious – no teamwork, no focus and no results!

Break down your competitive goals and identify clear milestones and targets. Create a structured working environment with clear requirements, expectations and responsibilities. Set deadlines, maintain clear lines of communication and request reports and updates so that you can stay in the loop. Update your people often and give feedback quickly. In short, keep everything running smoothly and you can move mountains.

If you can organize your manpower and resources better than your competitors then you can achieve a greater focus and superior results. Ten people working well together can achieve more than fifty people who cannot collaborate. Smaller groups of people are able to achieve more than larger groups and the differentiating factors are organization and communication.

For the optimum results, consider ways that you can confuse your competitor and their attempts to organize themselves with misguided information.

ORIGINAL TEXT:

故策之而知得失之計，
作之而知動靜之理，
形之而知死生之地，
角之而知有餘不足之處。
故形兵之極，至于無形；無形，
則深間不能窺，智者不能謀。
因形而措勝于眾，眾不能知，
人皆知我所以勝之形，
而莫知吾所以制勝之形；
故其戰勝不復，而應形於無窮。

TRANSLITERATION:

If you are able to analyze the enemy's situation and his battle plans you will be able to quickly discern his chances of victory. If you agitate the enemy, you will be able to observe his patterns of attack and defense. If you lure the enemy, you will be able to pick out the areas where he feels most vulnerable. If you count the number of horses and men that he has at his disposal, you will know his strengths and his weaknesses.

On the other side of the coin, the greatest art in warfare is to conceal your own tactics and capabilities from the enemy so that even the most cunning and devious of spies will not be able to discern your plans and even the greatest military minds will be unable to conspire against you. Even if you were to go on to make your tactics public and to explain that you won your victory through adapting your approach to the enemy's ever changing circumstances, they should still not be able to understand how you have achieved it. Though everyone may know your rationale, they will be unable to comprehend your application. The way to defeat the enemy must never be predictable, nor follow the tried and true. Instead, always change your strategy to match the mood of the moment and the enemy's particular situation at any given time.

COMMENTARY:

Knowledge is only potential power in a competition. Applied knowledge is true power. Analyze and study your competitor's track record, methods and thinking. Understand them so you can beat them.

When you have missing links in your knowledge, you can create test situations to see how your rivals react. Do something small to agitate them and see whether they bend or break. Create false leads and measure the speed, nature and effectiveness of their response to it. Try posing as a customer and working your way through their sales funnel to see how they do business. You might find areas where they are lacking that can be exploited. Infiltrate and investigate!

You must become unpredictable. Being unpredictable doesn't mean that you should make bad calls or do things which don't make sense. What it means is that you must conceal your intentions and your reasoning. Under a veil of enigma you can obtain results more readily and with less effort. You can divert attention from your weaknesses and shortcomings. With the element of surprise, the odds slide into your favor. Secrecy is a powerful weapon.

In order to become less predictable, dismiss your initial, second and third ideas. Think laterally. If you execute a plan successfully, don't re-use the same plan. Feign interest in one course of action then pursue another. Make it a point to create a culture of secrecy within your organization. This is the method Steve Jobs famously adopted during his tenure as CEO of Apple. Keep your true plans private until the last possible moment and keep your methods in-house. Legally, you can use non disclosure methods to enforce your wishes and privately you can ensure stealth by telling others only what they need to know. Companies often leak incorrect information or use code names and dummy projects to throw others off the trail – learn from their example. Distract, confuse, divert and unsettle your rivals! During his tenure, Steve Jobs would drive his competitors crazy with these simple tricks. Steve Jobs was apparently a master of Sun Tzu's warcraft and his results speak volumes!

Ideally, when you do finally make your move, it should appear as if it has come out of the blue to others. If you can seem enigmatic and adaptable to others then they will always be one step behind.

ORIGINAL TEXT:

夫兵形象水，水之形，
避高而趨下：兵之形，
避實而擊虛；水因地而制流，
兵因敵而制勝。故兵無常勢，
水無常形；能因敵變化而取勝，
謂之神。故五行無常勝，
四時無常位，日有短長，
月有死生。

TRANSLITERATION:

Military strategy may be compared to flowing water. Water follows a path from high to low. Similarly, a good military strategy always avoids attack of the enemy's strong points and instead aims lower to attack only his weak points. Just as water's course is dictated by the many different landforms, the course of successful military strategy is decided by the changing circumstances and capabilities of the enemy.

Accordingly, just as the flow of a river does not follow a constant path, the tactics a commander uses in battle must constantly evolve. The commander who is able to win victory by adapting his approach to the needs of the moment and the changing circumstances of his enemy is the one who shows the greatest skill and the most complete understanding of military operations. It is like the wuxing (5 Elements), in which no element is ever dominant or the four seasons, no one of which can ever last forever, the turning of days which may be longer or shorter dependent on the time of year and the great orb of the moon which goes through its cycle; waxing and waning.

COMMENTARY:

Competition is an ongoing matter. The market is ever evolving and changing. You must continuously update and reassess your tactics so that you move – almost like water – towards your destination in the most opportune way. If you see a short cut or easier way to reach your targets then you must take it, even if your original strategy did not prescribe it.

The only thing that is certain in life or business is change itself and so you must never become too rigid or stubborn about your chosen course or you risk falling behind as a result of change. You must be adaptive and flexible like water. If you tether yourself tightly to a predetermined plan, then you run the risk of becoming rigid and predictable. If you are predictable, your competitors can second guess you and undermine your efforts. If you employ timely tactical decision and revise your plans as you go, then you won't have to worry about being predictable or missing out. Make change work for you. Embracing change can also help you make headway against competitors who try in vain to work against it.

Anticipate change. Preliminary planning is of great importance, but you must give yourself tactical maneuvering room when drawing up your plans so that you can alter your course along the way. Don't assume too much and remember, if you cannot change your mind, you cannot change anything.

6

QI MEN DUN JIA :

In the preceding chapter, Sun Tzu spoke about the existence and utility of both the mundane (direct) and extraordinary (indirect) forces in life. He used the terms *Zheng* 正 to describe mundane force and *Qi* 奇 to describe extraordinary force.

In this chapter, Sun Tzu covers the principles of the *Substantial* 實 and the *Insubstantial* 虛. He details the wisdom of pitting strength against weakness in order to achieve competitive breakthroughs.

In Qi Men Dun Jia parlance, we can use the synonyms *Substance* and *Void* to refer to the Substantial and the Insubstantial. The underlying meaning remains the same.

In Qi Men, there is a concept known as *Kong Wang* 空亡 or "Death & Emptiness" which is relatable to Sun Tzu's teachings on the Substantial and Insubstantial, as you will see. Via consideration of this concept, we can use Qi Men in accordance with Sun Tzu's principles.

Within every Qi Men Dun Jia Chart, there are Palaces which are said to be "solid" or of "substance" and there are Palaces which are "void". Solid Palaces are those which are not affected by *Death & Emptiness*. Palaces which are affected by the *Death & Emptiness* are known as "void" Palaces. These Palaces are marked with "DE" on a Qi Men Chart, as shown on the following page for a Chart plotted on 15 May, 2014 at 5.30am.

Forecast Date: 15 May, 2014 at 5.30am

局 STRUCTURE:	日 DAY:	時 HOUR:
陽一局 YANG ONE	丙戌 Bing Xu **Fire Dog**	辛卯 Xin Mao **Metal Rabbit** (5am - 6.59am)

Death & Emptiness

SE 巽 4木 / 馬HS Horse	**S** 離 9火 / 空DE	/ 坤 2土 **SW**

庚 沖 符
Geng Chong Fu
  Destructor Chief
	辛 輔 蛇
	Xin Fu She
	  Assistant Snake
	辛 虎 真 地 雲
	刑 猖 詐 遁 遁
	Xin Hu Zhen Di Yun
	Xing Chang Zha Dun Dun
		乙 英 陰
		Yi Ying Yin
		  Hero Moon
		日 墓
		Ri Mu

辛 死 **9**
Xin Si
  Death
	乙 驚 **5**
	Yi Jing
	壬 Fear
	Ren
		己 開 **7**
		Ji Kai
		  Open

丙 任 天 Bing Ren Tian Ambassador Heaven 月 跌 天 權 癸 白 旺 穴 假 怡 Ying Yue Die Tian Quan Bai Wang Xue Jia Yi	壬 Ren	己 芮 合 Ji Rui He 壬 Grain Harmony Ren

E 震 3木 / 庚 景 **8**
Geng Jing
  Scenery
	壬 **Ren**	丁 休 **3**
		Ding Xiu
		  Rest / 兌 7金 **W**

戊 蓬 地
Wu Peng Di
  Grass Earth
籠 返
Long Fan
	癸 心 雀
	Gui Xin Que
	  Heart Phoenix
		丁 柱 陳
		Ding Zhu Chen
		  Pillar Hook
		朱 投
		Zhu Tou

丙 杜 **4**
Bing Du
  Delusion
	戊 傷 **6**
	Wu Shang
	  Harm
		癸 生 **2**
		Gui Sheng
		  Life

NE 艮 8土	**N** 坎 1水	6金 乾 **NW**

符首 **Lead Stem**	庚 Geng		馬HS **Horse Star**	空DE **Death & Emptiness**
直使 **Envoy**	傷門 Harm Door		巳 Si **Snake**	午 Wu **Horse**
直符 **Lead Star**	天沖星 Heavenly Destructor			未 Wei **Goat**

Joey Yap's Qi Men Dun Jia Sun Tzu Warcraft

When a Palace is affected by *Death & Emptiness* it indicates that the results of the action in question will be compromised, reduced or diminished in some way. In Qi Men parlance, it is said that the contents of the Palace (and what it represents) have "entered into Emptiness".

Although this sounds scary and ominous, it does not necessarily mean a negative outcome. *Death & Emptiness* renders any positive formation in the Palace moot but it can also render any negative formation moot too! It basically neutralizes the effects of the Palace.

Palaces which "enters into Emptiness" are seen as weak positions (or directions) in a Qi Men Dun Jia Chart. The influence of *Death & Emptiness* can be a help or hindrance depending on other characteristics of the forecast or reading.

Let's examine another example.

Example:

Forecast Date :	22 April, 1992 at 3.39pm	
局 STRUCTURE:	日 DAY :	時 HOUR :
陽五局 YANG FIVE	戊辰 Wu Chen **Earth Dragon**	庚申 Geng Shen **Metal Monkey** (3pm - 4.59pm)

SE 丁 芮 雀 / 乙 死 4 / 壬 英 陳 / 丙 景 3 / 辛 杜 8	**S** 庚 柱 地 / 壬 驚 9 / 戊 / 丙 沖 陰 / 癸 傷 1	**SW** 己 心 天 / 丁 開 2 / 癸 蓬 符 / 庚 休 7 / 己 生 6 **NW**

符首 **Lead Stem**	癸 Gui	馬 馬星 **Horse Star**	寅 Yin **Tiger**
直使 **Envoy**	休門 Rest Door	空 空亡 **Death & Emptiness**	子 Zi **Rat** / 丑 Chou **Ox**
直符 **Lead Star**	天蓬星 Heavenly Grass		

In this Chart, *Death & Emptiness* bears influence in both the Kan (North) and Gen (Northeast) Palaces. However, the presence of *Death & Emptiness* in these two different Palaces produces two very different results. In the North sector, there is a positive Structure. The presence of *Death & Emptiness* minimizes these positive effects, creating a less auspicious outlook.

Meanwhile in the Northeast sector, there is a configuration known as *The Green Dragon Escape (青龍逃走)* that creates a negative outcome. The presence of *Death & Emptiness* here subdues these negative effects and so its presence may be considered welcome, although the overall result is still far from ideal.

Sun Tzu said that "To advance without the possibility of being checked, you must strike fast at the enemy's weakest points." A Qi Men Dun Jia Chart is like an energy map that helps illustrate what the most auspicious – and most advantageous – course of action in regard to your goals. It can also help reveal weakness in others so you know where to attack.

Imagine a scenario in which your rival at work is seated in a sector affected by *Death & Emptiness* and you are sitting in a solid sector (with positive *Qi* 奇 Stems). In this situation, you already have the upper hand! Application of Qi Men Dun Jia is straightforward and easy in this situation. Pre-plot a Qi Men Hour Chart for your boardmeeting (or competitive event) in order to plan out exactly where you should be seated and if possible, where your rival should sit for the best outcome. As Sun Tzu advocated at the start of this chapter, it is always beneficial to arrive early at the battle field and Qi Men can help in this regard. With Qi Men, you can position yourself to operate in the most advantageous sector and thus win the battle!

Understanding the influence of the Void sector (the *Death & Emptiness* sector) in Qi Men Dun Jia will help improve your overall analysis and in turn generate more accurate actionable information.

FIGHTING FOR MILITARY ADVANTAGE 軍爭

ORIGINAL TEXT:

孫子曰：凡用兵之法，將受命於君，合軍聚眾，交和而舍，莫難於軍爭。軍爭之難者，以迂為直，以患為利。故迂其途，而誘之以利，後人發，先人至，此知迂直之計者也。

TRANSLITERATION:

Sun Tzu said: in military operations the commanding officer receives his instructions from the head of state and it then becomes his task to assemble his forces into units which can be mobilized in order to confront the enemy. During this process, nothing is more challenging than planning a strategy in order to maneuver himself and his troops into an advantageous position.

The central challenge in this process is to create a direct route to victory without revealing his intentions to the enemy. He must work to create a strategy that will create a tactical advantage even in the face of disadvantage. In most cases, he will attempt to deceive the enemy or to create a distraction in order to redirect their attention and force them to slow down or deviate, giving his own troops the opportunity to strike early while the enemy is unprepared. If he can achieve this then he has demonstrated that he understands the art of deception.

COMMENTARY:

As a leader, you will rarely get to work in ideal conditions or have access to all of the resources you would like. In many situations, the odds may be stacked decidedly against your success. Simply throwing yourself into direct competition against the odds and hoping for the best is ridiculous. You must find ways to put your opponents at a disadvantage even when you are weak.

According to Sun Tzu - Deception can let you do this. The word 'deception' however carries a negative connotation. While it is all right to deceive an enemy in War, but in the modern business world, deceiving is unethical and is frowned upon. The concept of deception in the modern context is better seen as the *ability to influence*, or the Art of Influencing. Strength, power and access to resources may not necessary be the deciding factors in competition unless you can master the art of influencing. In a negotiation where you have an upper hand, for instance, you could appear crestfallen in order to lure your opponents into overreaching. In this example, giving the false appearance of being incapable or incompetent would make it easier to defeat your opponent, as it will cause them to act with complacency.

When your nemesis has no idea what you plan to do, you have the advantage. When you can use misdirection to make them predict - and prepare for - your next move in error then it will be all for the better.

Misdirection and secrecy are also types of deception. They can surround you with an air of mystery and your rivals will have to second guess all of your decisions. The more powerful you are, the greater the psychological impact of using deception and secrecy - you can play mind games and win dominance psychologically, creating an advantage even before any real competition has taken place. Even if you fail to use deception, your competitors and rivals won't hesitate to mislead or deceive you if they can. Deception must be *expected* of others. Finally, remember that you should only use deception against your competitors, however, and never against your customers or allies.

ORIGINAL TEXT:

故軍爭為利，軍爭為危。
舉軍而爭利，則不及；
委軍而爭利，則輜重捐。
是故卷甲而趨，日夜不處，
倍道兼行，百里而爭利，
則擒三將軍，勁者先，疲者後，
其法十一而至；五十里而爭利，
則蹶上將軍，其法半至；
卅里而爭利，則三分之二至。
是故軍無輜重則亡，
無糧食則亡，無委積則亡。

TRANSLITERATION:

Although there are obvious advantages to arriving early at the scene of a battle, any potential hazards should not be ignored. For an entire army to move into position, they must mobilize not only themselves but also their weaponry and provisions. This may be time consuming and it is likely to slow them down. If they were to leave their weaponry and provisions behind, however, they would certainly lose them.

In marching day and night while loaded with provisions in order to reach their target rapidly, an army also runs the risk of being divided. Those who are strong and powerful may arrive ahead of their comrades and face the possibility of being captured, while the weaker and less vigorous among them will lag behind and lose their fellows. If an army were to march thirty li, it is possible that only two thirds of their number will arrive on schedule and these numbers will only deteriorate with greater distances. For a march of fifty li, around half will arrive on time and for a march of a hundred li, a tenth.

Everyone knows that an army that travels without weaponry and provisions will soon be defeated.

COMMENTARY:

Weigh up the costs and benefits of every course of action. For the benefit you identify in one area, there is often a drawback of some kind in another and you must weigh all things against each other before arriving at your conclusion. What makes sense in one situation might not in another and so it isn't always obvious what the most tactically advantageous route is. Here, Sun Tzu described the hidden perils of trying to grow too quickly or moving too fast in order to illustrate this point.

Let's consider the so-called "first mover advantage". The conventional wisdom is that arriving first in a new market is best. Even here, however, there are tradeoffs which must be considered. The returns in any new venture are uncertain and the difficulties you may face in a new market are unknowable in advance. In exchange for the possibility of attaining the profits usually gained by the first mover in the market, the business must definitely bear the full cost of researching, developing, refining and optimizing their new product, service and business model.

If there are any lessons that must be learned in the marketplace, the first business to enter will pay the cost of learning them alone. Any subsequent companies who begin offering the same service will both benefit from and avoid the cost of making the same mistakes. They will be able to take much of the same profit at a far smaller cost. Sometimes, it may be advantageous to let a rival take first place and bear the cost so that you can build upon their work.

Moving too quickly towards your goal without proper planning and the lack of a stress-tested strategy can lead to disaster. Conversely, moving too slowly can mean losing out on market share and thus, profit.

You need to look at all the facts when making tactical decisions.

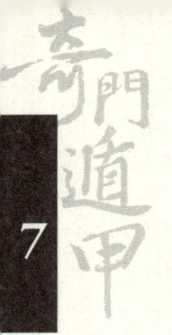

ORIGINAL TEXT:

故不知諸侯之謀者，不能豫交；
不知山林、險阻、沮澤之形者，
不能行軍，不能鄉導者，
不能得地利。

TRANSLITERATION:

A commanding officer who does not understand the intricacies of politics and diplomacy will not be able to work effectively with political leaders. A commander who is not familiar with the geography and topography of the land will not be able to plan a marching route or transport his troops safely. If he does not employ the help of local guides, it will not be possible for him to find a tactical advantage.

COMMENTARY:

An exceptional leader must have exceptional people skills. They must identify people who have power, connections and abilities of use and avoid those who are treacherous. Brilliant leaders must also have razor sharp communication abilities so that they can direct and manage people and their talent in accordance with their vision for the future. Maintaining ties with the correct people can create opportunities that are unavailable to others and so having political savvy is a tactical advantage. A true leader must never behave like a victim for an excuse to victimize others.

A keen awareness of your operational environment is just as important as social intelligence. In business, understanding current market conditions is vital. With an eye on the features of the market you can spot profitable gaps, trends and safe 'routes' towards your goals. The more you know about the environment you operate in, the better you can navigate it.

Ultimately, a greater level of understanding allows for superior tactical decision making.

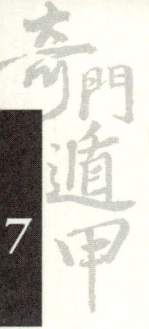

ORIGINAL TEXT:

故兵以詐立，以利動，
以分合爲變者也，故其疾如風，
其徐如林，侵掠如火，
不動如山，難知如陰，
動如雷霆。掠鄉分眾，
廓地分利，懸權而動，
先知迂直之計者勝，此軍爭之法也。

TRANSLITERATION:

In military operations, victory is gained through the use of effective strategy. Deception is your friend. You must seek tactical advantage and deploy your troops to make the most out of any given circumstances. You should be prepared to fly like the wind when rapid action is called for, be as unyielding and unshakable as the forest when marching in formation, be as fierce and unstoppable as a raging fire in times of battle, be as strong and stable as a mountain when fortifying your territory, be as mysterious as the mists in covert operations and strike like lighting when the moment is right. It is important to carefully observe the situation in order to direct your men towards the best possible course of action. A new territory may be plundered or defended at strategic points. The commander who is able to master both direct and indirect tactics will be sure to achieve victory. This is the art of strategy and manoeuvring against the enemy.

COMMENTARY:

In business, strategic planning dictates your long term goals. Tactical decision-making helps you move towards your goals under the given circumstances and Deception allows you to nullify your own shortcomings and misdirect the competition.

Your tactical approaches must be as varied as the conditions you encounter. Here, Sun Tzu described various tactical situations which require different responses.

Sometimes you must act quickly, even at increased cost, when there is a transient window of opportunity. For instance, when a vacuum is created in the market as an existing player leaves. Moving too quickly in the pursuit of your goals, however, can be just as ruinous as moving too slowly. Hasty attempts at growth can cause your team to fracture and you may find yourself skipping important steps and ignoring valid contributions in the name of "progress". Sometimes it may be smarter to walk the long route to success for a better long-term outlook.

Look at the facts and ask what it is called for. Only one thing is certain – there is no 'one size fits all' tactic that will always work, so you must be willing to mix it up. Different situations beg for different tactics and the way that you tailor your tactics will define your long term results. As a leader, it is up to you to choose the best route ahead for you and your organization, based on existing circumstances.

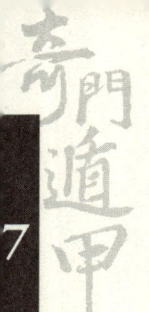

ORIGINAL TEXT:

軍政曰：「言不相聞，
故為金鼓；視不相見，
故為旌旗。」夫金鼓旌旗者，
所以一人之耳目也；
人既專一，則勇者不得獨進，
怯者不得獨退，此用眾之法也。
故夜戰多火鼓，晝戰多旌旗，
所以變人之耳目也。

TRANSLITERATION:

The book Military Management says that 'Gongs and Drums are used in battle because voices are not heard; banners and flags are used because soldiers cannot easily identify one another.'

In this way gongs, drums, flags and banners can be used to unify an army.

When forces have been brought together in this way, the courageous are less likely to try to advance ahead and the cowardly are less likely to retreat alone. Therefore, this is the way to direct a large army to maneuver as one.

During the night it is best to use drums and fires as signals while banners and flags should be used during the day instead. This also helps to hone soldiers' ability to see and hear.

COMMENTARY:

Leaders can use symbolism, metaphors and branding to unite their people and create a unified front to intimidate their rivals. The flag of a country is so much more than just a piece of cloth; it can be used as a tool to rouse patriotism, loyalty and spirits among the troops. A country's flag is used to remind people that they are a part of a larger team and instill a sense of obligation. Indeed, patriotism – created using imagery and branding – is so powerful that many people are willing to die for their country.

As human being, we can derive incredible strength from imagery. Capitalize on this fact: choose branding imagery that clearly represents and articulates your vision and the values of your organization. Use it to build team spirit and start a legacy. When people feel that they are a part of something bigger and that they have an idea to strive for, then they will give a greater portion of themselves to the cause.

ORIGINAL TEXT:

故三軍可奪氣，將軍可奪心。
是故朝氣銳，晝氣惰，暮氣歸；

TRANSLITERATION:

It is important to take action that reduces the morale of enemy forces and to dent their commanding officer's confidence. At the beginning of a conflict, both sides are generally very keen and optimistic. After a certain period of time, their energy will begin to wane and their conviction may be shaken. In the final stages of war, it may be so weak that the soldiers will lack for the spirit required to fight.

COMMENTARY:

Use psychological warfare techniques to get ahead. It is said that the battle is won in the mind and this is true when your opponent loses the will to fight, you can move in and claim your prize with ease.

In competitive boxing, fighters go to great lengths to brag and exaggerate their fighting prowess; they understand that reducing their opponents' conviction can assure victory. Muhammad Ali is as famous today for his quips as he is for his legendary fighting. Attacking the confidence of your rivals causes them to second guess their abilities, leading them to a state of indecision and inaction. With their inaction comes a golden chance for you to advance.

You can undermine your competitor's confidence in a number of ways. The first is by fighting a war of attrition – confidence naturally wanes over time. If you are able to hold out longer in a deadlock, then your opponent will eventually lose their conviction. The second way to deplete your opponent's morale is through the use of surprise and shock tactics to exhaust them. Get inside your rival's head. Familiarize yourself with your opponent's cycle of observation-orientation-decision-action and time your efforts to confuse and tire them out.

You can maintain your own mental strength even under harsh circumstances and great pressure by returning to and focusing on your original driving vision. Remind yourself why you set the goals you did. If you can maintain energy, confidence and belief in yourself and in your mission while others are losing theirs, you will come out on top. Just remember that you must act. Coming up with a great idea, and then assembling a team to bring that idea to life is the first step in creating a successful business venture. While creating a truly unique concept and business idea is rare enough, the ability and discipline to successfully execute this idea is what truly separates the dreamers from the leaders.

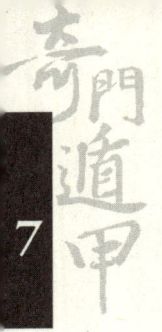

ORIGINAL TEXT:

故善用兵者，避其銳氣，
擊其惰歸，此治氣者也。
以治待亂，以靜待譁，此治心者
也。以近待遠，以佚待勞，
以飽待飢，此治力者也。
無邀正正之旗，勿擊堂堂之陣，
此治變者也；

TRANSLITERATION:

The skillful commander will not attack his enemy while the enemy is in good spirits and his morale is high. Instead, he will wait until his enemy is tired and weakened. He will aim to become the master of his enemy's morale. An effective commander will use discipline to gain control of disorder and face frenzy with calm and certainty. He will teach his troops the art of retaining self-control and emotional mastery. If he is able to gather his men in the battlefield to see his enemies still marching from afar, he can ensure that his men are well-fed and rested while the enemy troops will be hungry and tired upon their arrival. This is the best way to control military strength.

A skilful commander will never confront an enemy when his troops are lined up with their banners held high and their battle formations appearing strong and impressive. This demonstrates that he has a clear understanding of the use of tactics.

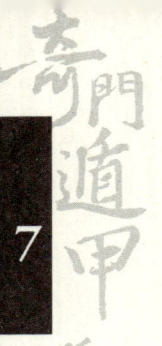

COMMENTARY:

If you try to overthrow your opponent while they are held in high esteem, you can expect a great deal of friction. In fact, your attempts can backfire completely, leading to a decline in your popularity and power. If, however, you make the decision to move forward when your opponent has fallen on hard times, then it will be much easier to do so and the journey to your new position will be much shorter. This wisdom lies at the heart of politics and the best politicians sync their ascent up the career ladder in time with the changing fortunes of their opposition.

Success in life, career or business can be attained more easily if we have prior knowledge of what can be expected in the future. This is the ability to anticipate and forecast the outcome of your own actions and decisions. This is especially necessary when you embark upon a new business venture and assemble a team. It is vital that you sell your team on your vision for the future. They must become invested in your dream. Even when you are leading a team in pursuit of your dream through uncharted waters with no clear guidance, you need to appear certain of your course as a leader. Remember that the way you act as a leader has a psychological impact on your organization. It is critical that your team develops confidence in you as well as your vision. One way to earn this confidence is to maintain your composure and strength under all circumstances. Your team will take their behavioral cues from you. So if you lead with strength, they will follow with strength.

Honesty and integrity are extremely important in leadership. When you become responsible for a team of people, you must raise the bar and your standards. Your business and your team are an extension and a reflection of yourself, so make sure you set a good example. If you display honesty and ethical behavior in some of your core values, rest assured that your team will do so too.

In the business world and in life, everything is uncertain. Oftentimes, the higher the risk of the task, the higher the pressure one will feel. This is where your ability to anticipate trouble - a leader's intuition - has to kick in. You need to listen to your instincts and guide your team through the challenges they face. When something unexpected occurs, or when your team is thrown into a new scenario, they will look to you for guidance. The ball will always be in your court and you will have to make tough calls and respond as the situation requires you to. Learning to trust yourself and fine-tune your instincts is as critical as earning your team's trust.

Your preparedness, confidence and good judgment will be returned by your staff in the form of respect, loyalty, work and obedience.

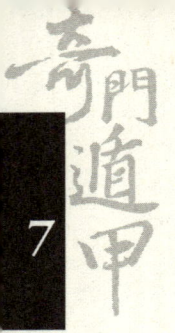

ORIGINAL TEXT:

故用兵之法，高陵勿向，
背邱勿逆，佯北勿從，
銳卒勿攻，餌兵勿食，
歸師勿遏，圍師必闕，
窮寇勿迫，此用兵之法也。

TRANSLITERATION:

Here are some principles of military operations:

Never launch an attack on an enemy who has the higher ground. Never attack an army head on when they can easily retreat to the higher ground of hills behind him. Never enter into a pursuit when he pretends to flee. Lastly, never attack when his forces are at the peak of their strength. Be cautious, do not immediately take any bait that is offered and do not seek to prevent the enemy from withdrawing from the battleground. If you are able to successfully surround your enemy, make sure that you give them a means of escape and do not press them too hard once they are in a desperate corner. Such is the art of waging war.

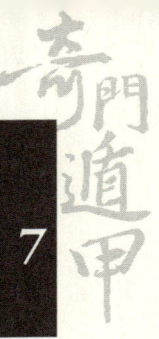

COMMENTARY:

You should never launch a front-on attack against an opponent who occupies a superior position when they have ample ability to defend themselves or hold the line. You must only attack when you either have clear superiority or when success can be decisively claimed. Don't bother fighting the battles you can't win.

Expect deception. Your competitors have a lot to gain by luring you into difficulty or throwing you off the trail. If it looks too good to be true, it usually is. Look for the catch and read the small print. Conduct research and determine who has vested interests and find out where the conflicts of interest lie. Due diligence is essential in business, don't skimp on it.

Once you corner the market and gain a monopoly over your opponent, you must handle their defeat with care. Allow them to save face. Give them the opportunity to leave on their own terms. Crushing your opponents entirely is a mistake. Anyone who has studied history knows that past enemies often become allies and it is wise to leave the door open for this possibility. In war, in politics and in business, there are neither permanent friends nor permanent enemies, only permanent interests.

QI MEN DUN JIA :

Sun Tzu said, "Victory belongs to he who has mastered the combination of the devious and the direct". Competitive tactics must never be fixed and immutable, they have to be timely and able to evolve as the situation unfolds. You must employ whatever tactic that will give you the upper hand at any given moment. Sometimes the best way to compete is by facing the enemy head on with superior numbers. On other occasions, the best course will be to scatter your forces and attack at multiple unexpected locations at once. The key to the success of all of these approaches is, of course, secrecy. Whatever you do, you must ensure that you can benefit from the element of surprise.

As explained in Chapter One, a Qi Men Dun Jia Chart is made up of four components: Heaven, Earth, Man and the Universe. Together, these can form combinations which may appear among the 10 Stems, 8 Doors, 8 Deities and 9 Stars which will lead to the formation of either positive or negative Structures within any given Palace. We can draw a parallel between Sun Tzu's teachings to a group of specific combinations in Qi Men Dun Jia known as the *3 Deceptions*, which are described on the following page.

Real Deception 眞詐						
地 Earth		人 Man	天 Heaven	神 Universe	宮 Palace	
天干 Heavenly Stem	地支 Earthly Stem	八門 8 Doors	九星 9 Stars	八神 8 Deities	
乙 Yi Yin Wood		休 Xiu Rest				
丙 Bing Yang Fire		生 Sheng Life		太陰 Great Moon	
丁 Ding Yin Fire		開 Kai Open				

Description

Favourable for concealing your tracks and to succeed in operations that are conducted under the radar as the Great Moon Deity represents concealment. Also suitable for retreating and seeking spiritual enhancement and worshipping.

This special formation causes the enemy to perceive you as being weak, unprepared or unconfident. This gives the appearance that you are incapable or incompetent. The purpose is to encourage complacency and slack in your competitors so that you can beat them more readily.

This is an example Chart plotted on 28 April, 2008 at 5.30am which shows the Real Deception Structure:

Forecast Date	28 April, 2008 at 5.30am

局 STRUCTURE:	日 DAY:	時 HOUR:
陽五局 YANG FIVE	戊戌 Wu Xu **Earth Dog**	乙卯 Yi Mao **Wood Rabbit** (5am - 6.59am)

Lead Stem	癸 Gui
Envoy	休門 Rest Door
Lead Star	天蓬星 Heavenly Grass

Horse Star	Death & Emptiness
巳 Si **Snake**	子 Zi **Rat** 丑 Chou **Ox**

In the Kun (Southwest) Palace, the Bing Heavenly Stem resides with both the Rest Door and the Great Moon, forming the *Real Deception* Structure.

Double Deception 重詐

Earth 地		Man 人	Heaven 天	Universe 神	Palace 宮
Heavenly Stem 天干	Earthly Stem 地支	8 Doors 八門	9 Stars 九星	8 Deities 八神	
乙 *Yi* Yin Wood		休 *Xiu* Rest			
丙 *Bing* Yang Fire		生 *Sheng* Life		九地 Nine Earth	
丁 *Ding* Yin Fire		開 *Kai* Open			

Description

This special formation is a form of misdirection and gives an aura of secrecy. It forces your rivals to second guess your decisions, become uncertain and fearful of your next move. The Double Deception formation gives an impression that you are more powerful than you really are. This causes great psychological impact on the enemy. With this formation, you can play mind games and win dominance psychologically, creating an advantage even before any real competition has taken place.

In other applications of this special formation, it is also favourable for personal development, improving one's attitude, exhibiting profound skills and physical strength because the Nine Earth Deity favours long-term, steady growth.

As the Nine Earth Deity also favours concealment, it is perfect for espionage and defense. This formation will also support money making activities, dealing with officers, assuming a new position or role and conceiving.

This is an example Chart plotted on 28 March, 2008 at 3.30pm which shows the Double Deception Structure:

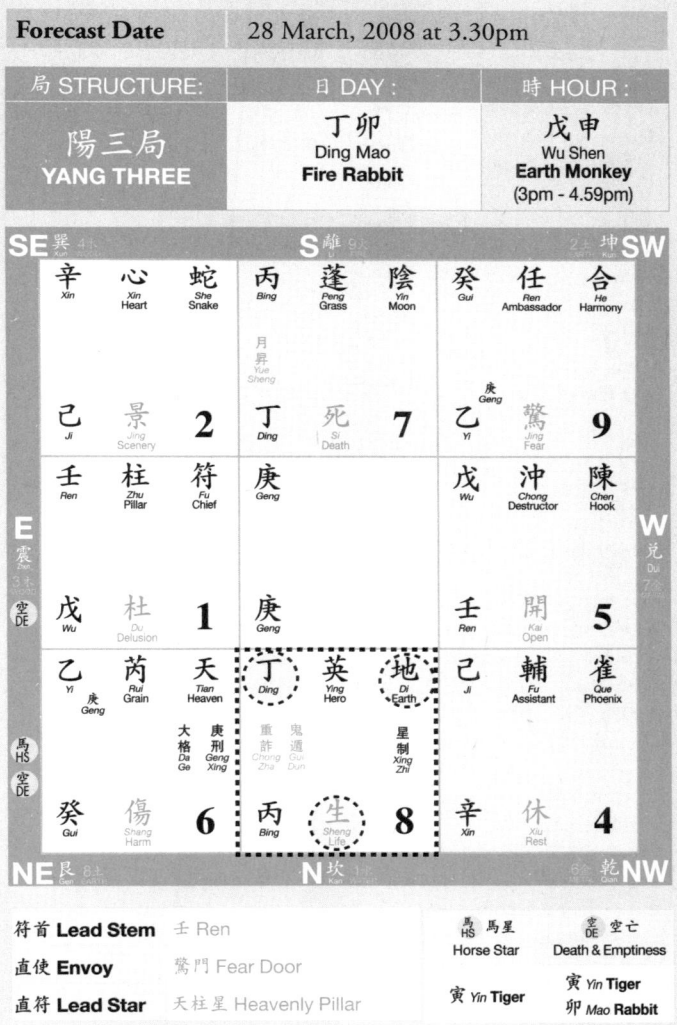

The Ding Stem, the Life Door and the Nine Heaven are all residing in the Kan (North) Palace. They form the auspicious *Double Deception* Structure.

Nobility Deception 休詐

地 Earth		人 Man	天 Heaven	神 Universe	宮 Palace
天干 Heavenly Stem	地支 Earthly Stem	八門 8 Doors	九星 9 Stars	八神 8 Deities	
乙 *Yi* Yin Wood 丙 *Bing* Yang Fire 丁 *Ding* Yin Fire		休 *Xiu* Rest 生 *Sheng* Life 開 *Kai* Open		六合 Six Harmony	

Description

This formation gives the impression to the enemy that you are non-aggressive and not interested in winning the battle. When your opponent has no idea what you plan to do, you are in a position of absolute advantage. This special formation can make the enemies predict – and prepare – for your next move in error. With this, you are at a greater advantage. You now become your enemies' puppeteers.

This formation is also very positive for forming subtle connections, winning other people's trust, convincing, influencing, mesmerizing or bonding with others as the Six Harmony Deity governs relationships and personal affairs. It is the master in all matters relating people and individual connections. It denotes good outcomes for seeking medication and asking for divine help.

This is an example Chart plotted on 3 November, 2009 at 7.30pm for the Nobility Deception Structure:

Forecast Date	3 November, 2009 at 7.30pm	
局 STRUCTURE:	日 DAY:	時 HOUR:
陽七局 YANG SEVEN	乙卯 Yi Mao **Wood Rabbit**	丙戌 Bing Xu **Fire Dog** (7pm - 8.59pm)

Lead Stem 符首	庚 Geng
Envoy 直使	景門 Scenery Door
Lead Star 直符	天英星 Heavenly Hero
Horse Star 馬星	申 Shen **Monkey**
Death & Emptiness 空亡	午 Wu **Horse** / 未 Wei **Goat**

The Yi Stem and the Six Harmony Deity are residing together here with the Open Door. This arrangement forms the *Nobility Deception* in the Kan (North) Palace.

When plotting a Qi Men Dun Jia Chart, having one or more of these formations present in the Chart is highly desirable when you seek to start something new. Though not every Chart will produce these kinds of formation, they are an indication of perfect timing when they do appear.

THE NINE VARIABLES 九變

8

ORIGINAL TEXT:

孫子曰：凡用兵之法，
將受命於君，合軍聚眾；
圮地無舍，衢地合交，
絕地無留，圍地則謀，
死地則戰，途有所不由，
軍有所不擊，城有所不攻，
地有所不爭，君命有所不受。

TRANSLITERATION:

Sun Tzu said: in war, the military commander will receive his orders from the ruler. It is then his task to marshal the forces available to him. It is best not to encamp where the terrain is unfavorable, instead aim to ally with the local princes whose territories are open in all directions. It is not wise to linger where the land is uninhabitable. If you must venture into an enclosed region, do so by keeping your wits about you and do not allow yourself to be drawn into a desperate battle where there is no way to advance or retreat. There are some roads that should not be followed, some enemies that should not be attacked, some cities and regions that should not be seized and some orders from the sovereign which need not to be obeyed.

COMMENTARY:

As a leader, it is your responsibility to get the job done with the resources available under the given circumstances. To this end, a combination of strategic and tactical intelligence and action is required. First, it is necessary to understand the difference between the two.

In business, both the short and the long term timeline must be considered. The time sensitivity of information is often what determines whether it is important strategically or tactically. A leader must seek out information of both tactical and strategic use so that he may have his eyes on the horizon and his hands on the wheel.

Strategically useful intelligence is what helps business leaders make estimations and predictions about the future in their industry or market. With this information, they can visualize the playing field of the future and begin to adjust themselves in order to do well when the time comes. Information about emerging trends, patterns or new technologies all have strategic utility.

Tactically useful intelligence should be gathered in real time. Customer feedback and sales figures are examples of this kind of information. Tactical intelligence helps drive real time improvement and indicates growth avenues that are conducive to businesses strategic objectives.

In most cases, strategic intelligence and planning should be handled by top management. It should then be left to middle management and those on the ground to handle tactical intelligence gathering and make tactical decisions. Through this division of labor and by delegating responsibility appropriately, a business can set and realize long term goals via constant, near real time adjustment and improvement.

As circumstances change and the situation 'on the ground' changes, your tactics must change too. Tactical flexibility is the hallmark of many successful organizations.

Successful organizations seek to both identify existing tactical advantages and create them. Often, the ability to do this comes with hard won experience but there are many common tricks that can be employed. Forming alliances with others can give you the added strength and leverage in a tough marketplace.

Choose your battles wisely. Some roads are dead ends and it is your job to know which without walking them all. Analyze the risks. Find out what the market wants. Look for the gaps. Pick the smartest strategic route.

Don't use the same tactics in all situations or you will become predictable. Being predictable is a weakness your rivals can exploit.

Finally, since the most informed person is the one on the ground, you must give those who have tactical responsibility the authority to act as they see fit in accordance with your wider goals. Similarly, in cases where you feel that tactically disobeying orders from above will preserve strategic viability, you must do so.

ORIGINAL TEXT:

故將通于九變之利者，
知用兵矣。
將不通于九變之利者，
雖知地形，
不能得地之利矣。
治兵不知九變之術，
雖知地利，
不能得人之用矣。

TRANSLITERATION:

There are nine variables that will make an impact on military strategy and it is incumbent upon a commanding officer to develop a thorough understanding of them all. Only he who knows these variables well will be able to have a complete comprehension of military operations. If he does not understand them, he will not be able to use the terrain to his advantage regardless of how well he knows the topography. If he does not take note of them, he will not be able to harness and direct the full power of his army no matter how well he knows the five advantages.

COMMENTARY:

Sun Tzu explained that any competent leader must be familiar with the "Nine Variables". These Nine Variables will help guide and shape strategic thinking. Without an understanding of them, you won't be able to correctly interpret circumstances in a strategic way, even if you understand the "Five Factors" (discussed in Chapter One).

Note that Sun Tzu did not literally mean that there are *nine* variables; this discrepancy can be attributed to a translation difficulty. One explanation is that the Chinese use the number "nine" to represent a non-determined large quantity. In other words, there are more than nine variables that must be considered and the general point being made here is that a leader must understand the strategy, generally speaking.

ORIGINAL TEXT:

是故智者之慮，
必雜于利害，
雜于利而務可信也，
雜于害而患可解也。
是故屈諸侯者以害，
役諸侯者以業，
趨諸侯者以利。

TRANSLITERATION:

A wise general will give thought to the positive factors that are working in his favor as well as any factors that may work against him. By pausing to consider the potential hazards that he may face, even when he is in an apparently advantageous position, he can be sure that he can stay one step ahead and achieve his goals. By taking time to identify the hidden advantages of a perilous situation, he may be able to resolve his difficulties.

In order to subdue hostile princes, it is necessary to threaten them with what they fear most. In order to compel them to do as you desire, you will need to keep them busy. In order to lead them wherever you wish, you will have to give them small advantages.

COMMENTARY:

In making your appraisal of an idea, be honest with yourself. Look at both the advantages and the disadvantages, equally. In any context, there is always an edge that you can exploit or that others can exploit against you. Never forget it or you can come undone.

When things are going according to plan, it's very easy to assume they always will. It is too tempting to forget the bitter taste of failure or how easily and rapidly things can change. This 'blindness' can create looming disaster, whereby a foolish person experiencing a period of transient success assumes that it will be constant and fails to prepare for change. Always cover yourself against a change in conditions of the unexpected. In business, this is called risk management. Think in a risk-averse way even when you are succeeding at your goals and hitting your targets. Ask yourself what might be around the corner, plan for it and you will have an advantage over your more reckless competitors who will get caught out. Put something aside for a rainy day and reinvest your profit in order to lay the foundation for continuing success.

Whatever is your competitive approach, it should be one that forges a new path which others must follow. Don't relegate yourself to a game of catch up – set your own rules. As a leader you can always be one step ahead and in a better position to misguide and misdirect your rivals as you see fit.

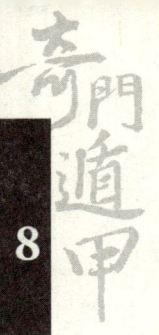

ORIGINAL TEXT:

故用兵之法，無恃其不來，
恃吾有以待之也；無恃其不攻，
恃吾有所不可攻也。

TRANSLITERATION:

In warfare, you should never rely on the likelihood of your enemy failing to arrive at the battlefield. Instead, you should rely on your own readiness to meet him. Do not expect your enemy to hold back or miss an opportunity to attack. Instead, know that you have made yourself invincible.

COMMENTARY:

Never assume that the competition isn't coming or that your position is entirely secure. You must always be ready to launch an offensive attack – it is not good enough to simply defend yourself against the competition. As they say, the best defense is a good offense!

In making preparation, you should focus on both reducing your own liabilities and further honing your specialized talents in order to stay ahead of the game. The degree to which you focus on one over the other is up to you and will be specific to your situation.

Take the fight to your rival or they will take it to you.

ORIGINAL TEXT:

故將有五危：
必死，可殺也；
必生，可虜也；
忿速，可侮也；
廉潔，可辱也；
愛民，可煩也。
凡此五危，將之過也，
用兵之災也。
覆軍殺將，必以五危，
不可不察也。

TRANSLITERATION:

There are five fatal weaknesses in a military commander. He who is brave but reckless, and knows only how to put up a desperate fight will easily be killed. He who is cowardly on the eve of battle will be captured. He who is quick tempered will be easily provoked into making rash decisions. He who has too delicate a sense of honor may be shamed into foolish action. He who is too benevolent and over-fond of his men may become hesitant and passive.

These five fatal weaknesses can be ruinous to military operations. The destruction of your army and the slaughter of your commanding officers are the inevitable results of these flaws.

COMMENTARY:

There are five weaknesses in a leader that generate failure. If you recognize them in yourself, try to remedy them and ensure that you don't advertise these shortcomings to others – even people who are close to you, as they create your wider reputation.

The first weakness is rashness, which is taking action without due consideration of the facts. When a rash leader succeeds, it probably has more to do with blind luck than anything else. The less purposefully and skillfully you direct your own efforts (and choose your results), the more that the outside world and other people will determine what you get instead. Unfortunately, nobody else has your best interests at heart, so you may not like what happens if you don't keep your hands on the wheel. You can capitalize on the recklessness of others by luring them into making costly mistakes.

The second weakness is excessive self-protection. A person who is so afraid of failure that they take no risks whatsoever will fail by default. Inaction is just as costly as taking the wrong course of action. If you identify such weakness in others you can take what you want from right under their nose – they won't do what is necessary to stop you.

The third weakness is anger. When you let any emotional state interfere with your decision making, your choices will be compromised. Don't allow yourself to make permanent mistakes because of a temporary feeling. Anger can cloud your judgment. A manager who shoots the messenger will surely stop receiving bad news, but they will also find themselves uninformed and unable to deal with problems. Do less when you are angry and if you can frustrate your opponent, then do so; anger diminishes performance in competition.

The fourth weakness is sensitivity. Do you take things too personally? Do you over-analyze the situation? Do you get defensive all the time? Excessive sensitivity can compel people to carry on doing something which isn't working because they don't want to endure embarrassment or shame. If you have sensitive competitors, you can push and pull them as you see fit by manipulating their emotions. If you are sensitive you must develop a thicker skin or you will remain unfit to lead in a competitive environment. Try to remove sensitivity, practice objectivity.

The final weakness in a leader is excessive kindness and empathy. These are positive traits but in a competitive environment they can hold you back. Other people will see that you are willing to give in easily and they will take from you until you have nothing left. Excessive attachment to others can prevent you from making the hard choices that create success such as redundant staff. The ways to exploit over-developed empathy in others are numerous; such people give too freely and take nothing in return – a profitable exchange for you!

QI MEN DUN JIA :

In this chapter, Sun Tzu discussed the importance of using a variety of tactical options in order to best respond to a variety of situations. He went on to discuss the need for adequate defensive plans and in having a realistic understanding of one's own strengths and weaknesses. He also outlines the incredible significance of good leadership skills in any successful group mobilisation.

As you will recall from the previous chapters, a Qi Men Dun Jia Chart is made up of a series of components including *Deities, Stars, Stems* and *Doors* which come together to form 'Structures 格局.' These Structures indicate the potential outcomes of different actions. We can think of each Structure as being associated with a different tactical option and so assessing the quality of each Structure lets you choose the best tactical option for the situation. Therefore, we can relate Qi Men Dun Jia to Sun Tzu's teachings in this Chapter via special Structures known as the Nine Dun 九遁. These 'Structures' indicate whether or not the conditions at the time considered support a proposed strategic operation.

Let's examine each on the Nine Dun 九遁 and their properties in turn.

Heavenly Dun 天遁 (Tian Dun)

地 Earth		人 Man	天 Heaven	神 Universe	宮 Palace
天干 Heavenly Stem	地支 Earthly Stem	八門 8 Doors	九星 9 Stars	八神 8 Deities	
丙 *Bing* Yang Fire	丁 *Ding* Yin Fire 戊 *Wu* Yang Earth	生 *Sheng* Life			
		開 *Kai* Open			

Description

This is the most favorable formation of the *Nine Dun*. It is auspicious for most activities. This is particularly suitable for keeping a steady pace, maintaining current wealth conditions, and even going into retirement. This formation will allow you to easily maintain that which you have already accumulated and achieved.

It is also beneficial for such affairs as giving an official statement or making an official announcement, career promotion, self-cultivation, reprimanding immoral people or those who are in the wrong, conducting new business deals, travel, marriage and moving house.

The following is an example Chart plotted on 27 December, 2006 at 5.30pm which shows the Structure for the Heavenly Dun appearing in the Kan (North) Palace.

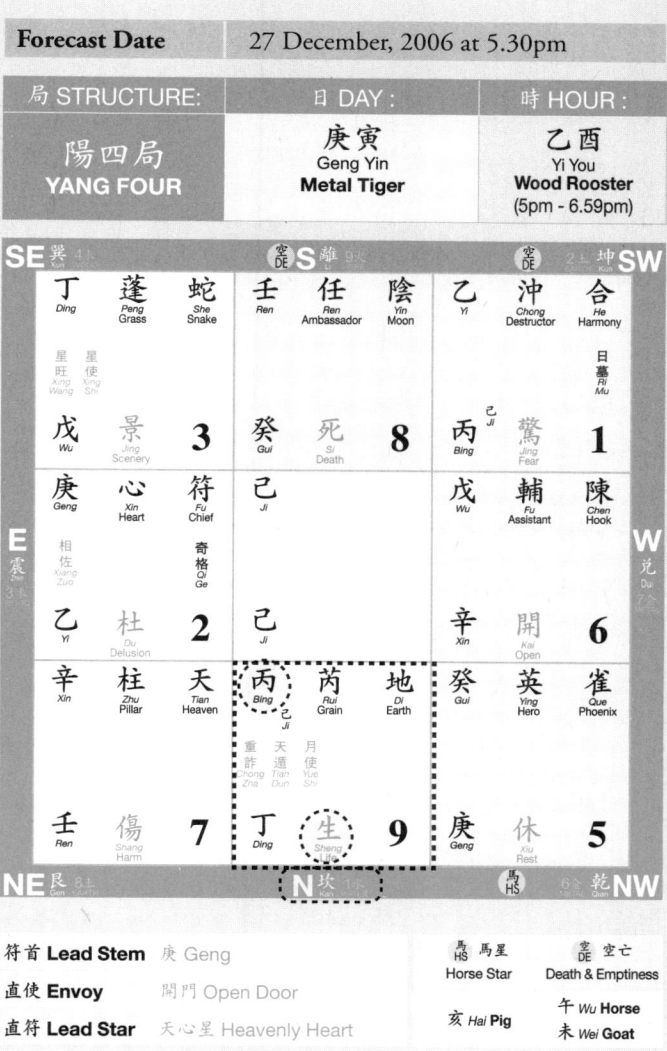

符首 **Lead Stem**	庚 Geng
直使 **Envoy**	開門 Open Door
直符 **Lead Star**	天心星 Heavenly Heart

| 馬星 Horse Star | 亥 Hai Pig |
| 空亡 Death & Emptiness | 午 Wu Horse / 未 Wei Goat |

In the Kan (North) Palace, the Bing Heavenly Stem, the Ding Earthly Stem and the Life Door form a combination of the Heavenly Dun.

Earthly Dun 地遁 (Di Dun)

地 Earth	人 Man	天 Heaven	神 Universe	宮 Palace
天干 Heavenly Stem	地支 Earthly Stem	八門 8 Doors	九星 9 Stars	八神 8 Deities
乙 *Yi* Yin Wood	己 *Ji* Yin Earth	開 *Kai* Open		

Description

This formation is great for setting up foundations or creating a system. It is also very positive for the construction or development of something from the ground up. Where something is chaotic and unstructured, this formation can help create order.

Examples of activities which will benefit from this formation include setting up camp, building a mansion or a warehouse, building walls, flattening a piece of land, opening or digging a mine, excavation, exploration or building something from scratch.

In some ways, this formation can also assist an individual in their quest for enlightenment via activities like soul-searching and meditation. The Earthly Dun enables someone to penetrate deep into the subconscious and explore the depths of their mind.

In ancient days, the Earth Dun formation was used for concealing, hiding and preparing troops for the purpose of carrying out a siege.

The following is an example Chart plotted on 21 April, 2007 at 11.30pm which shows the Structure for the Earthly Dun in the Zhen (East) Palace.

The Earthly Dun is formed by a combination of the Yi Heavenly Stem and the Ji Earthly Stem together with the Open Door in the Zhen (East) Palace.

Man Dun 人遁 (Ren Dun)

地 Earth		人 Man	天 Heaven	神 Universe	宮 Palace
天干 Heavenly Stem	地支 Earthly Stem	八門 8 Doors	九星 9 Stars	八神 8 Deities	
丁 *Ding* Yin Fire		休 *Xiu* Rest		太陰 *Tai Yin* Great Moon	

Description

This formation enables the right people with the right skills and right attitude to seek you out and aid you in your quest. This formation is about putting the right people in the right positions and maximizing their talents.

In modern practice, this formation is best used when hiring new staff, recruiting new blood or headhunting individuals with specific abilities.

The following is an example Chart plotted on 22 February, 2011 at 1.30am which shows the Structure for the Man Dun in the Kan (North) Palace.

Forecast Date	22 February, 2011 at 1.30am	
局 STRUCTURE:	日 DAY :	時 HOUR :
陽二局 YANG TWO	戊申 Wu Shen **Earth Monkey**	癸丑 Gui Chou **Water Ox** (1am - 2.59am)

丙 Bing	英 Ying Hero	雀 Que Phoenix	戊 Wu	芮 Rui Grain	地 Di Earth	癸 Gui	柱 Zhu Pillar	天 Tian Heaven
月旺 Yue Wang			辛 Xin 龍返 Long Fan			辛 Xin		
庚 Geng	杜 Du Delusion	**1**	丙 Bing	景 Jing Scenery	**6**	戊 Wu	死 Si Death	**8**
庚 Geng	輔 Fu Assistant	陳 Chen Hook	辛 Xin			壬 Ren	心 Xin Heart	符 Fu Chief
		刑格 Xing Ge						
空 DE	己 Ji	傷 Sheng Harm	**9**	辛 Xin			癸 Gui	驚 Jing Fear	**4**
	己 Ji	沖 Chong Destructor	合 He Harmony	丁 Ding	任 Ren Ambassador	陰 Yin Moon	乙 Yi	蓬 Peng Grass	蛇 She Snake
空 DE				真詐道 Zhen Ren Dun		星制 Xing Zhi	悖制 Quan Wu	日伏 Ri Shi	日制 Ri Zhi	日墓 Ri Mu
	丁 Ding	生 Sheng Life	**5**	乙 Yi	休 Xiu Rest	**7**	壬 Ren	開 Kai Open	**3**
							馬 HS		

符首 Lead Stem	壬 Ren		馬 HS 馬星 Horse Star	空 DE 空亡 Death & Emptiness
直使 Envoy	開門 Open Door		亥 Hai **Pig**	寅 Yin **Tiger**
直符 Lead Star	天心星 Heavenly Heart			卯 Mao **Rabbit**

The Ding Stem and the Rest Door with the Great Moon in the same Palace will form the Man Dun Structure.

Spirit Dun 神遁 (Shen Dun)

地 Earth		人 Man	天 Heaven	神 Universe	宮 Palace
天干 Heavenly Stem	地支 Earthly Stem	八門 8 Doors	九星 9 Stars	八神 8 Deities	
丙 *Bing* Yang Fire		生 *Sheng* Life		九天 Nine Heaven	
乙 *Yi* Yin Wood		休 *Xiu* Rest		九天 Nine Heaven	

Description

This is one of the most sought after formations in Qi Men Dun Jia. This formation connects you to the *spirit realm* or the Cosmic Plate and will help you get your prayers answered. If you seek Divine intervention, use this formation.

Its presence is also favorable for meditation, prayer and making wishes. In modern day application, this formation can be used to aid in subconscious mind programming, enabling a user to change his or her bad habits and manifest his or her desires.

The following is an example Chart plotted on 23 March, 2008 at 11.30pm which shows the Structure for the Spirit Dun in the Dui (West) Palace.

Forecast Date	23 March, 2008 at 11.30pm

局 STRUCTURE:	日 DAY:	時 HOUR:
陽四局 YANG FOUR	壬戌 Ren Xu **Water Dog**	庚子 Geng Zi **Metal Rat** (11pm - 12.59am)

SE 巽		S 離		SW 坤	
乙 Yi / 沖 Chong Destructor / 陳 Chen Hook	戊 Wu / 輔 Fu Assistant / 雀 Que Phoenix		癸 Gui / 英 Ying Hero / 地 Di Earth		
戊 Wu / 驚 Jing Fear **3**	癸 Gui / 開 Kai Open **8**		丙 Bing / 休 Xiu Rest **1** (己 Ji)		
壬 Ren / 任 Ren Ambassador / 合 He Harmony	己 Ji		丙 Bing (己 Ji) / 芮 Rui Grain / 天 Tian Heaven		
			跌穴 Die Xue / 權儀 Quan Yi / 神遁 Shen Dun		
乙 Yi / 死 Si Death **2**	己 Ji		辛 Xin / 生 Sheng Life **6**		
丁 Ding / 蓬 Peng Grass / 陰 Yin Moon	庚 Geng / 心 Xin Heart / 蛇 She Snake		辛 Xin / 柱 Zhu Pillar / 符 Fu Chief		
壬 Ren / 景 Jing Scenery **7**	丁 Ding / 杜 Du Delusion **9**		庚 Geng / 傷 Shang Harm **5**		
NE 艮		N 坎		NW 乾	

符首 Lead Stem	辛 Xin	馬 HS 馬星 Horse Star	空 DE 空亡 Death & Emptiness
直使 Envoy	驚門 Fear Door	寅 Yin **Tiger**	辰 Chen **Dragon**
直符 Lead Star	天柱星 Heavenly Pillar		巳 Si **Snake**

With the Bing Stem, the Life Door and the Nine Heaven residing in the Dui (West) Palace, the Spirit Dun can be formed.

Ghost Dun 鬼遁 (Gui Dun)

地 Earth		人 Man	天 Heaven	神 Universe	宮 Palace
天干 Heavenly Stem	地支 Earthly Stem	八門 8 Doors	九星 9 Stars	八神 8 Deities	
乙 *Yi* Yin Wood		杜 *Du* Delusion 開 *Kai* Open 生 *Sheng* Life		九地 Nine Earth	
丁 *Ding* Yin Fire		開 *Kai* Open 休 *Xiu* Rest 生 *Sheng* Life		九地 Nine Earth	

Description

The influence of this formation is perfect for arranging an ambush or a sudden, surprise attack on your enemies, carrying out investigative work, circulating rumors designed to confuse and mislead the enemy and when performing industrial espionage.

This formation is also highly potent when applied together with *focused wishes* (in modern day language, The Law of Attraction) and in a more esoteric sense - *spell casting*. In ancient days of war, offerings were made to appease the Gods to ensure that weather and environmental conditions would favor the battle. Such efforts were usually successful, according to the history books.

Dragon Dun 龍遁 (Long Dun)

地 Earth		人 Man	天 Heaven	神 Universe	宮 Palace
天干 Heavenly Stem	地支 Earthly Stem	八門 8 Doors	九星 9 Stars	八神 8 Deities	
乙 *Yi* Yin Wood	辛 *Xin* Yin Metal	休 *Xiu* Rest			坎 Kan (North)
		開 *Kai* Open			乾 Qian (Northwest)
乙 *Yi* Yin Wood		休 *Xiu* Rest			坎 Kan (North)
		生 *Sheng* Life			
		開 *Kai* Open			

Description

The presence of this formation is suitable for the practice and application of theological knowledge, increasing wealth, forming business or marketing strategies, aquatic activities, work related travel, starting work on large development projects, getting married, giving birth and attacking your enemies at sea or near rivers and water formations.

This formation highly favors any water related activities. Water activities can mean those literately involve the physical element of water, or the activities, businesses or tactics associated with water such as fishing.

The following is an example Chart plotted on 11 April 2007 at 7.05 pm which shows the Structure for the Dragon Dun:

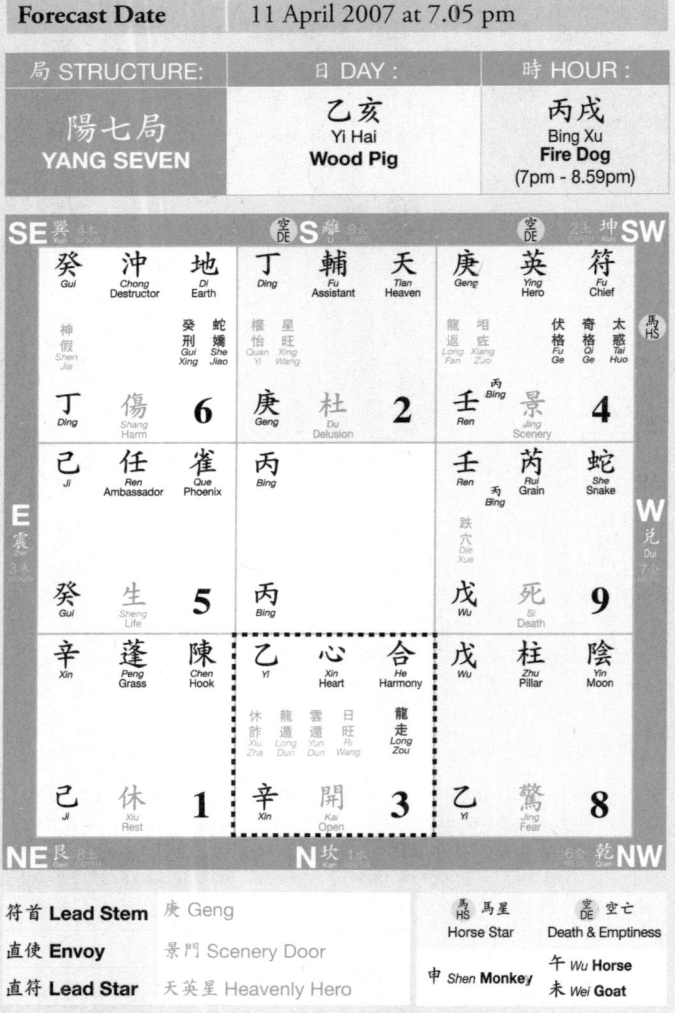

In the Kan (North) Palace, the Yi Stem resides with the Open Door forming the Dragon Dun.

Cloud Dun 雲遁 (Yun Dun)

地 Earth		人 Man	天 Heaven	神 Universe	宮 Palace
天干 Heavenly Stem	地支 Earthly Stem	八門 8 Doors	九星 9 Stars	八神 8 Deities	
乙 *Yi* Yin Wood	辛 *Xin* Yin Metal	休 *Xiu* Rest 生 *Sheng* Life 開 *Kai* Open			
乙 *Yi* Yin Wood		休 *Xiu* Rest 生 *Sheng* Life			坤 **Kun** (Southwest)

Description

Suitable for the practice and study of theology, for succeeding while maintaining a low profile, embarking long journeys and pursuing knowledge and skills. This formation highly favours self-cultivation and self-improvement. It can help to create positive self-transformation, remove bad habits and improve on attitude and character traits.

Tiger Dun 虎遁 (Hu Dun)

地 Earth		人 Man	天 Heaven	神 Universe	宮 Palace
天干 Heavenly Stem	地支 Earthly Stem	八門 8 Doors	九星 9 Stars	八神 8 Deities	
乙 Yi Yin Wood	辛 Xin Yin Metal	休 Xiu Rest			艮 Gen (Northeast)
乙 Yi Yin Wood		生 Sheng Life			艮 Gen (Northeast)
辛 Xin Yin Metal		生 Sheng Life			艮 Gen (Northeast)
庚 Geng Yang Metal		開 Kai Open			兌 Dui (West)

Description

This formation will help you to get what you want, usually by force or via intimidation. Suitable for hunting, asking for a promotion, when assuming a new role or title, forcing your enemies to surrender, going into exile, starting work at a construction site and plotting covert actions.

This formation enables you to operate undetected under the radar. With its influence, you can operate in a cover manor. Your enemies will be unable to see exactly what you are doing or why. The clouds (or mists) will hide your tracks.

The following is an example plotted on 4 November, 2013 at 11.30am which shows the Structure for the Cloud Dun and Tiger Dun.

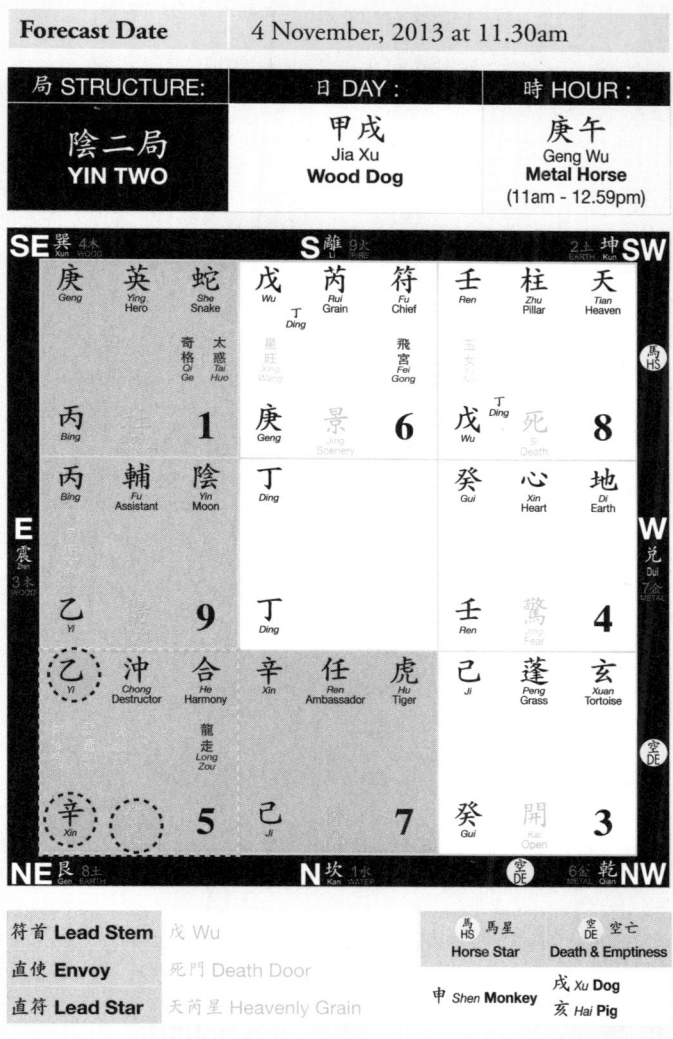

Forecast Date   4 November, 2013 at 11.30am

局 STRUCTURE:	日 DAY:	時 HOUR:
陰二局 YIN TWO	甲戌 Jia Xu **Wood Dog**	庚午 Geng Wu **Metal Horse** (11am - 12.59pm)

符首 **Lead Stem** 戊 Wu	馬 **Horse Star**	空 **Death & Emptiness**
直使 **Envoy** 死門 Death Door	申 Shen **Monkey**	戌 Xu **Dog**
直符 **Lead Star** 天芮星 Heavenly Grain		亥 Hai **Pig**

In the Gen (Northeast) Palace, the Yi Heavenly Stem resides with Xin Earthly Stem in the same Palace together with the Life Door. These components will form the Cloud Dun.

In the same Palace, the Tiger Dun is also formed by a combination of the Yi Heavenly Stem, and the Life Door in the Gen Palace.

Joey Yap's Qi Men Dun Jia Sun Tzu Warcraft

地 Earth		人 Man	天 Heaven	神 Universe	宮 Palace
天干 Heavenly Stem	地支 Earthly Stem	八門 8 Doors	九星 9 Stars	八神 8 Deities	
乙 *Yi* **Yin Wood**		杜 *Du* **Delusion**			
		生 *Sheng* **Life**			
		開 *Kai* **Open**			
丙 *Bing* **Yang Fire**		開 *Kai* **Open**			

Wind Dun 風遁 (Feng Dun)

Description

Publicity and popularity are the domain of this formation. It is best used for building a good name, spreading news or creating viral content on social media.

This formation, once activated, can help in promotional work, advertising, publicity, relationships and marriage (by restoring trust), long journeys (the Wind travels far), sending troops (swiftly) to battle and carrying out an arson attack.

As this formation only takes place in the Southeast Sector, traditionally, it is favorable for handling issues stemming from the Northwest area.

The following is an example Chart plotted on 8 March, 2008 at 1.30pm which shows the Structure for the Wind Dun.

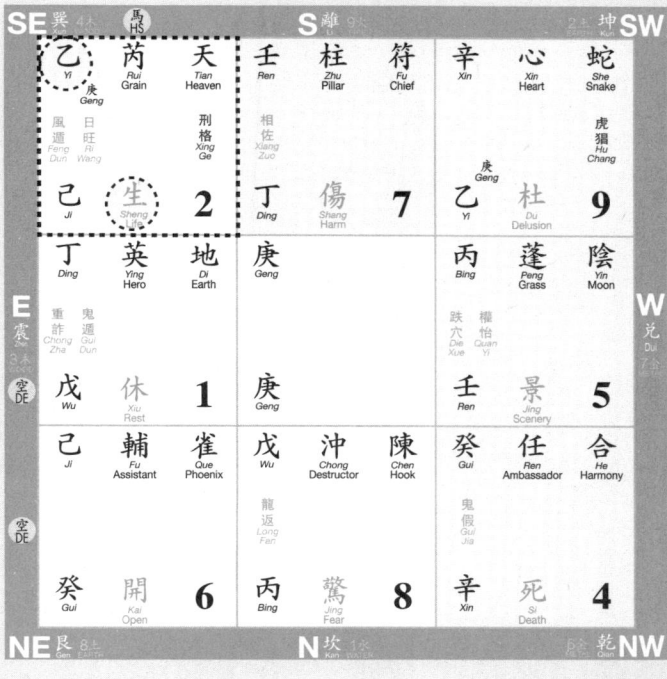

Forecast Date	8 March, 2008 at 1.30pm	
局 STRUCTURE:	日 DAY:	時 HOUR:
陽三局 YANG THREE	丁未 DingWei **Fire Goat**	丁未 Ding Wei **Fire Goat** (1pm - 2.59pm)

符首 **Lead Stem**	壬 Ren	馬 馬星 Horse Star	空 DE 空亡 Death & Emptiness
直使 **Envoy**	驚門 Fear Door	巳 Si **Snake**	寅 Yin **Tiger**
直符 **Lead Star**	天柱星 Heavenly Pillar		卯 Mao **Rabbit**

The Wind Dun is formed by a combination of the Yi Stem and the Life Door in the Xun (Southeast) Palace.

Sun Tzu said, "A general who thoroughly understands the Nine Variables will know how to use his armies". In the same way, it can be argued that those who have the *Nine Dun* on their side will have everything they need to overcome their opponents. Historically, these formations were believed to be particularly beneficial when waging war. In modern times, they can be used for those engaged in fierce business competition or by individuals who want to advance in their careers, ahead of everyone else.

Sun Tzu also said, "A commander may be well acquainted with the Five Factors but without understanding the Nine Variables, he will never use his men to their best effort". We earlier formed a comparison between Sun Tzu's Five Factors and the Five Components of Qi Men Dun Jia. The Nine Dun can therefore be seen as giving a deeper understanding of how various tactics can create the right strategic results.

MANEUVERING ARMIES 行軍

9

奇門遁甲 孫子兵法

ORIGINAL TEXT:

孫子曰：凡處軍相敵：絕山依谷，視生處高，戰隆無登，此處山之軍也。絕水必遠水，客絕水而來，勿迎于水內，令半濟而擊之利。欲戰者，無附于水而迎客，視生處高，無迎水流，此處水上之軍也。

TRANSLITERATION:

Sun Tzu said: a general must investigate the footing of his opponent before deploying troops and he must also pay regard to the following:

When traveling through mountainous regions, be sure to maintain a course that runs close to the valleys. Select a location that is on higher ground and which faces to the sunlight when choosing a place to camp, and do not ascend to fight a battle on higher ground. These are the rules for adopting a military position in the mountains.

After crossing a river, it is wise to travel further inland and keep your distance from it. If an enemy attacks from across a river, do not attack them while they are in the water, wait until at least half their number has reached the shore. If you wish to stage a battle, do not do so on the banks of the river; instead stage it on higher ground. This is also the case for setting up camp. Never camp in the lower reaches of a river, again choose the higher ground and make sure that you are not facing the sun. These are the rules for adopting a military position in the vicinity of rivers and waterways.

COMMENTARY:

Your position determines your power. Anyone who occupies a higher position has greater strength. Know where your competitors stand in the market and choose your own wisely. If you position yourself incorrectly you will fail to connect with the opportunities you are suited for. If you position yourself in a way that aligns with your unique core values, you can gain genuine traction that propels you to higher ground and allows you to displace others.

Never take on someone who occupies higher ground in the market on their terms. It is nearly impossible to beat a more entrenched and experienced opponent at their own game. You must carve out your own niche, create your own brand and compete in a non-direct way. Once you have grown in capability, then you can compete for market share head on. This is how you grow using your unique strengths and in safety.

Whenever you move forward to a new position – for example, once you've paid off a large loan or once you have been promoted – you should keep up your momentum so that you can fully consolidate and secure your new position. This prevents a minor setback from pushing you all the way back to your previous level. Avoid competitive action when you are in a weak position or diminished capacity.

Remember that you must only ever compete from strength, not against it. Until you are a viable contender, seek growth not conflict.

ORIGINAL TEXT:

絕斥澤，惟亟去勿留，
若交軍于斥澤之中，必依水草，
而背眾樹，此處斥澤之軍也。
平陸處易，右背高，前死後生，
此處平陸之軍也。
凡此四軍之利，
黃帝之所以勝四帝也。

TRANSLITERATION:

Don't delay when crossing salt marshes; make sure that operations in them are conducted as quickly as possible. If you are forced to face the enemy in a salt marsh, make sure that you keep to areas where there is plenty of grass and where there are trees at the rear. This is the rule for adopting a military position in and around salt marshes.

When choosing a location to set up camp on leveled ground, make sure that you select a spot which is easily accessible and that has some elevation to the rear and right and lower ground to the front and left. This is the rule for adopting a military position in and around leveled ground.

These four rules for encampment enabled the Yellow Emperor to conquer the four enemy emperors that he faced in battle during ancient times.

COMMENTARY:

Make it a top priority to get to higher, more lucrative operating ground in business as fast as possible.

There are two distinct types of 'space' you can do business in. There are existing market places and there are new markets. Most existing markets are crowded. Many businesses offer the same product resulting in them competing on price in order to distinguish themselves. Therefore, prices in the market drop as it becomes saturated. These businesses find themselves in a 'race to the bottom' as their margins dwindle and their once unique service or product becomes a commodity. Growth in these markets is all but impossible and it is not in your interest to enter into them. You must, in fact, grow and move beyond them quickly or you will perish.

New markets are full of untapped potential. When a business identifies a new market, they can setup shop without competition and charge a premium. New markets can emerge from existing ones; all you need to do is look for an untapped niche and fill it. As a leader seeking growth and profitability, it is up to you to look for these niches and act upon your findings before others do. Push the boundaries in your industry further then anyone else has. Distinguish yourself and do something new that stems from your unique core values. If you can identify a unique selling proposition (your competitive advantage) then nobody will be able to replicate your model and terms precisely. Convey your values to customers and build up your user base. The security this affords can fund new growth and allows you to gain the traction necessary for growth.

If you must put your growth plans on hold or if you are unsure of your next move, keep your eyes wide open while you stand still. Watch what your competitors are doing. Track new market developments, follow ongoing efforts. Learn. Look for the gaps. Copy winning ideas and strategies. When you spot a way to climb up, take it.

ORIGINAL TEXT:

凡軍好高而惡下，貴陽而賤陰，
養生處實，軍無百疾，
是謂必勝。邱陵隄防，
必處其陽，而右背之，
此兵之利，地之助也。

TRANSLITERATION:

When possible, any competent commander will prefer to station his troops on higher ground rather than on low ground, in the sunlight rather than the shade and where food crops can be grown. This will help keep their troops healthy and free of disease so that they can fight their way to victory. If you find yourself surrounded by hills or dykes, always station your troops on the sunny side with the hills and dykes to the rear. Choosing suitable ground for encampment can afford significant military advantages.

COMMENTARY:

You must aim high. The higher the position in the market you occupy, the greater the margins, security and brand loyalty you will enjoy. Despite the undeniable benefits of seeking the high ground, businesses too often scramble to compete at a low level, hoping to make up their profits in sheer volume. However, it is a plain truth that this is a losing game. It is much easier to sell once than it is to sell ten times, regardless of your pricing! If you wish to be the leader, your strategic goal must be to move into the highest position available in the market and to operate from a set of unique core values that others cannot replicate. If you want the champions profit, you must become the champion.

But wait – there are more benefits for those who become the market leaders! As circumstances change and the market is reshuffled, organizations which occupy the higher ground invariably end up capturing even more market share and enjoying all of the accompanying benefits. This dysfunction forces displaced competitors to compete harder for smaller positions that offer even smaller profits. In every industry, the simple act of moving up in market share also erodes the competitor's market share. If you don't seek growth in the market, you will move down in position by default as others advance. You must swim or you will sink.

Staging your efforts from the right place and at the right angle will determine how easily you are able to reach higher ground. Work within a supportive network and environment. It's much easier to create the momentum and power that will propel you up and ahead when you operate from a supportive base. For example, you can locate your business in a location where there are tax rebates or incentives that create a strong foundation for growth. In politics, aligning yourself with the powerful party and catering to their wishes will give you access to their support and influence, making your political goals easier to attain.

Make sure you launch for the stars with sufficient force and enough fuel!

ORIGINAL TEXT:

上雨，水沫至，欲涉者，待其定也。
凡地有絕澗，天井、天牢、天羅、天陷、天隙，必亟去之，勿近也。
吾遠之，敵近之；吾迎之，敵背之。
軍旁有險阻、潢井、葭葦、林木、翳薈者，必謹覆索之，
此伏奸之所處也。

TRANSLITERATION:

If heavy rainfall on the upper reaches of a river has caused a powerful torrent, never attempt to cross while the river is raging. Wait until the flood subsides and the currents are calmer.

When you encounter dangerous or difficult terrain do not advance, instead find an alternative route. Examples of locations that may indicate such a course include a deep ravine with a violent watercourse at the bottom, a deep chasm with steep cliffs all around, a hemmed-in position that is easily occupied but hard to escape from, a position that is overgrown with grasses and thickets, low laying marshy land and narrow passes between mountains.

It is wise to steer clear of these kinds of locations. Let the enemy approach them and then attack them so that they are forced to fight with their backs against them.

If a survey of the land near to your camp reveals dangerous defiles, low lying land overgrown with reeds or densely forested mountains covered in tangled undergrowth, be sure to search these areas thoroughly so that you can determine whether you are being watched or if anyone lies in wait to ambush you as you pass.

COMMENTARY:

You must learn to avoid risk. Wait until the danger has subsided before acting. Lay low until the storm has passed. We see this wisdom in practice every time there is a media backlash against a public figure or business – they seem to go into hiding until months later when their unpopular deeds are old news. The idea here is that with a little patience, danger and risk often shrink. Patience really is a virtue!

When you face an insurmountable challenge or an unreasonable level of risk, you usually have the option to readdress your approach in other way or look for an alternative path to your goals. There are no prizes for choosing hardship. Often, the safer route will take longer but it will involve far lesser risk. That's fine, because slow and steady usually wins the race, both in life and business.

The ideal competitive maneuver is to make your rivals shoulder risk to compete. If you are a small business, for example, you can afford to try out daring advertising strategies and experiment with risqué or unusual public relations messages. A larger business can lose a lot if they make a single error and so calling them out to compete against you in this risky way may cause them to lose focus and market share. At the very least, they will appear out of touch if they fail to take the bait.

Expect and prepare for the possibility that your opponent means you harm. Risk analysis and due diligence can help mitigate the harm.

ORIGINAL TEXT:

敵近而靜者，恃其險也。
遠而挑戰者，欲人之進也。
其所居易者，利也。

TRANSLITERATION:

If the enemy camp is near to yours and yet remain calm and composed then this is an indication that they are confident that their position gives them an advantage over you. If they are camped far from you and approach to challenge you at your own encampment, it is because they wish to dare you into making an advance. The enemy is likely to choose the location of his camp because there are practical and tactical reasons for so doing.

COMMENTARY:

You can gain insight into the strength and intentions of your opponent by looking at how brash they are towards you. Everyone chooses the way they position themselves and there are always reasons behind their decisions. It is possible to reverse engineer a third parties' likely intent towards you by looking at their placement within the market in relation to yourself. Therefore, it is easy to know your rival. Judge what he or she is doing on a daily basis and you can predict the nature, character and possibly, the future fortunes of that individual. The power to anticipate their next move allows you to best them in life, politics and business.

Let's consider an example in business to illustrate this concept. If a directly competing business moves close to your existing location, then they clearly feel that they can offer a viable alternative to your current service and that they also have the means to launch a viable bid to take your customers. Their confidence reveals that they are probably a legitimate competitive threat to you. If a normally distant or inconsequential rival goes far outside their normal boundaries to challenge you, consider the notion that they wish to lure you into a trap of some kind. You could also infer that they lack the means to compete head on with you and that they are trying to get ahead using a different approach. Proceed only with caution.

Question motives and assess threat by looking at what people do as well as what they say. A disparity between the two reveals deceit.

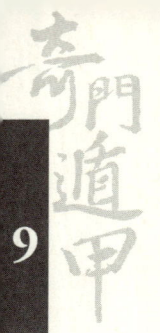

ORIGINAL TEXT:

眾樹動者，來也。眾草多障者，疑也。鳥起者，伏也。獸駭者，覆也。塵：高而銳者，車來也；卑而廣者，徒來也；散而條達者，樵採也；少而往來者，營軍也。

TRANSLITERATION:

Should you observe the trees moving at a distance, you can be sure that the enemy is advancing towards you. If you find obstacles hidden in the undergrowth, be aware that this is likely an enemy tactic. Birds suddenly rising in flight suggest a hidden enemy presence. Frightened animals scurrying away may be a forewarning of attack. Clouds of dust rising in columns may be compelled by the wheels of rapidly approaching chariots or low and wide spread dust clouds may have been stirred up by the tread of infantrymen. Scattered dust may be an indication that the enemy is cutting wood and low, small clouds that rise intermittently could show you where the enemy is setting up camp.

COMMENTARY:

Watch out for the writing on the wall. It's often said that hindsight is 20:20. After you have lost the battle, you can usually see that there were clear signs of your impending defeat that you either chose to ignore or didn't notice. You will probably never have 20:20 foresight but you can certainly adjust your thinking to improve it.

When things are about to change, there is almost always an advance warning or indicator of some kind. When new technologies make old ones obsolete, their existence is reported and discussed in depth as they are developed. Sales don't stop overnight – they usually slow down over a period of time. The question is, what don't you see that is causing this slow down? It is always the things you don't see that make or break the deal. Scrutinize the situation. There are always measurable metrics which allow you to track the trajectory of your business and forecast potential trouble. When your competitors are making plans to encroach upon your territory then you will be able observe such movement if you observe their operations with scrutiny.

Change is the law of life. The best way to deal with it is to adapt before you have to.

ORIGINAL TEXT:

辭卑而備者，進也；
辭強而進驅者，退也；
輕車先出居側者，陣也。
無約而請和者，謀也；
奔走而陣兵者，期也；
半進者，誘也。

TRANSLITERATION:

Should an enemy messenger appear humble while his country's war preparations continue, it is more than likely that they are prepared to advance. If the enemy speaks without compromise and threatens a further advance, in reality, he is more likely to be considering a retreat. Should the enemy's light chariots set out first and take up a flanking position, be aware that they are arranging their battle formation. If the enemy asks for a truce without first requesting an advance appointment, it suggests that he has been plotting. If enemy generals are engaged in arranging the position of troops and vehicles, take note, as they may be planning a decisive attack. Should half of the enemy troops advance while the other half retreat, beware; your opponent is attempting to deceive you.

COMMENTARY:

Never expect plain speaking from your competitors – remember the power of deception in competition and expect your rivals to use it against you. The good news is that you can predictably interpret the real intentions people have by reading between the lines and thinking about their motivations.

If your competitor is truly in a position to best you, what would they gain from telling you about it? How would they benefit from giving you forewarning? What is more likely is that they are attempting to bluff you. Conversely, when a rival gives you no reason to worry, ask what they might gain from hiding their intentions! The answer is: A lot.

One actionable indicator of aggressive intentions is change in the way your rival positions and aligns themselves. This usually precedes actual action. In business, a change in leadership or branding might indicate that a rival is considering making a move to a new position in the market – perhaps one where they will compete for your customers. Then again, you must also consider the possibility of deception and that they are trying to mislead you.

ORIGINAL TEXT:

仗而立者，飢也。汲而先飲者，渴也。見利而不進者，勞也。鳥集者，虛也。夜呼者，恐也。軍擾者，將不重也。旌旗動者，亂也。吏怒者，倦也。殺馬肉食者，軍無糧也。懸缶不返其舍者，窮寇也。

TRANSLITERATION:

When enemy soldiers are exhausted and lean heavily upon their weapons, it is often an indication that they are starving. When you see them drink from a water supply before they carry it back to their comrades, it is likely that they are suffering from thirst. If the enemy sees a chance for profit or advancement and does not take it, it is because they are exhausted and lack the energy to pursue it. If birds wheel above the site of the enemy camp, it is probable that they have fled. Agitation and noise at the enemy camp during the night is a sign that they are frightened and insecure. Uproar and insurrection at the enemy camp tells you that your opponents' men have lost respect for their commanders. The repeated movement of banners and flags suggests confusion and disorganization. When lower officers become irritable, it is probable that they are struggling to hide their weariness of the war. If the enemy feeds his horses with grain, kills his draught beasts in order to nourish his men, destroys his cooking utensils and appears to show no intention of returning again to his camp, know that he is already resolved to fight to the death.

COMMENTARY:

In order to size up the competition accurately, you must look for signs, signals and behaviors that act as a thermostat and tell you what the situation is in their camp.

When you ask other people directly about their condition, it is likely that you will get the answer they want you to hear, not the real one. Even a struggling opponent will put up the appearance of strength and vitality. If you ask your competitors how business is, they will tell you it's great, even if nothing could be further from the truth. Ultimately, however, people's actions betray their true state of mind and their true intentions. Watch what they do and don't do. This will betray the reality of their condition. Identify and act upon this information alone in order to gain a leg up in the market place.

ORIGINAL TEXT:

諄諄翕翕，徐與人言者，
失眾也。數賞者，窘也。
數罰者，困也。
先暴而後畏其眾者，
不精之至也。來委謝者，
欲休息也。

TRANSLITERATION:

When soldiers gather together to talk in hushed voices it can be taken as a sign that their commanding officer has already lost their support. A commander who rewards his men too often is likely to be in a difficult position and seen as attempting to buy their loyalty. A commander who punishes his troops too frequently is likely to be in serious distress. If he punishes them violently at first and then fears that they will betray him, he is weak and unintelligent. If the enemy sends a messenger who expresses their thanks in mild tones, it is likely an indication that they wish for a truce.

COMMENTARY:

Look for indicators of trouble and vulnerability. It is usually possible to infer that there is trouble afoot within an organization even when it is not directly observed. Read the signs.

An organization without faith in its leader is an organization on track for disaster. There are many, many ways that a leader can lose the support of his or her team but once it is lost, it's almost impossible for them to capture it again. Look for signs of dissent and you can predict what will come next – revolt.

Watch your opponents – you can often assess their strength accurately by looking at how aggressive and confrontational they are in the market or in their competition. If they become meek, there may be an opportunity to join forces as this implies they are in a weaker position and that you may able to subjugate them in some way.

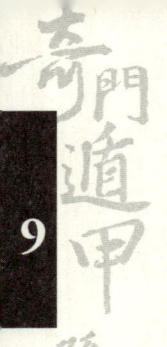

ORIGINAL TEXT:

兵怒而相迎，久而不合，
又不相去，必謹察之。

TRANSLITERATION:

If enemy troops approach enraged and confront your men, holding their attention but neither fighting nor retreating, be very wary of what their real intentions are.

COMMENTARY:

If a competitor directly calls you out, you must question their motives with great scrutiny. If their confidence doesn't align with their known capabilities, further investigation is required before you take any action. Beware of deceit, they may be trying to bring you down to their level in some way. This is a common tactic used by the underdog to help them reposition themselves better via comparison and association. Therefore, don't do your competitors the favor!

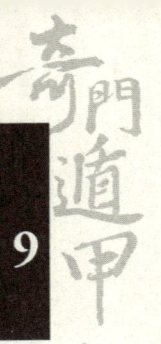

ORIGINAL TEXT:

兵非貴益多，惟無武進，
足以併力料敵取人而已。
夫惟無慮而易敵者，必擒于人。

TRANSLITERATION:

Simply having military might on your side is no guarantee of victory. Never advance recklessly, relying on the sheer force of numbers to drive success, always direct your troops in accordance with a careful assessment of the enemy's advantages and disposition. He who underestimates the enemy and fails to plan his strategy will surely be captured, regardless of the strength of his army.

COMMENTARY:

Sheer strength (financial, political, social) guarantees nothing. There must always be a strategy, focus and specific intent behind your spending. Before you take any competitive action, you must identify the purpose, correct targets and objectives. Carelessly throwing resources at a goal is plainly wasteful and if you insist upon it, you will run yourself or your business eventually. Instead, identify the optimum way of spending and acting based on your unique circumstances and tactical position. Reckless spending can cripple a business. You must curb all reckless spending.

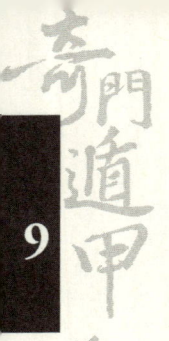

ORIGINAL TEXT:

卒未親附而罰之，則不服，不服則難用。卒已親附而罰不行，則不可用。故令之以文，齊之以武，是謂必取。令素行以教其民，則民服；令不素行以教其民，則民不服；令素行，與眾相得也。

TRANSLITERATION:

If soldiers are punished before you have been able to win their respect and loyalty, you should know that they will never obey you and that they will be tremendously difficult to command. However, you should also be aware that no matter how close the bond that you share with your men may be, if you never exercise discipline, you will not be able to command them to fight.

If you are able to command your troops with civility and humanity while simultaneously controlling and unifying them with martial discipline, you will be invincible in competition. Orders must always be strictly observed and discipline must be used to guide and instruct, otherwise the troops will never be obedient. When orders are consistently and conscientiously followed, it is an indication that the commander and his troops are able to trust one another.

COMMENTARY:

Remember, popularity is not a prerequisite for good leadership. A leader needs only do what is right and what needs to be done. A leader doesn't always have to be liked, but they do have to be respected and obeyed. As a leader, you must apply the same fair standards to everyone if you wish to instill a sense of loyalty. Meaningful loyalty cannot be created through brutal discipline. Lead justly. Set measurable standards and consistently reward those who meet them to create a culture of achievement. Fair, visionary leadership is the only way that you can win respect and create true compliance within your organization.

If you want to accomplish anything significant in life or business, you will need help from others. No one can do it alone, and so leaders require the loyalty of others. Money cannot buy absolute loyalty. You will also never be able to frighten people into helping you. You must inspire others to give their best efforts to you for the sake of a great cause. Your people want to know that their lives have meaning. They want to know that their work matters. It is your job to give them this meaning.

As your people's leader, you need to believe in the future. You must be able to paint a vivid picture of a different and much better reality. You must make it concrete, so your people can see it, feel it, sense it and taste it. You must give your followers the hope that things can and will be better, and that you know exactly how to make it so.

A good leader should be willing to do everything he or she ask his or her team to do and he or she will occasionally demonstrate that fact. He should be the first one to step into battle and the last one to leave. In this way, he can set the tone for his people. True leaders won't ask their people to do anything they are unwilling to do themselves. They will set the pace. An unfit leader only knows how to throw their weight around and expects to control their team by force rather than lead by example. A good leader should always be knowledgeable and wise; else he will not command the respect and admiration of his followers. When all is said and done, there will sometimes be a need to reprimand people in your organization who step out of line. Failing to do so displays weakness on your part and weakness encourages dissent and reduces people's confidence in you. You must not leave contempt unchecked. The key is to be fair in determining when discipline is called for and when it isn't.

Honest mistakes or failings shouldn't necessarily be punished – provided the person who made the mistake is aware of their wrongdoing and that their action was genuinely in error.

Your people are your greatest asset – treat them as such. A good leader gives people what they want within his abilities. You may be unable to give out raises if your business is not profitable but you must share the rewards if your business does well as a result of your team's effort. In cases where you cannot offer financial reward, there are many ways to reward your staff. Genuine praise, acknowledgment, recognition and the occasional "thank you" for a team member's contribution are all just as motivating and valuable. A great leader understands the importance of reward and knows that ignoring this advice may lead to dissent.

QI MEN DUN JIA:

In this chapter, Sun Tzu emphasized the importance of being familiar with the lay of the land so that you can avoid potentially hazardous routes. He advised commanders to find an alternative path when confronted with 'raging torrents', 'deep ravines', 'steep mountains', enclosed positions that may be 'tantamount to a prison', 'overgrown grasses' and 'narrow passes between mountains'. Similarly, in a Qi Men Dun Jia Chart, there are several formations which are considered to be very negative and are best avoided. These unfortunate formations, made of inauspicious components, indicate an undesirable outcome across a range of activities. It is always best to avoid any direction or location that has these negative Qi Men Structures. Thus, by identifying these formations, a leader can avoid the hazards entirely or take the necessary precautions to protect himself and his staff.

The negative Structures in a Qi Men Chart are listed below:

War Structure 戰格					
地 Earth		人 Man	天 Heaven	神 Universe	宮 Palace
天干 Heavenly Stem	地支 Earthly Stem	八門 8 Doors	九星 9 Stars	八神 8 Deities	
庚 Geng Yang Metal	庚 Geng Yang Metal				

Description

The ancient scripts describe this formation as " injuries sustained from a fight, or the death of a family member." This means that where this special formation is found in a Qi Men Chart, it indicates that the action in question will result in loss, disarray and failure. This formation denotes physical damage and possible bodily harm – in short, it represents danger and one must be extremely cautious if it is identified in a Qi Men Chart.

Big Structure 大格

地 Earth		人 Man	天 Heaven	神 Universe	宮 Palace
天干 Heavenly Stem	地支 Earthly Stem	八門 8 Doors	九星 9 Stars	八神 8 Deities	
庚 *Geng* **Yang Metal**	癸 *Gui* **Yim Water**				

Description

The ancient scripts say - the carriage will be broken and the horse will be dead. This is a very inauspicious indication that support (or transport) will not be available when it is needed. It means there is going to be a logistical problem causing an event or activity to fail. If you intend to create or establish something new, it is likely that there will be a great deal of hassle and significant setbacks under the influence of this formation. In addition, you are likely to struggle to win the support of your team or even your own relatives, leading to failure.

The following is an example Chart plotted on 16 February, 2008 at 1.30pm which shows the formation of the Big Structure:

Forecast Date	16 February, 2008 at 1.30pm	
局 **STRUCTURE:**	日 **DAY:**	時 **HOUR:**
陽五局 Yang Five	丙戌 Bing Xu **Fire Dog**	乙未 Yi Wei **Wood Goat** (1pm - 2.59pm)

Chart

SE 巽

- Palace (SE): 辛 Xin / 任 Ren Ambassador / 符 Fu Chief; 相佐 Xiang Zuo, 雲遁 Yun Dun (空DE); 虎猖 Hu Chang; 乙 Yi / 休 Xiu Rest — **4**
- Palace (S): 丙 Bing / 沖 Chong Destructor / 蛇 She Snake; 月昇 Yue Sheng; 壬 Ren / 生 Sheng Life — **9**
- Palace (SW): 乙 Yi / 輔 Fu Assistant / 陰 Yin Moon; 日葦 Ri Mu (戊Wu); 丁 Ding / 傷 Shang Harm — **2**
- Palace (E): 癸 Gui / 蓬 Peng Grass / 天 Tian Heaven; 戊 Wu; 壬 Ren / 英 Ying Hero / 合 He Harmony
- Palace (W): (戊Wu)
- Palace (E lower): 丙 Bing / 開 Kai Open — **3**; 戊 Wu; 庚 Geng / 杜 Du Delusion — **7**
- Palace (NE): 己 Ji / 心 Xin Heart / 地 Di Earth; **庚 Geng / 柱 Zhu Pillar / 雀 Que Phoenix** 大格 Da Ge; 丁 Ding / 芮 Rui Grain / 陳 Chen Hook (戊Wu)
- Palace (N): 辛 Xin / 驚 Jing Fear — **8**; **癸 Gui / 死 Si Death** — **1**; 己 Ji / 景 Jing Scenery — **6**

NE 艮 **N** 坎 **NW** 乾

符首 **Lead Stem**	辛 Xin	馬HS **Horse Star**	空DE **Death & Emptiness**
直使 **Envoy**	生門 Life Door	巳 Si **Snake**	辰 Chen **Dragon**
直符 **Lead Star**	天任星 Heavenly Ambassador		巳 Si **Snake**

In this Palace, the Heavenly Stem is Geng Metal while the Earthly Stem is Gui Water; this forms the Big Structure. This arrangement is inauspicious. It denotes that the land where battle is to take place is ladened with danger.

In business, that might mean that the chosen location of operation is not wise. Proceed with a high level of caution or, better yet, do not proceed at all. If this Chart is plotted for the hour of a very important meeting, you must avoid sitting in this sector at all cost during the meeting. Let your opponent sit there, if possible.

Flying Palace Structure 飛宮格					
地 Earth		人 Man	天 Heaven	神 Universe	宮 Palace
天干 Heavenly Stem	地支 Earthly Stem	八門 8 Doors	九星 9 Stars	八神 8 Deities	
符首 *Fu Shou* Lead Stem 甲 *Jia* Yang Wood	庚 *Geng* Yang Metal				

Description

This special formation forecasts trouble caused by new conditions in the market as well as undesirable new economic or political circumstances that are beyond control. Such sudden changes in your external environment can throw you off course or scupper your plans. You are advised to brace yourself for the worst. There will also be hidden dangers in the environment that may derail your competitive plans.

The following is an example Chart plotted on 19 March 2006 at 11.30pm which shows the Flying Palace Structure.

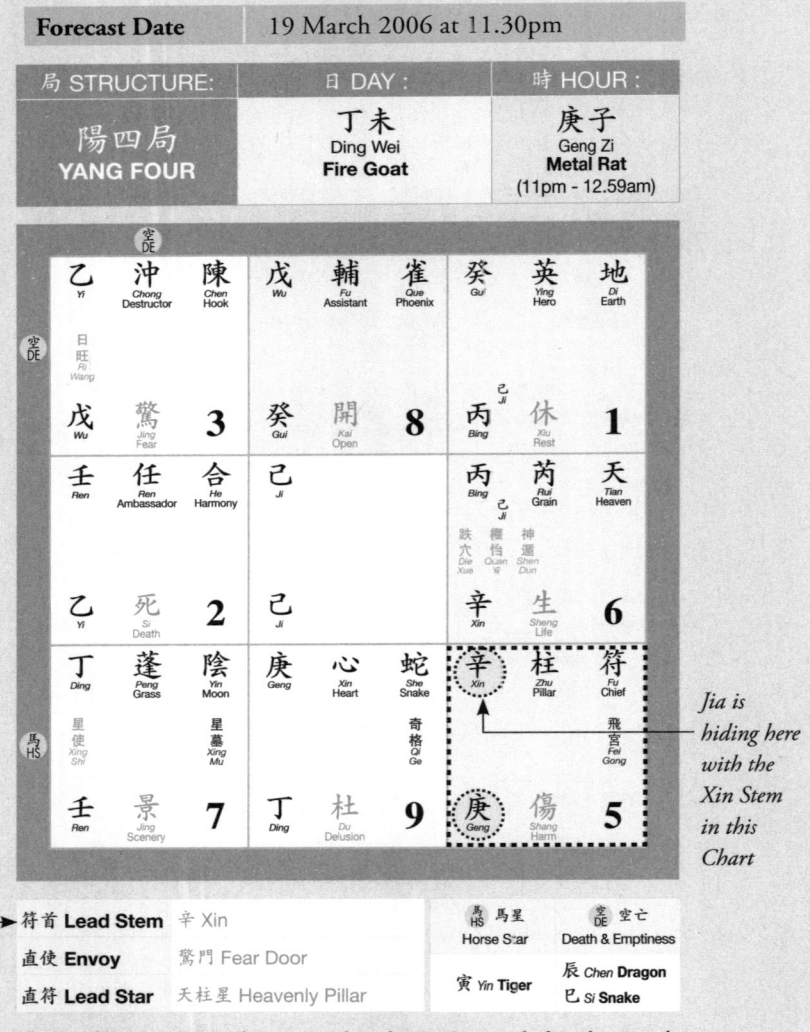

Lead Stem 辛 Xin
Envoy 驚門 Fear Door
Lead Star 天柱星 Heavenly Pillar

Horse Star: 寅 Yin Tiger
Death & Emptiness: 辰 Chen Dragon, 巳 Si Snake

The Lead Stem is Xin. This means that the Jia Stem is hiding here in the Chart.

In the Qian (Northwest) Palace, the Heavenly Stem is Xin (which hides the Jia) and the Earthly Stem is Geng. This forms the Flying Palace Structure. This is a highly unfavorable direction. Avoid pursuing in this direction. In a business meeting with such a chart, avoid sitting in this sector.

Sitting Palace Structure 伏宮格

地 Earth		人 Man	天 Heaven	神 Universe	宮 Palace
天干 Heavenly Stem	地支 Earthly Stem	八門 8 Doors	九星 9 Stars	八神 8 Deities	
庚 *Geng* Yang Metal	符首 *Fu Shou* Lead Stem 甲 *Jia* Yang Wood				

Description

The ancient scripts say that this formation signifies the "Loss of a General and the need to defend oneself vigorously". This means that the formation predicts a loss of leadership or that a serious leadership related problem is about to occur. It could also mean that your subordinates have lost their faith in you, or that they no longer believe in your vision. With no support, it is likely that you will be plagued with uncertainty. It will be best to avoid making hasty decisions at this time.

天羅地網 Heavenly Web Earthly Net	Heavenly Net Four Spreads 天網四張
	Earthly Net Shelter 地網遮蔽

Description

The ancient texts advices that where this formation is found, it is *"Unsuitable for dispatching troops"*.

1. The *Heavenly Net Four Spreads* formation is formed when the Gui Crest 癸義 is on the Heavenly and Earthly Stem. This formation indicates that there are traps ahead and that you should not advance.

2. The *Earthly Net Entanglement* formation is formed when the Ren Crest 壬義 is on the Heavenly Plate with the Gui Crest 癸義 in the Earth Plate. This indicates that there are spies in your camp and that your security is breached.

The appearance of any of these Structures is highly inauspicious as they suggest a strong likelihood of difficulty. It is recommended that you do not proceed in this direction when these formations are present.

TERRAIN

ORIGINAL TEXT:

孫子曰：地形有通者，有挂者，有支者，有隘者，有險者，有遠者。我可以往，彼可以來，曰通；通形者，先居高陽，利糧道以戰，則利。

TRANSLITERATION:

Sun Tzu said: nature will present you with many different kinds of terrain. Some terrain is easily accessible while some is enclosed and entrapping. Some will slow you down and some will restrict you, some slopes will be steep and arduous and some terrain will be secluded.

What makes for accessible ground? Terrain that is easy for both you and the enemy to negotiate is considered accessible. If you enter into such an area of land, make sure to take up a high and well lit position and work to make sure that your supply lines are protected. This kind of area makes for a simple and convenient battleground.

COMMENTARY:

The competitive market and economic conditions that you must operate in are much like the terrain upon which a general wages his war. For the sake of clarity, we will refer to the amalgamation of such conditions as the "environment" from here on. You must work with, not against, the characteristics and realities of your environment.

The features of your environment can either serve or hinder your plans, just as the terrain can impede or serve a general's plans in a military campaign. Sometimes, your environment will be conducive to success and at other times it may present you with risk and challenges. As an example, think about the different financial markets that exist and the barriers to entry and consider the risk/reward ratios associated with each. People tend to approach these markets with different objectives and different levels of risk tolerance.

Learning to understand your environment is the first step towards operating profitably within it. A leader should go to great lengths to get a 'feel' for the environment and to stay abreast of the current events. Get close to your prospects, find out what they want and then investigate what is available to understand the existing features of the 'terrain'. Without an intuitive understanding of the environment, you are flying blind. Even the smartest people make stupid mistakes when they don't have a good understanding of the circumstances.

As market conditions change over time, your plans and operating methods must change too. New conditions call for renewed tactics. It is up to you to avoid what can be avoided while capitalizing on the opportunities that the terrain presents to you.

Sun Tzu described several common operating 'environments' and their characteristics. Each demands a different way of thinking. The first is accessible ground.

Accessible ground refers to any open arena with low barriers to entry. The problem with any open competitive environment is that *anyone* can compete – you will be in a thousand, vying for the prize. The way to get the edge in this context is to look for the high ground; find ways to distinguish yourself if you want to get ahead. Otherwise, you will find yourself in a race to the bottom. Make sure that you have plenty of funds and resources that support your attempts to do this. With a secure foundation you can afford to take the bold risks necessary to make a name for yourself.

ORIGINAL TEXT:

可以往,難以返,曰挂;
挂形者,敵無備,出而勝之,
敵若有備,出而不勝,難以返,
不利。

TRANSLITERATION:

Enclosed ground may be easy to enter but it can be hard to find a suitable exit point. The advantage here is that if your enemy is unprepared and you stage an ambush at such a location, you will stand a good chance of defeating him. However, the risk is that if your enemy is prepared, you may not be able to defeat him and it may be hard for you to fight your way back out to safety.

COMMENTARY:

Beware of enclosed ground. In niche markets and careers, there is often very little competition and it is easy to set up a business. Think, for example, of the pursuit of a highly specialized career. You can rise to the top in a narrow niche with relative ease and charge a hefty fee but the rug can be pulled from under your feet if demand for your expertise decreases or technology makes your skills obsolete. In addition, it is also harder to achieve horizontal growth in a limited space. If circumstances change, you might find it hard to transfer your abilities and resources into a more generalized career or environment.

If your opponent does business in an enclosed ground, the decision to attack them directly must hinge on whether or not you have the element of surprise on your side. This means looking for ways to make them irrelevant in the market.

ORIGINAL TEXT:

我出而不利，彼出而不利，
曰支；支形者，敵雖利我，
我無出也；引而去之，
令敵半出而擊之，利。

TRANSLITERATION:

Ground that slows you down is of no help and it is an unwise place to stage a battle or plan an ambush. If the enemy tries to goad you into battle on such terrain, you should not rise to the bait. Instead, you should feign a retreat. Once half their number has emerged in pursuit, you may then strike them with the problematic terrain at their rear. This way you will be able to secure an advantage.

COMMENTARY:

Don't bother competing in environments where growth will be excessively difficult. Some industries simply have limited growth capacity. Excessive competition or tepid promotion opportunities both fit into this scenario. Leadership is all about avoiding the avoidable and choosing only to fight the battles you can win. If there is no profit to be had, why not look elsewhere?

If your opponent tries to coax you into a competition which will be prolonged and costly, feign weakness and retreat. This may make them overextend themselves, thinking they have an opportunity for advancement. You will be able to compete profitably on your own terms when they come to you in weakness. Instead of accepting their invitation, make them come to you where you have an advantage.

ORIGINAL TEXT:

隘形者,我先居之,
必盈以待敵;若敵先居之,
盈而勿從,不盈而從之。

TRANSLITERATION:

If you find yourself occupying narrow or restrictive territories, you should make sure to block each of the passes with strong garrisons and wait for the enemy there. If the enemy has taken such a location and they have already secured it with garrisons, you should be discouraged from launching an attack. If, however, they have failed to garrison the territory and the passes are open, you may feel free to pursue them.

COMMENTARY:

When you operate in a niche market or you are highly specialized, defend your position above all else to protect your revenue stream. You need to raise the barriers to entry in your game. In order to compete, you must immediately strengthen and consolidate your current capabilities as well as your position before taunting your competitors. They will be forced to try and beat you at your own game, with rules set by you. It has been mentioned several times so far that it is exceedingly difficult to try and displace an opponent from their own position. This rings true the more specialized you are and the narrower the environment you occupy is.

When the shoe is on the other foot and you see that your competitors have entrenched themselves in a strong position, it would be foolish and wasteful to overthrow or overpower them directly. Therefore, find another way to get what you want; look for an edge or opening that capitalizes on your unique abilities which they cannot defend against. Find out what you can do better and engage in a non-direct competition.

ORIGINAL TEXT:

險形者，我先居之，
必居高陽以待敵；
若敵先居之，引而去之，
勿從也。

TRANSLITERATION:

If you occupy steep and precipitous ground you should aim to take a high point with good light and await the enemy. If the enemy troops race to try and take control of such territory, allow your troops to fall back and do not attempt to face the enemy at this location.

COMMENTARY:

In high risk environments where you have a lot to lose, you must acknowledge the dangers in order to stay alive. Sometimes a good leader needs to know when to cut losses and save the race for another day. Keep a close eye on the horizon and avoid taking any competitive risks that you don't have to. Be ready to maintain your bottom line, even if that means withdrawing to preserve yourself in the face of opposition.

ORIGINAL TEXT:

遠形者，勢均，難以挑戰，
戰而不利。凡此六者，
地之道也，將之至任，
不可不察也。

TRANSLITERATION:

If the enemy stations himself on a distant and secluded piece of land and his strength is equal to yours, it will not be easy to provoke him into battle. Doing so will place you at a disadvantage.

These are the different kinds of terrain that you may face and the advantages and disadvantages that they represent. It is the responsibility of the commanders of the armed forces to determine which they face and act accordingly.

COMMENTARY:

In situations where your opponent is distant in some way, you are at a disadvantage, even with all things being equal. There are many kinds of 'distance' to be considered here. You might be distant in experience, distant in capability, distant in location, distant in leadership, distant in knowledge or distant in manpower. It will take a lot of energy to grab their attention, influence them and to compete on their level. They will always enjoy the upper hand so long as you are content to chasing them.

When you find yourself in this kind of scenario, think about the unique opportunities and risks that each of these environment creates. Adopt the appropriate defensive and offensive tactics to maintain the edge. As a leader, it is your responsibility to act in accordance with the situation you are in and the realities of your own position in relation to your competitors.

ORIGINAL TEXT:

故兵有走者,有弛者,有陷者,
有崩者,有亂者,有北者;
凡此六者,非天地之災,
將之過也。

TRANSLITERATION:

There are six indications that an army may soon be defeated and a good general should be able to spot each of them: the first is when soldiers take flight, the second is when the men are lazy and disobedient, the third is when the army as a whole is held back by men who are weak and cowardly, the fourth is when it collapses under insurgency, the fifth is when it is disorganized and the sixth is when it is routed. None of these situations can be attributed to natural disasters and all can be avoided. Should these situations arise, they are indicative of poor leadership. They should not be regarded as inevitable.

COMMENTARY:

These six indicators signal impending disaster. Watch out for them and you will be able to anticipate defeat. All six of them stemmed from the result of mismanagement and a lack of direction. Therefore, all six of these indicators can be avoided if specific measures are taken.

People close to the action see the writing on the wall long before institutional problems are made public. When more and more people think that their best course of action is to cut their losses and walk away, that's a sign that things are about to fall apart. If you see people abandoning ship then you should assume it's about to sink.

Organization and obedience within a group often disintegrate when people's faith and trust in their leader fails. If you catch wind of dissent within a competitor's ranks, then you can guess what will happen next. Spot these things in your own organization or team and you will know that you are experiencing a breakdown in command.

If your competitor has a reputation for cowardice or they display an inability to act as required, they are held responsible for their own downfall or ruin. Indecision and fear always lead to defeat.

Rebellion from within is a reflection of troubled leadership. It only grows over time and, if left unchecked, it is a sure precursor to failure.

If you identify any of these within your own organization, know that they are the result of your own failures as a leader. You need to wake up and act fast to rectify the situation. Employ counter measures and review your methods. Turn things around before it's too late to prevent total failure. Some people will say that they are aware when they see these signs appearing in their own environment, but they don't know what to do. If you don't know what to do, the answer is simple – go and learn what to do.

ORIGINAL TEXT:

夫勢均，以一擊十，曰走。
卒強吏弱，曰陷。
大吏怒而不服，遇敵懟而自戰，
將不知其能，曰崩。將弱不嚴，
教道不明，吏卒無常，
陳兵縱橫，曰亂。將不能料敵，
以少合眾，以弱擊強，
兵無選鋒，曰北。
凡此六者，敗之道也。
將之至任，不可不察也。

TRANSLITERATION:

If you confront an enemy with an army ten times the size of your own, you will inevitably be forced to retreat, all other things being equal. If your officers are weak and incompetent, even brave and skilled soldiers will lack discipline. Valiant and wise officers cannot operate with speed and efficiency if their soldiers are weak or lacking in training. When the senior officers have a poor relationship with their commanders they will be insubordinate and they may rush into battle without authorization. If the commanders lack an appreciation of the abilities of their men and fail to utilize their skills accordingly, the entire army may well collapse into disorder. If all of these problems arise and the senior commanders are weak and fail to command respect, while the lieutenants and infantrymen are undisciplined and untrained, the army will fall into disarray. Indeed, if a commander fails to estimate the enemy's strength and sends a small force to defeat a large army or a weak force to defeat a powerful army or if he fails to send in his best and brightest as vanguard, the result will be annihilation.

All of these circumstances will inevitably lead to defeat. It is of the utmost importance that any commanding officer studies these scenarios with great care.

COMMENTARY:

Here, Sun Tzu identified a number of institutional and strategic errors that lead to failure and defeat. If any one of these problems is present, you cannot succeed.

If your competitor vastly outsizes you in some way you will fail every single time you take them head-on, even if you are evenly matched in other ways. Trying to compete in this way represents a failure in strategic understanding.

Even the most talented and eager people will flounder without the correct training and leadership or when they operate under a poor standard of leadership. Therefore, select the correct people. The best leaders cannot create a compelling force when they are assigned with the wrong people for the job. Choose candidates with appropriate skill-set and mindset. Then delegate intelligently to leverage those skills.

When communication is lacking throughout your organization, people will pull in different directions and mistakes will be made and loyalties will crumble. Keep communication flowing in both directions within your organization but prioritize and summarize information as it moves between people to prevent confusion. Allow sufficient autonomy within your organization so people can make tactical choices in real time that support strategic goals. The key here is to minimize bureaucracy.

When you fail to challenge your people or reward them sufficiently, you will find their results lacking. Set clear goals and targets and create a culture of accountability. Offer incentives for success as a matter of policy to encourage desirable results. But you need to weed out the non-performers quickly before their negative attitude contaminates the others.

To summarize, what is shown here is that all other things being equal, it only takes one hole to sink a ship. Ignore these variables at your peril. Learn from the precedent of leaders and past rivals who have fallen so you don't repeat their mistakes and meet the same end. More importantly, learn from your own failed ventures too!

ORIGINAL TEXT:

夫地形者，兵之助也。
料敵制勝，計險阨遠近，
上將之道也。
知此而用戰者，必勝；
不知此而用戰者必敗。
故戰道必勝；主曰：無戰；
必戰可也。戰道不勝，
主曰必戰，無戰可也。
故進不求名，退不避罪，
唯民是保，而利于主，
國之寶也。

TRANSLITERATION:

The understanding and use of terrain to your advantage is of great importance in military operations. It is one of the central duties of any commander to have a thorough knowledge of the geography and topography of the land as well as the distances involved. They should work to estimate the situation and deployments of the enemy in order to create a route that will expedite his own success in battle. He who understands this and knows how to apply this knowledge is sure to win a great victory and he who fails to acquire this knowledge and puts it to use will surely suffer a miserable defeat.

In light of the above, a wise commander may elect to go into battle even against the instructions of his sovereign if he sees certain victory. Equally, he may refuse to engage in battle if all he sees is certain defeat. A great commander should always act to protect the safety of the people and promote the agenda of the sovereign while paying no heed to his own interests. He should advance without thought of personal fame or reputation and he should retreat without ever shirking his responsibility. Such a man is nothing short of a treasure to his state.

COMMENTARY:

Understanding and working within the confines of your environment will allow you to shape the nature of your results. As a leader, it is your job to understand the circumstances you face intuitively.

Evaluate the competition and the market conditions, and see what else is going on outside your bubble. Research and obtain news, surveys and connections in your field can all help you see the bigger picture. The clearer you are in your perspective, the more you will be able to tailor your thinking to the facts and the better your results will be. A true understanding of the landscape can determine who will win and who will lose. Your customers will probably encounter both your competitor and yourself when searching for products or services. To win their custom, you must identify and accentuate your unique strengths.

There will be situations in which you answer to a higher authority and it is your job to ensure that their needs are met and their wishes fulfilled. The difficulty is that the situation on the ground can change rapidly. When you see a timely opportunity to do something against their instructions or without their authority, then you should act as long as it is in line with the greater goals. Conversely, you should remember that you have the option not to carry out instructions when you know that they are misguided or harmful. This is called being proactive and it is a prized and rare trait. Most people just sit by the fence and have no courage to take the initiative. This means you need to be able to make a 'judgment call' when it becomes necessary to do so. If you can demonstrate that you possess this ability, you will be rewarded.

The two differentiating factors that separate the initiatives from the plain disobedient are a true understanding of what your company's overall goals are and the ability to take the right action based on the given circumstances and move towards these goals. Without this understanding, you can easily overstep the mark, creating more problems for everyone. If your actions are proven wise and worthwhile, however, you will be rewarded with respect and admiration, which eventually will lead to greater responsibilities and power. Each time you make the right judgment call, you gain more recognition from your peers and superiors. Keep doing this and eventually you will be a respected figure in your team. You will become indispensable to your team and company.

ORIGINAL TEXT:

視卒如嬰兒，故可與之赴深谿；
視卒如愛子，故可與之俱死。
厚而不能使，愛而不能令，
亂而不能治，譬若驕子，
不可用也。

TRANSLITERATION:

If a general cares for his men in the same way that he would care for his own children, they will follow him through thick and thin. If he loves his men as dearly as he loves his own sons, they will be willing to die with him and for him on the fields of battle. However, if a general indulges his men yet does not know how to challenge them or use their strengths, if he loves them but cannot command them, if he fails to punish them when they transgress or break the rules, then they will become like spoiled children and they will lack the strength required for battle.

COMMENTARY:

The way you treat your staff determines how far they are willing to go and how much they will do for you. Treating people in the correct way will produce the desired results. To gain their strength and support, you must win their hearts. Many leaders mistakenly think that they must be harsh, stern and unforgiving in their leadership to get what they want and create respect. What they didn't know is that better results are achieved through sincere appreciation and empathy. A true leader strives to serve his people by leading them effectively. A true leader does not yearn to be served, for he is not a tyrant. However, if you are too kind and you don't demand results and challenge your team, then you will fail to bring out their full potential. When discipline is required, you must be willing to act. If you cannot or you will not, then you have lost your power and authority. You are no longer a leader and you cannot lead.

Getting too close to the people you direct will make it hard to do what is necessary which is why professional distance is required. Maintain it.

ORIGINAL TEXT:

知吾卒之可以擊,
而不知敵之不可擊,勝之半也;
知敵之可擊,
而不知吾卒之不可擊,
勝之半也。知敵之可擊,
知吾卒之可以擊,
而不知地形之不可以戰,
勝之半也。故知兵者,
動而不迷,舉而不窮。故曰:
知彼知己,勝乃不殆;
知天知地,勝乃可全。

地形

10

TRANSLITERATION:

A general who understands the strength of his own men but does not appreciate the strength of his enemy will only have half the chance of victory and the same is true of he who knows the weaknesses of the enemy and yet is blind to the weaknesses of his own troops. Equally, he who knows the weaknesses of the enemy and knows how to use the skills of his troops to strike but does not know the lay of the land will be unable to navigate its features and thus has only half the chance of winning.

A great general should have unlimited strategies and adaptations at his disposal. He should be able to move his troops without ever losing his direction or purpose. It is said that if you know the enemy as well as you know yourself then you are sure to be victorious. It is also true to say that if you have an understanding of the weather and the geographical conditions then you will be always be victorious.

COMMENTARY:

Leadership is all about understanding people, bringing out the best in them, leveraging their strengths, using their talents and minimizing the impact of their weaknesses on the collective output. Know your own people and you will know your potential power.

Counter-intuitively, you will get far further and receive far more in life if you strive to be the giver, not the taker. This means that you must have something to give, something of value you can offer to others. In business, this concept can mean that you must have a valuable service or product if you want custom. The same principle applies in life generally. Someone who is personable and kind will have a lot of friends and good job prospects, because they have a lot to offer. If you want results in life, you must create value.

Sun Tzu emphasized the need to thoroughly know yourself because if you know who you are (your character and your strengths), you will know what you have, what you can offer to the world, and how you can make a change. Conversely, if you do not know who you are (meaning you do not know your character and strengths), then you will not know what value you can give others. If you have nothing to offer, you will not be very attractive to others as a friend or an employee. And if you do not have anything to give in life, you inadvertently become a taker in life, always hoping someone out there can help you or do favors for you. Be a giver, not a taker. Extending this principle, the more value your business can offer, the more custom it will receive.

In a competitive situation, you must know what values your rivals are offering. If they have more value to offer, you will potentially lose the market to them.

When you combine this kind of knowledge with an understanding of the circumstances of competition, then you will have all the information you need to form a winning strategy that puts you in a position of strength and takes advantage of the weaknesses of your competitors. It is simply a matter of who has more value to offer.

The more you know about the people, the better your control over them because you will know which buttons to push. Things that motivate one person may not motivate another. A strategy that allows you to overpower one person may do nothing against the next. Be adaptable.

QI MEN DUN JIA:

In Chapter Ten, Sun Tzu stressed the importance of understanding the terrain when directing troops and developing strategies. He argued that possessing such knowledge can mean the difference between success and failure. Sun Tzu detailed six specific types of terrain: accessible, enclosed, entangling, restrictive, steep and secluded.

A student of Qi Men Dun Jia will quickly be able to draw a parallel between these and the Six Crescents already mentioned in Chapter Five, brought together under the concept of *Zheng* 正. In each Palace of a Qi Men Chart there is both a Heavenly Stem and an Earthly Stem. When the Six Crescents appear in any given Palace, their interactions with that Palace can be indicative of land shapes and formations. This fact is commonly used by Qi Men masters performing Feng Shui analysis in order to gain an understanding of landforms, contour and mountain ranges. The presence and configuration of these Six Crescents within the Stem Plates allows a Qi Men Feng Shui practitioner to remotely 'see' (or visualize) the characteristics of the land.

In addition to the six kinds of terrain, Sun Tzu also made reference to six degrees of disorder and disorganization that can occur within an army if it is not led effectively. If a general is unable to maintain order in his own ranks, he has no hope of being able to command them in battle. The six degrees of disorder are: flight, insubordination, decline, collapse, chaos and rout and these may be connected to the concept of the *Six Crest Striking Punishment* 六儀擊刑 in Qi Men Dun Jia.

The Six Crest Striking Punishments can be seen below:

Six Crest Striking Punishment 六儀擊刑					宮 Palace
地 Earth		人 Man	天 Heaven	神 Universe	
天干 Heavenly Stem	地支 Earthly Stem	八門 8 Doors	九星 9 Stars	八神 8 Deities	
戊儀擊刑 Wu Crest Striking Punishment	戊 *Wu* Yang Earth				震 Zhen East
己儀擊刑 Ji Crest Striking Punishment	己 *Ren* Yin Earth				坤 Kun (Southwest)
庚儀擊刑 Geng Crest Striking Punishment	庚 *Geng* Yang Metal				艮 Gen Northeast
辛儀擊刑 Xi Crest Striking Punishment	辛 *Xin* Yin Metal				離 Li South
壬儀擊刑 Ren Crest Striking Punishment	壬 *Ren* Yang Water				巽 Xun Southeast
癸儀擊刑 Gui Crest Striking Punishment	癸 *Gui* Yin Water				巽 Xun Southeast

Description

- The Wu Crest Striking Punishment: Zi punishes Mao.
- The Ji Crest Striking Punishment: Xu punishes Wei.
- The Geng Crest Striking Punishment: Shen punishes Yin.
- The Xin Crest Striking Punishment: Wu punishes itself.
- The Ren Crest Striking Punishment: Yin punishes Si.

The Six Crests Striking Punishment is vicious and can induce feelings of pressure and fear.

Example 1:

This is a Chart plotted on 6 March, 2010 at 11.40am.

Forecast Date	6 March, 2010 at 11.40am

局 STRUCTURE:	日 DAY:	時 HOUR:
陽七局 YANG SEVEN	乙卯 Yi Mao **Wood Rabbit**	壬午 Ren Wu **Water Horse** (11am - 12.59pm)

SE	S	SW
乙 Yi / 心 Xin Heart / 地 Di Earth 日旺 Ri Wang 丁 Ding / 驚 Jing Fear — **6**	辛 Xin / 蓬 Peng Grass / 天 Tian Heaven 辛刑 Xin Xing 庚 Geng / 開 Kai Open — **2**	己 Ji / 任 Ren Ambassador / 符 Fu Chief 龍返 Long Fan / 相佐 Xiang Zuo / 己刑 Ji Xing 壬 Ren / 休 Xiu Rest — **4**
戊 Wu / 柱 Zhu Pillar / 雀 Que Phoenix 戊刑 Wu Xing 癸 Gui / 死 Si Death — **5**	丙 Bing 丙 Bing	癸 Gui / 沖 Chong Destructor / 蛇 She Snake 戊 Wu / 生 Sheng Life — **9**
壬 Ren / 芮 Rui Grain / 陳 Chen Hook 丙 Bing / 跌穴 Die Xue / 權怡 Quan Yi 己 Ji / 景 Jing Scenery — **1**	庚 Geng / 英 Ying Hero / 合 He Harmony 辛 Xin / 杜 Du Delusion — **3**	丁 Ding / 輔 Fu Assistant / 陰 Yin Moon 神侵 Shen Jia 乙 Yi / 傷 Shang Harm — **8**
NE	N	NW

符首 **Lead Stem**	己 Ji
直使 **Envoy**	生門 Life Door
直符 **Lead Star**	天任星 Heavenly Ambassador

馬HS Horse Star	空DE Death & Emptiness
申 Shen **Monkey**	申 Shen **Monkey** 酉 You **Rooster**

When the Wu 戊 Stem enters the Zhen (East) Palace, it forms the *Wu Crest Striking Punishment* 戊儀擊刑. In this same Chart, you will also see that the Xin 辛 Stem is in the Li (South) Palace where it too forms a *Striking Punishment* formation. This goes for the Ji Stem which is residing in the Kun (Southwest) Palace as well. The Ji 己 Stem in the Kun (Southwest) Palace automatically forms the *Ji Crest Striking Punishment* 己儀擊刑. This Chart contains 3 of the 6 Crescent Striking Punishment formations – clearly indicating that there are many undesirable terrain or 'situations' up head.

Example 2:

This is a Chart plotted on 24 April 2011 at 5.30pm where the Heavenly Stem Geng Metal is residing in the Gen (Northeast) Palace. Take note of the Heavenly Stem Gui Water which is residing in the Xun (Southeast) Palace.

Forecast Date	24 April 2011 at 5.30pm	
局 STRUCTURE:	日 DAY:	時 HOUR:
陽五局 YANG FIVE	己酉 Ji You **Earth Rooster**	癸酉 Gui You **Water Rooster** (5pm - 6.59pm)

Chart

SE 巽 4木

癸 Gui / 蓬 Peng Grass / 合 He Harmony 地假 Di Jia / 癸刑 Gui Xing 乙 Yi / 杜 Du Delusion / **4**	辛 Xin / 任 Ren Ambassador / 陳 Chen Hook 辛刑 Xin Xing 壬 Ren / 景 Jing Scenery / **9**	丙 Bing / 沖 Chong Destructor / 雀 Que Phoenix 跌穴 Die Xue / 權怡 Quan Yi / 月使 Yue Shi / 戊 Wu 丁 Ding / 死 Si Death / **2**
己 Ji / 心 Xin Heart / 陰 Yin Moon 神假 Shen Jia 丙 Bing / 傷 Shang Harm / **3**	戊 Wu 戊 Wu	乙 Yi / 輔 Fu Assistant / 地 Di Earth 日制 Ri Zhi 庚 Geng / 驚 Jing Fear / **7**
庚 Geng / 柱 Zhu Pillar / 蛇 She Snake 庚刑 Geng Xing 辛 Xin / 生 Sheng Life / **8**	丁 Ding / 芮 Rui Grain / 符 Fu Chief 戊 Wu / 禽 Qin Bird / 星制 Xing Zhi / 朱投 Zhu Tou 癸 Gui / 休 Xiu Rest / **1**	壬 Ren / 英 Ying Hero / 天 Tian Heaven 己 Ji / 開 Kai Open / **6**

E 震 3木 (left) · **W 兌 7金** (right)
NE 艮 8土 · **N 坎 1水** · **NW 乾 6金**
SW 坤 2土 (top right) · 空 DE (right middle)
馬 HS 空 DE (bottom)

符首 **Lead Stem**	戊 Wu
直使 **Envoy**	死門 Death Door
直符 **Lead Star**	天禽星 Heavenly Bird

馬 馬星 Horse Star	空 空亡 Death & Emptiness
亥 Hai **Pig**	戌 Xu **Dog** 亥 Hai **Pig**

In the Chart above, the Geng Stem is residing in the Gen (Northeast) Palace. This arrangement forms the *Geng Crest Striking Punishment* formation 庚儀擊刑. At the same time, the Gui Stem resides in the Xun (Southeast) Palace. This arrangement also forms the *Gui Crest Striking Punishment* formation 癸儀擊刑.

Using a Qi Men Chart, a practitioner is able to remotely view or understand the features of the environment in every direction. When read properly, a Qi Men Chart can serve, quite literally, as a map. With this map in hand, a practitioner can figure out how to best navigate these features or choose a new route altogether. Armed with this knowledge, he is able to make effective strategic plans and thus increase his odds in winning the battle.

Now, in a modern context, this technique is also extended to help a Qi Men strategist 'remotely' view and gauge a property's Feng Shui. As a Feng Shui practitioner I use this technique a lot in helping clients evaluate their property's Feng Shui remotely.

Here is an actual example based on a Chart plotted on 2 March 2014 at 3.00pm from one of the many cases I've worked on:

時 Hour	日 Day	月 Month	年 Year	
戊 (7K) Wu Yang Earth	壬 (DM) Ren Yang Water	丙 (IW) Bing Yang Fire	甲 (EG) Jia Yang Wood	天干 Heavenly Stems
申 Shen Monkey Yang Metal	申 Shen Monkey Yang Metal	寅 Yin Tiger Yang Wood	午 Wu Horse Yang Fire	地支 Earthly Branches
戊 庚 壬 +Earth +Metal +Water 殺7K 卩IR 比F	戊 庚 壬 +Earth +Metal +Water 殺7K 卩IR 比F	戊 甲 丙 +Earth +Wood +Fire 殺7K 食EG 才IW	丁 己 -Fire -Earth 財DW 官DO	藏干 Hidden Stems

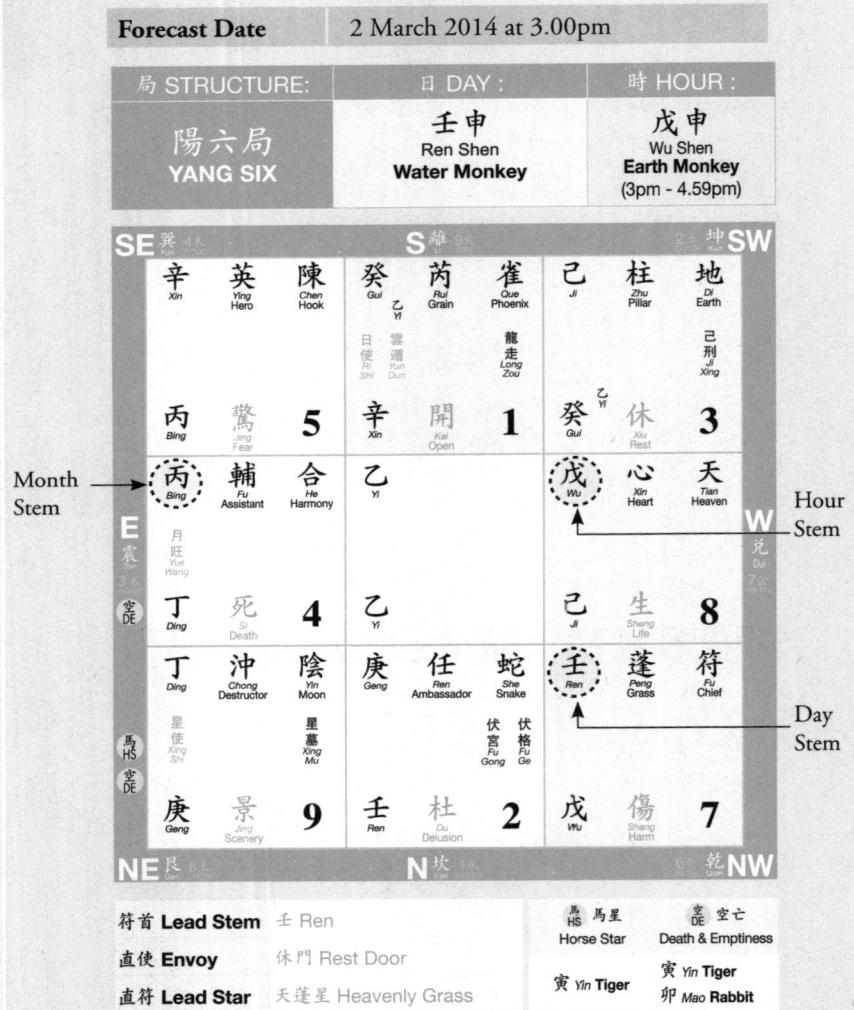

The Purchase of Land for Development

On the afternoon of March 2, 2014, I was descending from the town of Niseko to Sapporo in Hokkaido, Japan, after my snowboarding retreat. Just before reaching my hotel at about 3.15 pm, a VIP client called me from Malaysia. He works as a successful property developer and is also a good friend of mine. He told me that he was eyeing on a new 120-acre site and that he wanted to acquire it for a new development project.

The land was formerly used for agricultural purposes and had only recently become earmarked for residential development. Before making the purchase, my client wanted to determine if the land had good Feng Shui. From our work together in the past, he knew that it would be possible for myself to give him a quick assessment using Qi Men Dun Jia and without the need for a physical site visit. Of course, nothing can replace an onsite examination but sometimes clients need quick answers as they must act quickly before someone else does. A more thorough Feng Shui consultation can then take place after they have procured the site or property.

What follows is a break down of the Qi Men Dun Jia analysis I performed for my client, based on the given information.

The Qi Men Analysis:

I plotted the Qi Men Chart for March 2, 2014 at 3.15pm as this was the exact local time in Sapporo that the client called. Hence, the Chart plotted for this time formed the basis of my forecast.

In any Qi Men analysis, the first step, as you will recall, is to determine where the Useful God 用神 lies. This is the *focal point* of the Chart. A proper analysis cannot take place until this point has been identified. In Land Assessment forecasts, the Useful God is the Death Door 死門, which represents a 'piece of land'. I checked to find the location of the Death Door in the Qi Men Chart and found that it was located in the Zhen (East) Palace in the Chart.

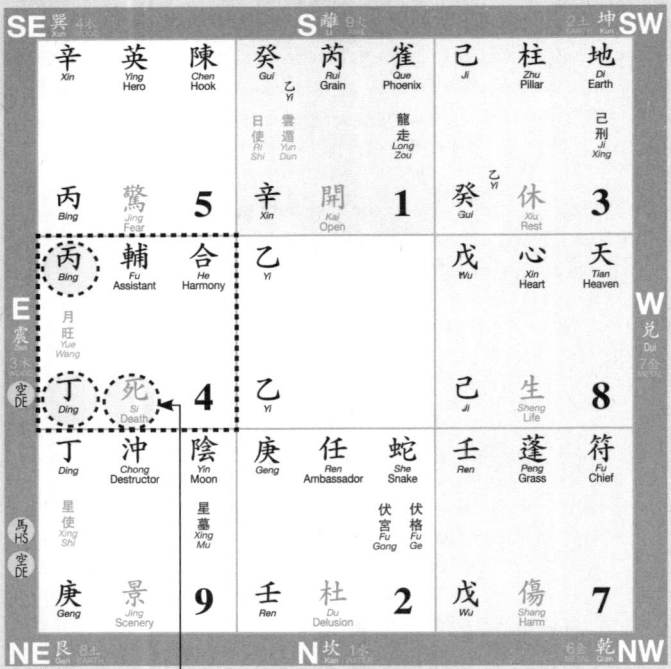

The Death Door represents the Land in this analysis.

In advanced Qi Men readings, it is necessary to consider the season or the month in which a forecast is made. I made this forecast in March 2014. In the month of March, the Wood element is prosperous. Knowing this, I continued my analysis.

Inside the Zhen (East) Palace lies a Bing Heavenly Stem 丙奇. This is considered highly auspicious as Bing Stem is one of the **3 Nobles** which protects Jia 甲. The Bing Stem, generally speaking, is representative of trait, such as grandeur, majestic, and splendour. In addition, there is also the Ding Earthly Stem 丁奇, also known as the *Jade Maiden* 玉女 which is representative of elegance and beauty. This arrangement is considered as highly auspicious because both the Bing and Ding Stems are part of the 3 Nobles which protect the Jia 甲. Both belong to the Fire element and are thus prosperous in the Zhen (East) Palace (Wood Element) according to the 5 Element relationships. Furthermore, the presence of the Bing Stem in the East sector forms the auspicious formation known as the *Moon Prosperous Structure* 月旺. In addition, both the Bing and Ding Stems as a combination also form the auspicious Structure known as the *Moon Noble Red Phoenix Formation* 月奇朱雀.

Noting all of the above, I told my client that according to the Qi Men Chart I had plotted, the landform of the land was beautiful and elegant, with a masculine type of land contour similar to a Sun and Moon shaped hill formations in the vicinity. This is owing to the nature of the Bing and Ding Stems. The Chart suggested that this land had a pleasant view with strong, calm, flowing hills, creating a good Qi flow, which is highly desirable in Feng Shui. Upon hearing this feedback, my client sounded shocked. He agreed that the property had a very 'majestic' feel and so he wished to know even more. I obliged and took my analysis to the next level.

In a Qi Men reading, the Hour Stem represents the *subject matter* in question during the forecast. In this case, the Hour Stem could be said to represent the decision of whether or not to buy the piece of land. In other words, the quality of the Hour Stem's contents could reveal whether or not the decision to buy was a sound one. In this Chart, the Hour Stem is the *Wu* 戊 Stem. It resides in the Dui (West) Palace. In this Palace, there is an auspicious Life Door 生門, which, in an environmental analysis, represents a Qi Mouth, an Incoming Dragon (source of Qi of the area) and/or open spaces. The Feng Shui in this environment was therefore very good!

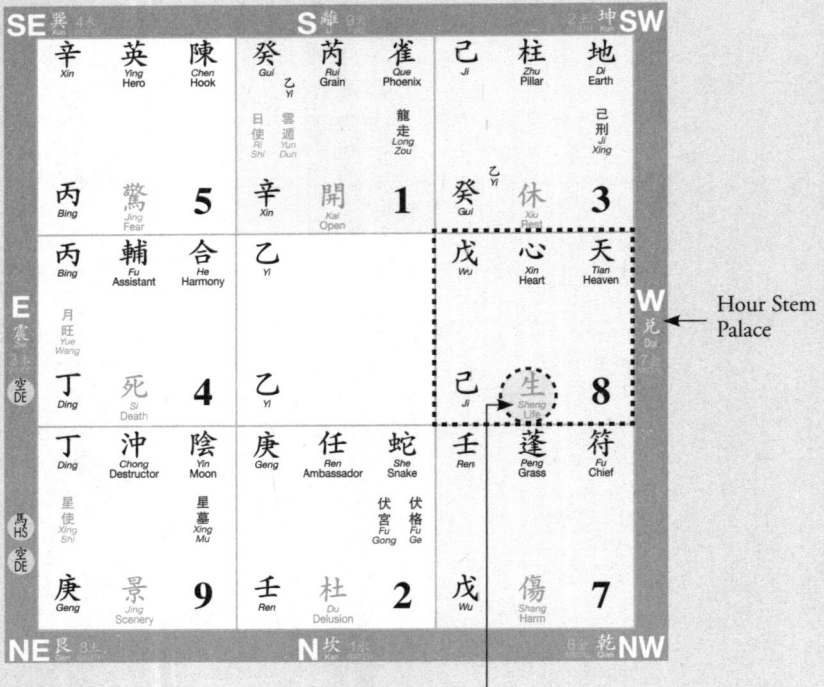

The Life Door represents the Qi source, Qi Mouth or Incoming Dragon

Knowing this, I told my client that the land he was deliberating over had higher mountain ranges on the West and that the land contour was moving towards the East, with its source of energy (Qi Mouth) within that vicinity. The land itself exuded a gentle airy feel as it was surrounded and embraced by mountains and buildings of decent height. However, these mountains or buildings would not obstruct the horizon. He confirmed, from his firsthand experience, that all of this information was true.

This is where the story becomes interesting. I told my client that his approval for the development of high-rise condominiums on this piece of land will not be granted. He was surprised and in shock. He asked me how I knew about his intention for this piece of land and more importantly how did I know that the approval would not be granted for a high-rise.

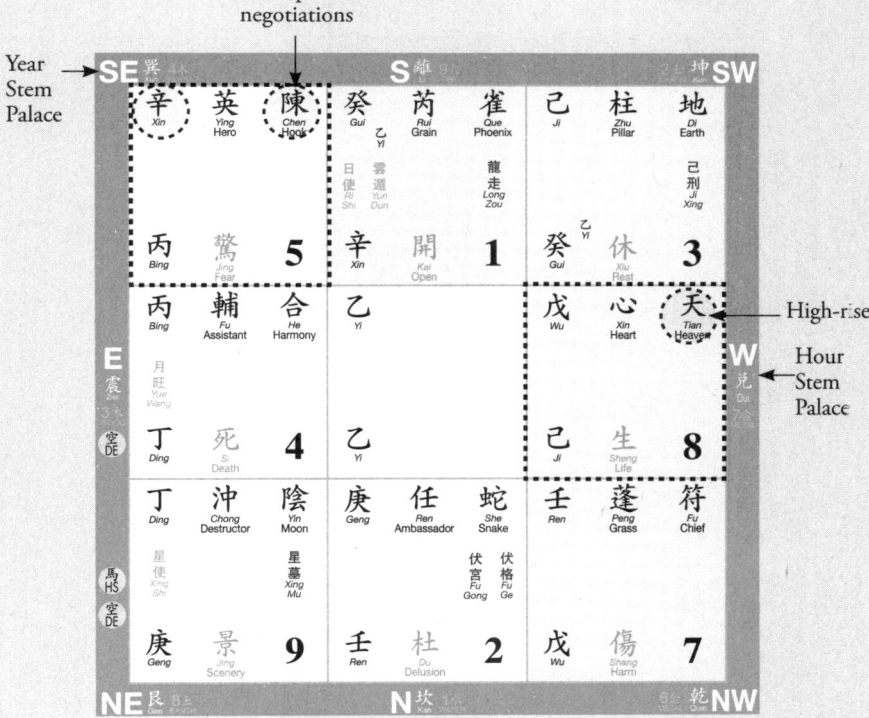

Now, how could I determine this information just by looking at the Qi Men Chart? The answer is simple. First, the Hour Stem Palace represents the subject matter, and in this case, it represents the intention to purchase and develop this piece of land. In this Palace, there is the Nine Heaven 九天 Deity. This Deity represents tall, high, sky-scrapping related features. There is also the Heavenly Heart Star 天心, which represents status and authority. Putting these two pieces of information together, I deduced that he wanted to build luxury high rise condominiums.

I also checked the Year Stem during my analysis. The Year Stem is Jia Wu 甲午. The Jia Wu's *Lead Stem* resides with the *Xin Stem* 辛*. The Year Stem is often representative of someone senior. In Chapter One, as you can recall, we discussed the way in which the Year Stem can represent the highest leadership, the Tao, or the Way in a Chart. In my analysis, I chose to interpret the Year Stem as being representative of someone senior - like the government officials or someone with authority on land development.

All fine and well, but how did I know he would not be able to obtain approval for his high-rise construction? In this Chart, the Xin Stem resides in the Xun (Southeast) Palace. In this Palace we see the Deity – Grappling Hook 勾陳 which represents cumbersome red tape and protracted negotiations. In this Palace, the Heavenly Hero Star 天英 together with the Fear Door 驚門 forms an '*all-talk-but-no-action*' scenario. Lastly, this Palace is countered elementally by both the Hour Stem Palace and the Day Stem Palace, which means they are not compatible.

By deliberating all of this information, I reached my conclusion that he would not get his approval for the high-rise easily. My client confirmed that he had friends who were in touch with the authorities and they had indeed indicated that such application for high-rise would most likely be declined.

* For this Hour Chart analysis, you must be able to differentiate between the **Jia Wu's Lead Stem** and the **Lead Stem of this Chart**, which is the Ren Stem. The Ren Stem is the Lead Stem for the Wu Shen Hour Pillar, since this is an Hour Chart. To find out the right Lead Stem for Jia Wu, you must refer to the Six Jia Streams Table, available in the **Joey Yap's Qi Men Dun Jia Ten Thousand Year Calendar**. In this case, the Lead Stem for Jia Wu is Xin.

After my client recovered from his initial shock, I then broke the news that it wouldn't be possible for him to purchase this piece of land in the first place anyway, as someone else had already placed a deposit on it.

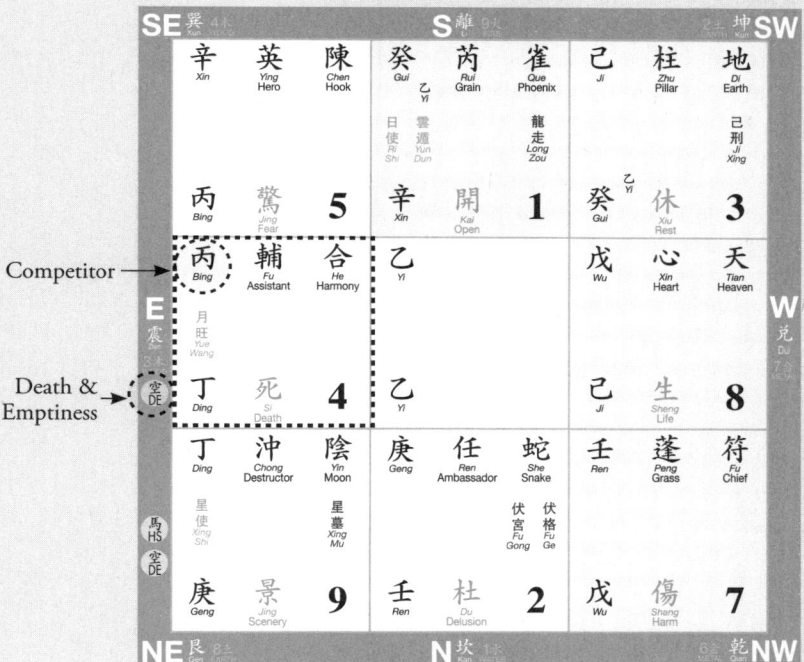

I knew this because the Six Harmony Deity 六合 also lies in the Zhen (East) Palace. The Death Door is also in the Zhen (East) Palace. This Door represents the piece of land in question and its Palace falls in the *Death & Emptiness* 空亡 (Void) state. Unfortunately, this means that the piece of land was no longer available. Furthermore, the Six Harmony denotes a joint-venture, a partnership or deal. Together with the Heavenly Assistant 天輔星 (Wood) and the Ding 丁 (Fire) Stem – this combination represents a deal or "contract". Considering both of these facts, I could infer that someone else had already made a move on the land.

To confirm this point, I also studied the Month Stem. The Month Stem, as indicated in Chapter One, represents the competitor. In this particular Forecast Chart, the Month Stem is Bing 丙. Now, Bing was also residing in the Zhen (East) Palace with the Death Door (the piece of land). This means that the Bing Stem, the competitor, was ALREADY on the piece of land. With a little bit of imagination here, I deduced that the competitor had already made a deposit for the purchase of the land!

The final nail in the coffin was that the Hour Stem (West) Palace counters the Death Door's Palace (East Palace), suggesting that my client could not get what he wanted – the land. Any how you dice it, it was all bad news for my client.

Immediately, my client knew of the person I was referring to. He got off the line and promised to call me again tomorrow. As I had predicted, a third party had indeed got his hands on the land first.

In the end, it just wasn't meant to be for my client.

---

* I included this story in the hopes of demonstrating how extensive a modern Qi Men Dun Jia analysis can be, although granted this is a complex example. Regrettably at this stage if you are very new to Qi Men Dun Jia, some of these technical terminologies may be alien to you. If you have been inspired by it, you can refer to some of the earlier books in my Qi Men Dun Jia series or watch some of the free introductory videos of my Qi Men workshops from my website in order to strengthen your understanding on Qi Men overall. Then come back and re-read this chapter and it will make more sense.

NINE GROUNDS 九地

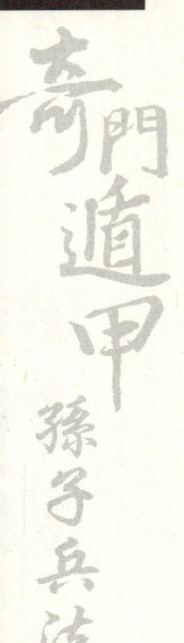

ORIGINAL TEXT:

孫子曰：用兵之法，有散地，
有輕地，有爭地，有交地，
有衢地，有重地，有圮地，
有圍地，有死地。

TRANSLITERATION:

Sun Tzu said: in connection with military operations, ground and territory can be divided into nine different classifications. The nine types of ground are dispersive, frontier, contentious, open, focal, serious, difficult, encircled and desperate ground.

COMMENTARY:

There are nine possible 'battlegrounds' that you can find yourself doing business or working in. On a smaller scale, one of these nine battlegrounds might, for example, be representative of the work environment you share with a rival colleague.

Each of these nine environments has different characteristics; some place you at an advantage, some at a disadvantage. Each of these 'battlegrounds' calls for different thinking and tactics; what works well in one may not in another. You must employ the most suitable management tactics for the battleground you fight on. If you are in a position to choose the area of competition you will be able to select the most advantageous battlefield, based on your understanding of these nine possibilities.

Since you can't control what you don't understand, and yet control and dominance of the 'battlefield' is the real end game in competition, it is wise to educate yourself on the characteristics of all nine possible competitive environments.

11

ORIGINAL TEXT:

諸侯自戰其地者，爲散地。
入人之地而不深者，爲輕地。
我得則利，彼得亦利者，
爲爭地。我可以往，
彼可以來者，爲交地。
諸侯之地三屬，
先至而得天下之眾者，爲衢地。
入人之地深，背城邑多者，
爲重地。山林、險阻、沮澤，
凡難行之道者，爲圮地。
所由入者隘，所從歸者迂，
彼寡可以擊吾之眾者，爲圍地。
疾戰則存，不疾戰則亡者，
爲死地。

TRANSLITERATION:

When a commander leads a campaign within the borders of his own territories, the ground may be referred to as dispersive.

When an army crosses enemy borders without travelling too far into enemy territory, the land they fight upon may be referred to as frontier ground.

A position that is favourable to both sides in a conflict is called contentious ground.

A position that is accessible to both sides is called open ground.

Should the position be the meeting point of the territorial borders of three neighbouring states and the occupation of this territory by one of these powers is the key to winning the support of the other two, then the ground is known as focal ground.

If an army penetrates deeply into hostile territory, having passed a series of enemy towns and cities, they can be said to be on serious ground.

An area that is dominated by interlocking mountains, tangled forests and impenetrable marshes or indeed any area that is challenging to traverse or navigate is known as difficult ground.

Land which is restricted or closed off or enclosed (and where there is a high risk of ambush) is known as encircled ground.

Any place where battle will be fierce and the outcome will make or break you is referred to as desperate ground.

COMMENTARY:

When you conduct business or compete in your own backyard under familiar circumstances, that is: within a market or niche you are already well established in, you do so on dispersive ground.

When you encroach slightly on a rival's territory to compete, you are on frontier ground. For instance, if you launch a new product or new project that competes indirectly with your competitor's current line then you are doing business on frontier ground.

Competitive efforts that take place in a new or neutral territory or market where neither side has a footing are said to take place on contentious ground.

Competition in a large environment or market with a great deal of competition and many existing players is said to take place on open ground. There will be a lot of room for manoeuvring, but it can be hard to distinguish yourself.

If you wish to operate in an environment where three existing players vie for dominance, you do so on focal ground. Your goal must be to win the support or allegiance of two existing players because there is rarely room for four serious warring contenders.

When you enter into competitive action directly against a rival on their terms, then you will find that you are on serious ground.

When you attempt to do business or compete against the odds under difficult circumstances with narrow criteria for victory, then you are on difficult ground.

Competition in a narrow niche or within a confined space takes place on encircled ground.

When the outcome of competition is absolutely critical, you are competing on desperate ground.

ORIGINAL TEXT:

是故散地則無戰，輕地則無止，
爭地則無攻，交地則無絕，
衢地則合交，重地則掠，
圮地則行，圍地則謀，
死地則戰。

TRANSLITERATION:

It is always unwise to fight on dispersive ground; one should never stop long on frontier ground; never attack the enemy who arrives first at an area of contentious ground; never allow your lines of communication to be blocked on open ground; always work to form alliances with neighbouring princes when on focal ground; make plans to plunder provisions once on serious ground; pass through difficult ground as quickly as possible, devise plans to escape should you find yourself trapped in encircled ground and when you find yourself on desperate ground, give everything you've got.

COMMENTARY:

Avoid competing in a way that can threaten your existing and established assets and revenue. Keep your risky competitive activities separate from your stable and productive operations in order to insulate and insure yourself against catastrophe if they fail.

If your rival is already well placed and successful then it is unwise to try to compete directly – he occupies an advantageous position by virtue of having arrived first. It is very difficult to try and displace an entrenched market player by beating him at his own game. If you try to engage an opponent on his home turf, on his terms, the best you can usually hope for is second place.

On open ground, maintain strong communication links. Teamwork is the link that can keep your organization together under difficult circumstances.

On focal ground, where you face multiple competitors, your first priority should be to create strategic alliances and combine forces and resources with existing players so that you can secure your footing and grow in strength.

If you find that you must do business or operate within your rivals' realm of experience and in their market, then look for what they have left untouched or scavenged. Identify specific services that they aren't currently providing and provide those to your shared user base so you can gain a better footing and grow in size and strength.

When you must operate under a high level of risk, make it your top priority to reach a more sustainable way of operating, and then seek growth.

Look for ways to get to a safer position and limit damage when you are in encircled ground. Don't get drawn into battles you can't win – they will only weaken you and there are no prizes for bravery in business, only victory.

Finally, on desperate ground, adopt a "win at all costs" mindset. Otherwise, it will only prolong your certain demise. Desperate times really do call for desperate measures; so turn up the pressure and set high goals for your people. The will to survive can be a powerful motivator. Hopefully, harnessing this instinct can create the power necessary to propel you to safety.

ORIGINAL TEXT:

古之所謂善用兵者，
能使敵人前後不相及，
眾寡不相恃，貴賤不相救，
上下不相收，卒離而不集，
兵合而不齊。合于利而動，
不合于利而止。
敢問：「敵眾整而將來，
待之若何？」
曰：「先奪其所愛，則聽矣；　」

TRANSLITERATION:

In ancient times, generals who were skilled in military operations knew exactly how to block enemy communications and scatter their forces. They would be able to prevent an initial vanguard from communicating their findings to the troops who were following at the rear. They would prevent the main body of the army from coordinating their operations with smaller frontier groups. They would make it impossible for superiors and subordinates to support one another. They would divide units so that they would not be able to reunite and keep them in disorder even while they were assembled.

Great generals would advance only when it was in their best interests to do so and they would halt their advance the moment the circumstances changed.

In response to the question: 'If the enemy comes to attack with a mighty and well-ordered army, how can you hope to defeat them?' The answer is that you must seize what he cherishes and he will conform to your desires.

COMMENTARY:

You can greatly diminish your competitors' effectiveness by creating chaos and confusion within their organisation. Since teamwork is power, any kind of disruptive strategy can reduce your opponents' capabilities greatly. Intercept their organisational lines of communication so that important information and instructions are either lost or misunderstood. Interrupt and distract them using any means, legally, at your disposal.

A great leader only fights the battles they can win. If they can't, they will find a way to take the battle to a place where they can. In business, this thinking can take many forms, for example, in choosing to negotiate only under a set of favourable conditions.

One way of gaining control over your opponents or work rivals is to seize something of importance to them. This will put you in a bargaining position where you can dictate terms. Thus, it is often worth acquiring things for which you don't have direct use if they are of interest to others. In the real estate industry, one developer might buy land that infringes upon a rival developers' expansion plans. The savvy developer could then sell the land in question for a greatly increased price or trade it for an agreed return on the expansion project which could otherwise not go ahead at all. In this example, the shrewd developer gained twice at the expense of his rival.

ORIGINAL TEXT:

兵之情主速，乘人之不及，
由不虞之道，攻其所不戒也。

TRANSLITERATION:

The essence of military operations is speed and taking advantage of the enemy while they are unprepared. In order to achieve this, you must take routes that they do not expect and attack them while they are defenceless.

COMMENTARY:

Speed gives you a disruptive competitive advantage. When you execute quickly at every level, your rival has no time to mount any kind of defence or employ counter measures. In some situations, quick action allows you to exclude your rival altogether – for example, following up quickly with prospects can help you close the deal before your rival has even had the chance to make a counter offer.

Smaller businesses which have a differentiating model but move rapidly in the market can compete effectively against much larger businesses which cannot move quickly due to bureaucracy. If you wish to take on a larger rival on new ground, then speed is a force multiplier that can make up for any deficiency you have in strength. Think, and act fast!

ORIGINAL TEXT:

凡爲客之道，深入則專，
主人不克，掠于饒野，
三軍足食，謹養而無勞，
併氣積力，運兵計謀，
爲不可測，投之無所往，
死且不北，死焉不得，
士人盡力。兵士甚陷則不懼，
無所往則固，深入則拘，
不得已則鬥。是故，
其兵不修而戒，不求而得，
不約而親，不令而信，
禁祥去疑，至死無所之。

TRANSLITERATION:

The following tactics should be employed when you do battle on enemy land. Be aware that when you penetrate deep into enemy territories, it will have the effect of uniting your men and bringing them together as a single mind. This should make it hard for the opposition to defeat you. Make use of ingenious and unpredictable tactics so that the enemy will never be able to anticipate you, keep your men well fed and rested, do not exhaust them, keep their morale up and plunder any fertile land for food and resources when you encounter it.

If you place your men in a position from which they cannot retreat and where there is no way to flee, even in the face of death, they will overcome their fears. Free of the fear of death, both soldiers and officers will fight with all their might. In this way, soldiers who are deep within enemy territory become fierce and fearless. With no avenue of retreat, they will stand firm. Alone in enemy territory, they will stand together. With no other choice, they will fight to their last.

In this kind of environment, the men will not need to be taught to be vigilant. They will do as you wish without being told, they will cooperate without being conditioned to do so and they will follow your orders before you even give them. If you prohibit superstition and dispel rumours and suspicions as soon as they arise, your men will be loyal in the face of death.

COMMENTARY:

You can get masterful results from your team by creating the right kind of pressure.

Set high expectations and make them known. Put them in writing and set dates, and then make sure every one of your team members internalises this expectation. You must coax their full hearty enrolment. You must get the 'buy-ins' from their own accord. Challenge your team and create accountability for results. A high-pressured environment and superstar status for the winners can serve to unite your staff, build a sense of camaraderie and give them purpose. Get them excited about your vision and make them hunger for the prize. If you block any avenue for 'retreat' and make it known that failure is not an option then your people will have no choice but to rise to the occasion – and they will!

Celebrate your team's winnings publicly. Create a system that rewards those who go the 'extra mile'. Recognise the superstars in your team! Treat your people well when they do well. Nip defeatist ideas or pessimistic talk that creeps into your organisation in the bud or it can poison morale and derail your plans.

Finally, as a growing organisation in a new market, you have the element of surprise on your side. You can make a strong debut if you are unpredictable and elusive from the word go. Move quickly so that you can't be crushed by more established players.

ORIGINAL TEXT:

吾士無餘財，非惡貨也；
無餘命，非惡壽也。
令發之日，士卒坐者涕沾襟，
偃臥者涕交頤，投之無所往，
則諸劌之勇也。

TRANSLITERATION:

Soldiers often have little wealth but don't believe that. This is because they do not like to have possessions. Similarly, soldiers who do not fear death still aspire longevity.

On the day that an army is ordered to fight a decisive battle, soldiers may shed many tears. They may sit and cry until their garments are soaked with their tears. They may lie down and do nothing but allow their tears to run down their cheeks. Nevertheless, if you throw them into a position where there is no way for them to retreat, they will be as brave as Zhuan Zhu or Cao Gui.

COMMENTARY:

Even though people don't always show it, they have the same basic fears and insecurities. Nobody wants to lose. Everyone wants to win.

You can count on this psychological truth when you manage your staff by setting lofty targets – the greater the challenge and the higher the cost of failure, the more that people will rise to the occasion because they will feel compelled to beat the odds. The extraordinary "survival instinct" that everyone is born with can be harnessed in order to create extraordinary results. Let your people know that failure is not an option. Block opportunities for retreat. Set fantastic, yet achievable goals for your people and you will find out just how capable they can really be. You will often be surprised in this regard. As the saying goes - even if you fall short of the moon, you will still land among the stars.

The best leaders set big (but plausible) goals for big, real results.

ORIGINAL TEXT:

故善用兵者，譬如率然；
率然者，常山之蛇也，擊其首，
則尾至，擊其尾，則首至，
擊其中，則首尾俱至。
敢問：「兵可使如率然乎？」
曰：「可。」夫吳人與越人相惡也，
當其同舟濟而遇風，
其相救也如左右手。
是故，方馬埋輪，未足恃也，
齊勇若一，政之道也；
剛柔皆得，地之理也。
故善用兵者，攜手若使一人，
不得已也。

TRANSLITERATION:

Those who are skilled in military operations should be as flexible and nimble as the shuairan snake of Mount Chang. If you strike its head, it will swing at you with its tail. If you strike its tail, it will attack you with its head and if you beat its body, the head will attack while the tail swings.

You may ask, "Is it possible for troops to achieve instant coordination like that?" I will tell you that the answer is possible.

It is common knowledge that the territories of Wu and Yue are sworn enemies but if they are travelling on the same boat and they are caught in a storm, they will still cooperate with one another just as the left hand cooperates with the right. However, tying their war horses *together and burying their chariot wheels is not a reliable way to bring men together. Uniting soldiers to fight bravely as a team is a matter of good management. The correct use of landforms will support the soldiers and bring their courage to the fore.*

A skillful commander will be able to command thousands upon thousands of horses and men as if he were instructing one man who has no choice but to obey.

COMMENTARY:

Whenever you are challenged, you must come up with a counter-strategy or solution so that your rivals understand you are not to be trifled with. React quickly; speed is your ally when under attack.

To unite people as a leader - even enemies - you must know how to motivate and influence. Leadership is after all an art of influencing. When seeking to unite competing factions, identify shared objectives that are close to their hearts and you will be able to direct them as one. Speak their language and help them internalise your vision. To direct many people as one force, you will need an absolute 'buy-in' for your vision and the ability to obtain this is a hallmark of strong leadership. The loftier the goal, the more pressing the need to make sure that your vision is communicated in terms that everyone can relate to. You must present your goal in an 'achievable' manner. People need to believe that they can do what you want them to do.

If you can master these principles, you can lead a thousand people from a thousand backgrounds just as easily as one.

ORIGINAL TEXT:

將軍之事，靜以幽，正以治，
能愚士卒之耳目，使之無知。
易其事，革其謀，使人無識，
易其居，迂其途，使人不得慮。
帥與之期，如登高而去其梯，
帥與之深，入諸侯之地而發其機。
若驅群羊，驅而往，驅而來，
莫知所之。聚三軍之眾，
投之于險，此將軍之事也。
九地之變，屈伸之利，
人情之理，不可不察也。

TRANSLITERATION:

A general in charge of an army should be as serene as he is unfathomable. He should manage his men with an upright impartiality and he should keep his military strategies a secret from his soldiers and officers alike. He should be free to alter his strategies without his men being aware of his decision to do so. He should have the option to change the location of his campsite or take a circuitous route to his destination without being questioned.

A general who leads his troops to fight a decisive battle should cut off any means of retreat as surely as he would have kicked down the ladder after his men have scaled a great wall. When leading his troops into enemy territories, he should have the momentum of an arrow that flies loose from the bow. He may burn boats and break cauldrons to make his men certain and resolute. He may drive his men the same *way as a shepherd drives his flock and his men should be no more aware of the future course of their journey or of their destination. He must be able to put his people into dangerous situations. That is what a commander must do.*

How to vary tactics in order to benefit from geographical locations, when to advance or retreat in order to secure the best possible advantage and the laws of human nature are the subjects a general must study with great care.

COMMENTARY:

A leader must seem sure of himself and his choices at all times. As the boss, your decisions must be seen to come from certainty and you must conceal any doubts or fears you have. Keep your internal decision making process a secret; all the people need to know are the conclusions you reach, not how you reach them or with what confidence. The more certain you appear to know where you are going, the more readily your people will follow you. Although nobody can be entirely sure of anything, you must give the impression that you alone are capable of doing so to your team. Unflappable confidence is magnetic.

Emotion must never drive your decision making and you must never appear swayed by your emotions in front of others. Your team follows your example and if they see that you are angry or scared they will take their cue from you. Negative emotions spread like wildfire and set the stage for disobedience, which cannot be tolerated.

Be brave and commit fully to your plans. You must leave no stone unturned. This is your prerogative as a leader. Remove any possibility of 'escape' and create pressure where there is none for high calibre results. When there is no choice but to make things work, people will find a way: their natural survival instincts will kick in. Without true pressure, this response cannot take place – it cannot be faked. Choose objectives and a working speed that force you to give it your all – push yourself!

ORIGINAL TEXT:

凡爲客之道，深則專，淺則散；
去國越境而師者，絕地也；
四達者，衢地也；
入深者，重地也；
入淺者，輕地也；背固前隘者，
圍地也；無所往者，死地也。

TRANSLITERATION:

If you penetrate only a short distance into enemy territory, your soldiers will fight with minimal intensity. If you penetrate deep into enemy territory, they will concentrate their efforts and you will ignite their fighting spirit. Crossing a neighbouring territory to a battleground where there is no way for the soldiers to return means that you are on critical ground. If you are at a juncture between territories then you are on focal ground. If you have penetrated deep into enemy territory then you are on serious ground. If you have penetrated only a short distance instead, you are on frontier ground. When you arrive at a place with rugged terrain at your back and a narrow pass before you, you are in encircled ground. When you enter a region where there is no way to retreat, you are on desperate ground.

COMMENTARY:

Here, Sun Tzu spoke also about the different types of ground you can find yourself on and different conditions call for different management tactics and levels of caution. These 'grounds' are metaphorical representations for the different competitive environments that you can encounter in life and business. On a smaller scale, they represent internal work politics that you must navigate in order to advance.

As a leader, never underestimate how competition can bring out the fighting spirit in your team. Pit your people against the opponent.

The more you encroach upon a rival and his operating territory, the greater the resistance you will encounter as they defend themselves and their interests more vigorously. It is worth considering this increased difficulty and the increased costs associated with it when deciding the scope and nature of your competitive campaigns. Indirect competition can often generate greater profit and allow you to grow. Be optimistic by all means, but don't over-reach.

ORIGINAL TEXT:

是故散地吾將一其志，
輕地吾將使之屬，
爭地吾將趨其後，
交地吾將謹其守，
衢地吾將固其結，
重地吾將繼其食，
圮地吾將進其途，
圍地吾將塞其闕，
死地吾將示之以不活。
故兵之情，圍則禦，
不得已則鬥，逼則從。

TRANSLITERATION:

When you are on dispersive ground, you should unify the will of your soldiers. When you are on frontier ground, you should shore up the lines of communications between the vanguard and the rear. When you are on contentious ground, you should hasten the movement of troops at the rear. When you are on open ground, you should take care to defend your encampment. When you are on focal ground, you should be sure to win the allegiance of neighbouring princes. When you are on serious ground, you should press on and aim to cross it rapidly. When you are in encircled ground, you should block the points of access. When you are on desperate ground, you must convince your soldiers that they have no choice but to fight with ferocity.

A general must understand the psychology state of his soldiers in order to lead them. They will resist when they are surrounded, they will fight with desperate passion when there is no chance of escape and they will follow the general with complete trust when they are in danger.

COMMENTARY:

Know which management techniques are best suited for the situation.

When you are on dispersive ground, your top priority is to keep your team working closely together. Set bold objectives and make them known so that your team is inspired to come together to work as a tight-knit group.

When you're on frontier ground, ensure that communication flows freely in both directions within your organization. Filter information so that confusion does not arise and everyone is kept in the loop and your team will fight as one, ensuring that your competitor doesn't have the chance to divide your people.

On open ground, defence is your top priority. Protect your existing revenue streams and maintain your connections.

On focal ground, you must work quickly to find allies and build beneficial partnerships – approach existing movers and shakers in your field with a worthwhile proposal so they can help shield you in the harsh conditions.

On serious ground, you must move quickly to secure better operating position and reduce your losses. Make sure that you take active measures to reduce your liabilities or others will find ways to take advantage of them.

On desperate ground, you must throw all your energy into making a strong, final attempt to succeed – anything less will result in certain failure. Apply pressure to your team and direct their intense force towards goals that will generate immediate returns.

People react in predictable ways. You can count upon them to resist when they are surrounded, become aggressive when they are desperate and trust anyone who promises them a safe passage through a difficult situation. You can use these facts of human nature to serve you in your leadership role.

ORIGINAL TEXT:

是故不知諸侯之謀者,
不能預交,
不知山林險阻沮澤之形者,
不能行軍,不用鄉導者,
不能得地利,此三者不知一,
非霸王之兵也。

TRANSLITERATION:

A general who is ignorant of the motivations and intentions of neighbouring princes will not be able to form alliances with them; he who does not know the location of interlocking mountains and tangled forests, the deepest abyss, the highest precipice, the swamps and the marshes will not be able to move his troops; he who fails to employ local guides will struggle to find a favourable location to camp; he who is ignorant of the advantages and disadvantages inherent in a variety of different battle positions will not be able to command an army in a way that befits his sovereign.

COMMENTARY:

Understand what drives and motivates other players in the market as well as your customers so that you can speak their language. Identify your own unique selling proposition, your core values and what you have in order to offer something better than anyone else. Know how business is usually done in your market and play ball. When you know how the game is played, you can determine what value you have to offer and thus you can partner or align with others for mutual benefit and greater combined strength in the market.

Understanding the characteristics of the situation you are operating in will prevent disaster. Asking and collaborating with people who are more experienced and better informed than you will make it easier to reach your goals. It's okay to seek advice and consultation; doing so can make up for what you may lack in raw experience.

ORIGINAL TEXT:

夫霸王之兵，
伐大國則其眾不得聚，
威加于敵，則其交不得合。
是故不爭天下之交，
不養天下之權，信己之私，
威加于敵，故其城可拔，
其國可墮。

TRANSLITERATION:

A truly powerful sovereign and overlord will have such an army that even when he attacks a strong state, the latter will not be able to collect their strength to resist. Wherever such an army goes, it will awe the enemy and prevent him from convincing his allies to stand beside him in battle.

A state with a truly invincible army will not need to seek alliances in order to gain political power. The evidence of its strength will be enough to inspire fear and it will easily be able to capture its enemy's cities and destroy the opponent's state.

COMMENTARY:

When you have reached the highest position in the market and when you are the supreme industry leader you will no longer need to seek allies – you will be unstoppable and your reputation will precede you. Others will seek you out, pleading to be your ally. When this rings true, it means that you have reached complete market domination. You have become the powerful sovereign that Sun Tzu had described. This is, of course, the ideal state to strive for. However, reaching this level is not the hardest part of the game. Sustaining and maintaining your position at the top will be the real challenge from then on.

To get to the top, you need to achieve consistent, strategic growth and build a loyal following. On a personal level, you must simultaneously build your own skills as a compassionate leader. Once you have reached to the top of the game, you can benefit from having a cult-like following and you will enjoy the respect and adoration of your followers. Your followers will then continue to build and maintain your reputation for you and spread the word. They will do this because you are their hero, their sovereign. At this point, your reputation is your primary asset. So as you build your business, seek to build your reputation. It will become a valuable asset that defends your interests around the clock, even in your absence.

Remember that staying in power requires ongoing effort. To maintain your position as the great leader you must continue to serve your followers by leading them intelligently and helping them obtain what they want. You must help your followers become better, happier and more successful. Remember, pride is your enemy when you are at the top. Do not let it consume you. Counter pride with humility. Pride is concerned with being right; humility on the other hand is concerned with what is right. Never let pride turn you into a tyrant. Once you become a tyrant, your reign will come to an end. This is why you must seek to build your compassion and skills as a leader.

11

ORIGINAL TEXT:

施無法之賞，懸無政之令，
犯三軍之眾，若使一人。
犯之以事，勿告以言；
犯之以利，勿告以害；
投之亡地然後存，
陷之死地然後生。
夫眾陷于害，然後能爲勝敗，

TRANSLITERATION:

If you are leading the army of an overlord, you will have the power to bestow rewards and honours irrespective of custom and issue orders irrespective of convention. You will have the influence to command thousands upon thousands of men and horses as if they were a single man. You will be able to compel your troops to act without advising them of your purpose and you will be able to use them to gain advantage without explaining your motives or the dangers that may be involved. You will understand that by throwing your men into a perilous situation, you can motivate them to survive and by forcing them to face death, you can give them the courage to live. If it is in true jeopardy, an army will be able to turn a sure defeat into a victory.

COMMENTARY:

Once you have fully consolidated your leadership, you will have the power to move mountains. Your opinions will take on such immense gravity that people will be willing to go to the ends of the earth to satisfy your whims. The rewards and punishments you dispense will be truly effective in creating motivation and instilling discipline simply because they came from you. When you give instructions, they will be carried out without hesitation or question. In this kind of position, you can get your people to take great risks and handle extreme challenges as a result of their loyalty to you. What's more, when they do so, they will succeed at any cost because they cannot bear the thought of failing you.

Possessing this kind of power will allow you to do great things and attaining it should be an aim of any leader. Create your vision. Build your following.

11

ORIGINAL TEXT:

故爲兵之事,在于順詳敵之意,
併力一向,千里殺將,
是謂巧能成事。

TRANSLITERATION:

Success in military operations often lies in pretending to be drawn into enemy plans while, in fact, concentrating your troops to attack. If you adopt this method you may be able to bring down the enemy commander even if you are a thousand li away from him. By using such artful tactics, you will be able to accomplish great tasks.

COMMENTARY:

Become a master of deception and you can create tactical windows as you see fit. Give the appearance that you are unprepared and conceal your strategic intentions from the competition until the last possible moment. In this way, you can simultaneously lure the opponent into pursuing the wrong course of action while giving yourself the element of surprise. This is how you can force your enemy's hand as you see fit.

ORIGINAL TEXT:

是故政舉之日，夷關折符，
無通其使，属于廊廟之上，
以誅其事，敵人開闔，
必亟入之。先其所愛，
微與之期，賤墨隨敵，
以決戰爭。是故始如處女，
敵人開戶，後如脫兔，
敵不及拒。

TRANSLITERATION:

On the day that war is declared, you should close all passes to and from the enemy territory, revoke all accounts and break off any military ties. You should carefully examine your plans in the temple. If you are able to locate your enemy's weakness, you must rapidly exploit that knowledge. Aim first to seize that which is valuable to the opponent without betraying the time of your intended attack. In pursuing your plans, be sure to modify them in accordance with the changing circumstances presented to you by the enemy so that you can keep the upper hand. In the first instance, assume the coyness of a maiden and then, once your opponent is exposed, attack as swiftly as a running hare. This will render the enemy powerless to resist your onslaught.

COMMENTARY:

When you decide that you are going to launch an attack against your opponent, you must take steps that will help shield you against any fallout. Cut ties and end any reliance on your opponent as necessary. Create plausible deniability and concoct insurance policies. Minimise the risk to yourself.

Speedy execution is vital. Once your plans are underway there can be no delay or hesitation in seeing them through to completion. Don't give your rival a chance to better defend against your efforts or to strike back. If you can identify any predatory measures that will help support your plans without drawing attention then do so – the shorter the actual aggressive action you have in mind, the greater the chance that it will succeed. For example, in business, you should have your supply and distribution channels already in place before you announce a new competing product. Once you have done so, you should get it to market as quickly as possible to maximise profit. Remember to adapt and tailor your tactics as events unfold and when you get feedback. When you harness the power of surprise as well as the power of speed then you will have an undisputable advantage.

11

QI MEN DUN JIA:

In this chapter, Sun Tzu described the nine possible types of battleground: dispersive, frontier, contentious, open, focal, serious, difficult, encircled and desperate. Parallels can be drawn between these and the Nine Palaces (known as Jiu Gong 九宮) in a Qi Men Dun Jia Chart, each one of these Nine Palaces represents a direction on the compass with the exception of the Taiji which is the central reference point. Think of a Qi Men Chart as being akin to a map. There are North, Northeast, East, Southeast, Southwest, West and Northwest Palaces. Each Palace, or sector as some call them, describes the battleground you will encounter if you head in the given direction.

Distributed within the Nine Palaces of every Qi Men Chart are the Eight Mystical Doors also known as *Ba Men* 八門. These Doors represent the conditions and circumstances associated with the Palace in which they appear. In other words, these 'Doors' allow us to get an insight into the kind of battleground you will encounter in the given direction.

Each of the Eight Doors has its own special attributes. Take, for instance, the Open Door 開門. Its presence denotes that the direction or sector in which it resides will match Sun Tzu's description of an 'open' battleground. Armed with this intelligence, you can tailor your tactics in accordance with Sun Tzu's teachings for this kind of battleground.

It is important to understand the relationship between the Eight Doors and the Nine Palaces. These interactions fall into the following categories: *harmony* 和, *produce* 生 and *counter* 制 or *compel* 迫. The Door may *counter* the Palace or the Palace may *produce* the Door. These relationships are governed by the interactions of the elements that represent each Door or Palace as shown below and these unique conditions will indicate what kind of tactics are best.

Five Elements	The 9 Palaces		The 8 Doors
金 Metal	乾 Qian (Northwest)	兌 Dui (West)	開 Open
			驚 Fear
水 Water	坎 Kan (North)		休 Rest
木 Wood	震 Zhen (East)	巽 Xun (Southeast)	杜 Delusion
			傷 Harm
火 Fire	離 Li (South)		景 Scenery
土 Earth	坤 Kun (Southwest)	艮 Gen (Northeast)	生 Life
			死 Death

The Eight Doors' attributes are as follow :

8 Doors	Attributes
開 **Open**	This is known as the *Door of Recognition* and is considered an auspicious Door. It can represent an open field, open area, clear space, the clear skies after a rain, farmlands and flat land. In Qi Men forecasting, it represents career. In legal related matters, it represents the court.
休 **Rest**	This Door indicates rejuvenation, healing, nurturing, growth and vitality; hence it is an auspicious Door. It can represent water, rain, clouds, dew, markets and the ocean.
生 **Life**	This is the Door of wealth, prosperity, opportunity, growth and life, and is one of the most auspicious Doors in Qi Men. It can represent advantage for having financial resources, financial assistance, vibrant life-force energy, good spirit, strong wind, yellow sand, grassland and mountains.
傷 **Harm**	This is Door is considered a moderately auspicious Door. It can represent thunder, aggression, fighting spirit, violent behaviour, brute strength, disease, hunting grounds and forests.

8 Doors	Attributes
杜 **Delusion**	This is also known as the Door of Obstruction or the Door of Hiding. It is considered moderately auspicious depending on which side of the battle camp you are in. It can represent sunny weather, gentle breeze, tunnels, caves, seclusion, blockages and obstructions. It also represents a safe hiding place or a comfort zone. It also represents the training camp.
景 **Scenery**	This is known as the Door of Liaison. It is considered a moderately auspicious Door. It represents beauty, elegance, class, sunset, city, streets and bright lights. It can also represent bickering, jealousy, suspicion and misgivings.
死 **Death**	This is known as the Door of Punishment and is considered an inauspicious Door. It can represent death, funeral, murder, hopeless situations, frost, polluted air, toxic gasses, wilderness and graveyards. The life-force energy is low from this Door's direction. It predicts likely losses.
驚 **Fear**	This is known as the Door of Scheming and Sorrow. It is moderately inauspicious. It can represent fear, injury, intimidation, danger, thunderstorm, hail storm, lightning, cliffs and rocky hills. It denotes a tense situation where everyone is under stress.

* **Note**: Any Door's effects can change from negative to positive and vice versa depending on their relationship with the element of the Palace in which they reside. So, while a Fear Door is generally an inauspicious Door, its effects can be turned positive if it resides in a Palace where it is considered elementally favourable with a positive Star and Stems present.

The following example Chart plotted on 23 April, 2010 at 7.30pm illustrates the effect:

In the following Chart, the Scenery Door in the Kun (Southwest) Palace is in a "Door Produces Palace" scenario. This is because the Scenery Door belongs to the Fire Element and the Kun Palace is of the Earth Element.

Fire produces Earth and so the "Door Produces Palace". This denotes that the battleground favours the Host in battle (the Host being the defender and the Guest being the attacker).

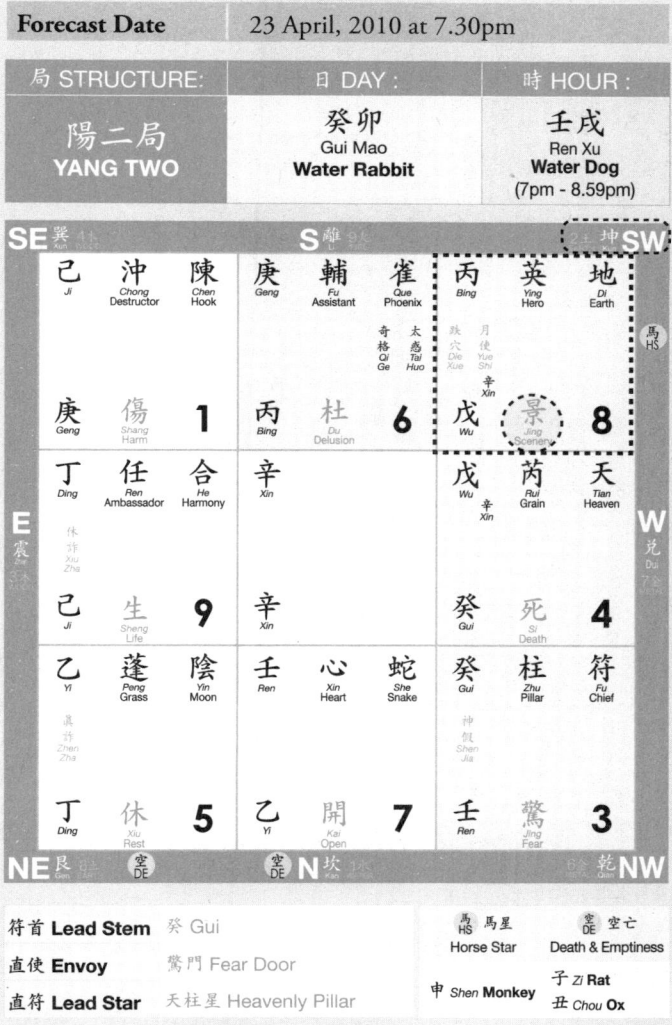

Let's consider another example which is plotted on 20 April, 2011 at 5.47pm.

Forecast Date	20 April, 2011 at 5.47pm

局 STRUCTURE:	日 DAY :	時 HOUR :
陽七局 YANG SEVEN	乙巳 Yi Si **Wood Snake**	乙酉 Yi You **Wood Rooster** (5pm - 6.59pm)

	SE	S		SW	
辛 Xin	蓬 Peng Grass	陳 Chen Hook	己 Ji	任 Ren Ambassador	雀 Que Phoenix	癸 Gui	沖 Chong Destructor	地 Di Earth
丁 Ding	開 Kai Open	6	庚 Geng	休 Xiu Rest	2	壬 Ren	丙 Bing / 生 Sheng Life	4
乙 Yi	心 Xin Heart	合 He Harmony	丙 Bing			丁 Ding	輔 Fu Assistant	天 Tian Heaven
E	日昇 Ri Sheng					星昇 Xing Sheng		W
癸 Gui	驚 Jing Fear	5	丙 Bing			戊 Wu	傷 Shang Harm	9
戊 Wu	柱 Zhu Pillar	陰 Yin Moon	壬 Ren	芮 Rui Grain / 丙 Bing	蛇 She Snake	庚 Geng	英 Ying Hero	符 Fu Chief
				月使 Yue Shi			相佐 Xiang Zuo	奇格 Qi Ge
己 Ji	死 Si Death	1	辛 Xin	景 Jing Scenery	3	乙 Yi	杜 Du Delusion	8
	NE	N		NW	

符首 **Lead Stem**	庚 Geng	馬星 Horse Star	空亡 Death & Emptiness
直使 **Envoy**	景門 Scenery Door	亥 Hai Pig	午 Wu Horse
直符 **Lead Star**	天英星 Heavenly Hero		未 Wei Goat

In this second example, the Open Door in the Xun (Southeast) Palace is "Door Counters Palace" as the Open Door is of the Metal Element and the Xun Palace is of the Wood Element. Metal counters Wood hence the "Door Counters Palace". While the attributes of the Open Door are generally positive, in this case it is *countering* the Palace and so these positive attributes are rendered moot. This means the battleground is unfavourable to the Host of the battle.

In this particular interaction, we can anticipate that the Guest will likely win. Armed with this knowledge, you can take steps to position yourself as the "guest" in any upcoming confrontation (or in the business world, a negotiation) instead of the "host". This will give you the winning edge. One way you can achieve this is to ask your opponent to host the event. By doing so, he becomes the Host and you now become the Guest. As the Chart indicates, you will leave the negotiating table in a better position.

Here is another example plotted on 18 March, 2008 at 3.47am:

Forecast Date	18 March, 2008 at 3.47am	
局 STRUCTURE:	日 DAY :	時 HOUR :
陽七局 YANG SEVEN	丁巳 Ding Si Fire Snake	壬寅 Ren Yin Water Tiger (3am - 4.59am)

SE 巽		S 離		SW 坤
戊 柱 地 Wu Zhu Di Pillar Earth 空DE 丁 開 **6** Ding Kai Open	乙 心 天 Yi Xin Tian Heart Heaven 日使Shi 庚 休 **2** Geng Xiu Rest		辛 蓬 符 Xin Peng Fu Grass Chief 龍相 返佐 Long Xiang Fan Zuo 壬 丙 生 **4** Ren Bing Sheng Life	馬HS
E 震	壬 芮 雀 Ren Rui Que 丙 Grain Phoenix Bing 月旺 Yue Wang 癸 驚 **5** Gui Jing Fear	丙 Bing 丙 Bing	己 任 蛇 Ji Ren She Ambassador Snake 戊 傷 **9** Wu Shang Harm	W 兌 空DE
	庚 英 陳 Geng Ying Chen Hero Hook 刑格 庚刑 Xing Ge Geng Xing 己 死 **1** Ji Si Death	丁 輔 合 Ding Fu He Assistant Harmony 權怡 Quan Yi 辛 景 **3** Xin Jing Scenery	癸 沖 陰 Gui Chong Yin Destructor Moon 地假 Di Jia 乙 杜 **8** Yi Du Delusion	
NE 艮		N 坎		NW 乾

符首 **Lead Stem**	辛 Xin		馬HS 馬星 Horse Star	空DE 空亡 Death & Emptiness
直使 **Envoy**	休門 Rest Door			辰 Chen **Dragon**
直符 **Lead Star**	天蓬星 Heavenly Grass		申 Shen **Monkey**	巳 Si **Snake**

In this third example, the Life Door in the Kun (Southwest) Palace is in a "Door Palace Harmony" formation as both the Life Door and the Kun Palace are the same element, which is Earth.

Since both the Door and Palace are of the same element, we know that the Southwest battleground is favourable. It also means that moving in this direction in competition will lead to a positive outcome for both the Host and the Guest. When something is beneficial to both the Host and the Guest, this means the war can be won without any conflict. This is the most desirable outcome according to Sun Tzu – to 'win' without having to fight or destroy the enemy. In a modern context this might mean a mutually beneficial merger or strategic alliance. Whenever this formation is found in a Qi Men Chart, a win-win result is possible.

FIRE ATTACK

12

ORIGINAL TEXT:

孫子曰：凡火攻有五：
一曰火人，二曰火積，
三曰火輜，四曰火庫，
五曰火隊。行火必有因，
煙火必素具。發火有時，
起火有日。時者，天之燥也。
日者，月在箕壁翼軫也。
凡此四宿者，風起之日也。

TRANSLITERATION:

Sun Tzu said: There are five ways that an army may use fire to attack their enemies. The first is to use fire to burn the enemy troops, the second is to burn their food and provisions, the third is to burn their equipment, the fourth is to burn their arsenal and weaponry and the fifth is to burn their means of transportation and communication.

In order to attack with fire, you will need the right materials and kindling. It is wise to always have these things available. It is also important that you select a suitable day in a suitable season for such an attack. You must choose a season when the weather is dry and a day when the moon is in alignment with the constellations of the basket, the wall, the wing or the carriage, for it is on these days that the strongest winds are likely to arise and help to drive the fire.

COMMENTARY:

You can direct a breakthrough attack against your competitor in one of five basic ways. First, you can attack them directly (publicly question the quality of their service, for example). Second, you can attack the source of their revenue (pinch their customers or undermine their business model). Third, you can attack their hardware and equipment (develop something new that makes their existing technology or service obsolete). Fourth, you can diminish their ability to damage you (gain compromising information on them) and finally you can attack their methods of communication and organisation so that they cannot operate effectively. The ways in which you can directly attack your rivals are almost limitless in nature and scope. Use some imagination!

In order to launch the most effective attack, you must choose your moment wisely. Find out what your opponent's comfortable operating patterns are by observing the routine. Time your attack so it is massively inconvenient and extremely disruptive for your rival.

Whatever is your chosen plan of attack, it is critical that you execute your plan with overwhelming force. Your strike must be extraordinary. Devote sufficient resources and attention to your attack plan and against a supportive background. If you strike with some kind of wider support behind you, your attack can be more devastating. Politicians often use topical issues as the basis for their attacks on their opposition for maximum political damage. They base their case around a trending topic and so benefit from great support and exposure. It is all about flawless timing.

Keep in mind that in the modern world, your 'fire attacks' must never be crass, malicious or offensive. You must, at all times, maintain a professional and courteous behaviour. Leading a negative campaign in today's social media landscape where scandal can spread instantly is a recipe for disaster. Relate your attack to your own positive message in some way and aim for the greater good to achieve a true breakthrough. You must never been seen to be rude, malicious, unethical or unprofessional.

ORIGINAL TEXT:

凡火攻，必因五火之變而應之，
火發于內，則早應之于外。
火發而其兵靜者，待而勿攻。
極其火力，可從而從之，
不可從而止。火可發于外，
無待于內，以時發之。
火發上風，無攻下風，晝風久，
夜風止。凡軍必知五火之變，
以數守之。故以火佐攻者明，
以水佐攻者強，水可以絕，
不可以奪。

TRANSLITERATION:

If you choose to make use of fire then you need to be prepared to act as events unfold, depending on which one of the five types of fire attack that you have chosen. When a fire is set within the enemy camp, it will be necessary to have the coordinated efforts of your people both behind enemy lines and on the front lines. It will be important for your troops on the outside to bide their time and not launch an attack while the enemy remains calm and unaware, only once the flames have grown and gotten out of hand may they advance to strike. If the fire has been set outside of the enemy camp, it is not necessary to wait until the flames have spread to their inner sanctum, however, it will be important to choose the right moment to launch the main body of your attack. You should be aware that heavy winds during the day often subside at night and that if you have set the fire at an upwind location, it will be vital that you do not attack from a down-wind location.

Every army should be proficient in the five types of fire attack and they should have an understanding of the various consequences that may result from their use. They should craft their plans around this understanding.

A general who uses fire to strengthen his attack is sure to win while a general who uses water will merely display his strength. Water may halt the enemy's progress but it will not deprive them of their weapons, armour, chariots and provisions.

COMMENTARY:

If you choose to attack, your organization must do so at great speed and with great unity to prevent your competitors from defending themselves or launching some kind of counter attack. Also, be prepared for the possibility of collateral damage; which is unintended fallout from your actions. Just as the use of fire in conflict poses a danger to both sides, so do aggressive tactics. There can always be a backlash and the risk of direct retaliation must be considered too. Allies who might be affected must be informed of your plans in advance so they can shelter themselves from harm or you will lose their support in the future. Your reputation may also be called into question, as you will be seen as having betrayed their trust.

If you are in the habit of making bold, competitive claims then you must follow up with action at least occasionally so that your future claims and threats are taken seriously. You can't bluff through every hand. Consolidate your position periodically. Doing so will imbue you with a formidable reputation - people will know that you are capable of walking the walk as well as talking the talk and they will think twice before they try to take you head on.

ORIGINAL TEXT:

夫戰勝攻取，而不修其攻者凶，
命曰費留。故曰：明主慮之，
良將修之，非利不動，
非得不用，非危不戰。
主不可以怒而興師，
將不可以慍而致戰；
合于利而動，不合于利而止。
怒可以復喜，慍可以復悅，
亡國不可以復存，
死者不可以復生。故明君慎之，
良將警之，此安國全軍之道也。

TRANSLITERATION:

To win a battle, raid the land and capture the spoils of war but failing to consolidate your victory fully in order to maintain your new strength is waste of time and effort. It is seldom wise to send in your troops where there is no advantage to be gained, you should not use your men if the victory will not yield success and you should never fight a hasty battle under any circumstances unless there is significant danger if you fail to do so. An enlightened sovereign will think carefully about these matters and an able general will take action to address them.

A wise ruler should never wage war in anger any more than a gifted general should dispatch his troops to fight purely out of indignation. When there is an advantage to be gained, take action; when there is no advantage to be gained, hold back. Remember that fury and indignation are only emotions and they will pass in time, making it possible for happiness and pleasure to be restored. However, a state that had been destroyed may never return to strength and a man who loses his life too young cannot be brought back from the dead.

A sagacious leader will always be prudent when it comes to warfare and a good general will always treat any military expedition with caution. In this way, it may be hoped, that the state will live in harmony and security, and the army will remain intact.

COMMENTARY:

After you topple your competitors from their position with a well timed 'blow', it is vital that you move in and consolidate your new position in the aftermath, otherwise you will gain nothing and you will slide back to your previous level of power. There must be follow up. If there is no opportunity to improve your own position through competitive action then you must not act. Never attack an enemy much stronger than you. If and when an opportunity is finally revealed, tie your attack with your own branding plans so that you stand to benefit directly from your opponents' weaknesses. For example, subtly launch a campaign that may clearly reflect your opponents' obvious shortcomings and convert their customers to your brand. This is an attack that will eventually lead to a clear payoff for you.

Remember that action must never come from a place of anger or shame. There must always be a strategic purpose to it; emotions have no place in decision making whatsoever and succumbing to them will allow your competitors to control and manipulate you. Think very carefully about the tangible benefits of any aggressive action before deciding whether or not to proceed. Are the benefits truly worth the risk? The answer must be a resounding yes.

QI MEN DUN JIA:

In order to reconcile the subject matter of this chapter - attacking your enemies with fire – with Qi Men Dun Jia, it is necessary to take a step back and look at the theory of Qi Men Dun Jia itself. The name Qi Men Dun Jia translates as 'Mystical Door, Hiding Jia'. The word 'Mystical' in Chinese is "奇 Qi", which represents the *Three Nobles* (三奇 San Qi) in the Qi Men Dun Jia system. The word 'Door' represents the 8 Doors in each sector of the Qi Men Chart and the term 'hiding Jia' refers to the Grand Marshall, known as Jia 甲, which is hidden in one of the 8 Palaces in the Qi Men Chart. The arch enemy of the Jia (Yang Wood) is Geng 庚 (Yang Metal) and wherever the Geng Stem is located in a Qi Men Chart, trouble and strife are sure to follow.

If we think of a Qi Men Chart as a Qi Map of the battlefield, the location of the Geng Stem can be taken to indicate the location of the enemy or the hidden dangers that may result in defeat. In Qi Men, it is always desirable to protect the Jia from being harmed by the Geng so that good can prevail. One of the ways to protect the Jia is to make sure that the Geng is countered, or attacked. Metal element is not vulnerable to much. Water and Earth elements will do little damage to a sword, but Geng *may* be vulnerable to Fire element.

As Fire is produced by Wood and Jia is Yang Wood, we can determine that Fire is the ally of the Jia – it allows the positive effects of Jia to fully manifest, creating desirable outcomes. There are *Three Nobles* that can come to the rescue of the Jia. Two of these belong to the Fire elements which are **Bing**丙 ***(Yang Fire)*** and **Ding**丁 ***(Yin Fire).*** Bing, the *Yang* Fire, is the stronger of the two and it is more likely to be able to succeed in a direct attack on Geng Metal, while the Ding, the Yin polarity Fire, may be able to outsmart the Geng in more subtle ways. There are two specific formations in Qi Men Dun Jia which make effective use of Bing: the **Green Dragon Returns** 青龍返首 Formation and the **Flying Bird Falls Into The Cave** 飛鳥跌穴 Formation.

12

Green Dragon Returns 青龍返首					宮 Palace
地 Earth		人 Man	天 Heaven	神 Universe	
天干 Heavenly Stem	地支 Earthly Stem	八門 8 Doors	九星 9 Stars	八神 8 Deities	
甲 Jia Yang Wood	丙 Bing Yang Fire				

Description

This is an extremely auspicious Structure which denotes a positive outcome in all endeavours. Think smooth sailing and clear skies! It suggests positive, vibrant energy and its influence is excellent for the pursuit of wealth, career progression, and for subduing enemies. It has the effect of creating positive outcomes in negative situations, turning enemies into friends and obstacles into opportunities.

Example:

This is a Chart plotted on 10 August, 2013 at 7.30am.

Forecast Date	10 August, 2013 at 7.30am

局 STRUCTURE:	日 DAY:	時 HOUR:
陰四局 YIN FOUR	戊申 Wu Shen **Earth Monkey**	丙辰 Bing Chen **Fire Dragon** (7am - 8.59am)

SE 巽			S 離				SW 坤
庚 Geng	芮 Rui Grain	虎 Hu Tiger	丁 Ding	柱 Zhu Pillar	合 He Harmony	丙 Bing	心 Xin Heart	陰 Yin Moon
戊 Wu	死 Si Death	**3**	壬 Ren	驚 Jing Fear	**8**	庚 Geng	開 Kai Open	**1**
壬 Ren	英 Ying Hero	玄 Xuan Tortoise	乙 Yi			辛 Xin	蓬 Peng Grass	蛇 She Snake
己 Ji	景 Jing Scenery	**2**	乙 Yi			丁 Ding	休 Xiu Rest	**6**
戊 Wu	輔 Fu Assistant	地 Di Earth	己 Ji	沖 Chong Destructor	天 Tian Heaven	癸 Gui	任 Ren Ambassador	符 Fu Chief
癸 Gui	柱 Du Delusion	**7**	辛 Xin	傷 Shang Harm	**9**	丙 Bing	生 Sheng Life	**5**
NE 艮			N 坎				NW 乾

The Jia Stem is hiding here in the Chart with the Gui Stem.

符首 Lead Stem	癸 Gui
直使 Envoy	生門 Life Door
直符 Lead Star	天任星 Heavenly Ambassador

| 馬 HS 馬星 Horse Star | 寅 Yin Tiger |
| 空 空亡 Death & Emptiness | 子 Zi Rat
丑 Chou Ox |

The Lead Stem is the Gui Stem. It is where the Jia Stem is hiding.

In the Qian (Northwest) Palace, the Jia Stem, hides within the Gui Heavenly Stem. In the same sector we can also see the Bing Earthly Stem. This forms the **Green Dragon Returns** Structure. This means that this sector possesses the power of this benevolent Structure. I personally like to find such formations whenever I perform a major presentation. Standing in this sector always gives me the strength to positively influence my audience and transform lives.

12

Flying Bird Fall Into Cave 飛鳥跌穴

地 Earth	人 Man	天 Heaven	神 Universe	宮 Palace
天干 Heavenly Stem	地支 Earthly Stem	八門 8 Doors	九星 9 Stars	八神 8 Deities
丙 Bing Yang Fire	甲 Jia Yang Wood			

Description

As Jia 甲 is the parent (Resource Element) of Bing Fire 丙火. It appears that Bing Fire returns to its parent in this combination, evoking imagery of a bird flying back to its cave. This is why it has been given the name Flying Bird Fall into Cave 飛鳥跌穴.

This is one of the most desirable 10 Stem Combinations to be found in Qi Men Dun Jia. Its appearance is usually an indication that everything will fall into place naturally and beneficially. It suggests that good fortune will come looking for you and that success will come easily. In addition, this formation also has the effect of bringing the help and support of well-placed and influential mentors into your circle. It helps in the development of strong working relationships and partnerships. It is positive for accruing wealth, moving houses, taking extended trips, trading, borrowing or lending money, dispatching troops, launching new campaigns or projects and winning court cases.

Example:

This Chart is plotted on 30 April, 2004 at 3.47pm.

Forecast Date	30 April, 2004 at 3.47pm

局 STRUCTURE:	日 DAY :	時 HOUR :
陽四局 **YANG FOUR**	己卯 Ji Mao **Earth Rabbit**	壬申 Ren Shen **Water Monkey** (3pm - 4.59pm)

This is where the Jia Stem is hiding in the Chart.

Qi Men Chart (SE Xun 4木 / S Li 9火 / SW Kun 2土 / E Zhen 3木 / W Dui 7金 / NE Gen 8土 / N Kan 1水 / NW Qian 6金)

SE Palace: 丙 Bing (己 Ji), 芮 Rui Grain, 陰 Yin Moon; 跌穴 Die Xue, 權怡 Quan Yi, 月旺 Yue Wang; 戊 Wu, 景 Jing Scenery — **3**

S Palace: 辛 Xin, 柱 Zhu Pillar, 合 He Harmony; 辛刑 Xin Xing; 癸 Gui, 死 Si Death — **8**

SW Palace: 庚 Geng, 心 Xin Heart, 陳 Chen Hook; 太惑 Tai Huo, 刑格 Xing Ge, 奇格 Qi Ge; 丙 Bing (己 Ji), 驚 Jing Fear — **1**

E Palace: 癸 Gui, 英 Ying Hero, 蛇 She Snake; 己 Ji

W Palace: 丁 Ding, 蓬 Peng Grass, 雀 Que Phoenix; 星昇 Xing Sheng

E Palace (lower): 乙 Yi, 杜 Du Delusion — **2**; 己 Ji

W Palace (lower): 辛 Xin, 開 Kai Open — **6**

NE Palace: 戊 Wu, 輔 Fu Assistant, 符 Fu Chief; 乙 Yi, 沖 Chong Destructor, 天 Tian Heaven; 龍遁 Long Dun, 日旺 Ri Wang; 壬 Ren, 任 Ren Ambassador; 地 Di Earth

NE lower: 壬 Ren, 傷 Shang Harm — **7**; 丁 Ding, 生 Sheng Life — **9**; 庚 Geng, 休 Xiu Rest — **5**

空 DE (NW 6金 Qian)

符首 **Lead Stem**	戊 Wu	馬 **Horse Star**	空亡 **Death & Emptiness**
直使 **Envoy**	杜門 Delusion Door		戊 Xu **Dog**
直符 **Lead Star**	天輔星 Heavenly Assistant	寅 Yin **Tiger**	亥 Hai **Pig**

The Wu Stem is the Lead Stem. It is where the Jia Stem is hiding.

The Bing 丙 Stem is residing with the Wu 戊 Stem in the Xun (Southeast) Palace. If you look at the bottom of the chart where it says 'Lead Stem', you will see that it is Wu 戊. This means that the Jia 甲 for this Qi Men Chart is hiding with the Wu. We now have a Bing and Jia combination in the Xun (Southeast) Palace, forming the ***Flying Bird Fall Into Cave*** Structure. This is a highly desirable formation in Qi Men Dun Jia.

There is another Fire structure which makes effective use of Ding and it is also highly favorable in Qi Men Dun Jia. This again, is a form of 'Fire Attack' as discussed by Sun Tzu in Chapter 12. This Structure is called "Jade Maiden Watching The Door 玉女守門" formation.

Jade Maiden Watching The Door 玉女守門					
地 Earth	人 Man	天 Heaven	神 Universe	宮 Palace	
天干 Heavenly Stem	地支 Earthly Stem	八門 8 Doors	九星 9 Stars	八神 8 Deities	
丁 *Ding* Yin Fire		直 使 Envoy			
	丁 *Ding* Yin Fire				

Description

This is a highly favourable and desirable formation in Qi Men Dun Jia. It is auspicious for all endeavours, especially those relating to interpersonal relationships, feelings and connections with others. As an extension of this, it may also assist in the mediation of disputes and in the pursuit of knowledge. For this reason it is also thought to be very beneficial for the successful completion of examinations. This formation generally rewards any intelligent strategic planning with results.

Example:

This is a Chart plotted on 17 March, 2010 at 5.30pm.

Forecast Date	17 March, 2010 at 5.30pm	
局 STRUCTURE:	日 DAY:	時 HOUR:
陽三局 YANG THREE	丙寅 Bing Yin **Fire Tiger**	丁酉 Ding You **Fire Rooster** (5pm - 6.59pm)

	Lead Stem	辛 Xin
→	Envoy	開門 Open Door
	Lead Star	天心星 Heavenly Heart

馬星 Horse Star	空亡 Death & Emptiness
亥 Hai **Pig**	辰 Chen **Dragon** 巳 Si **Snake**

The Envoy for this Chart is Open Door.

The Earthly Stem Ding resides in the Li (South) Palace with the Envoy, which is the Open Door, forming the Jade Maiden Watching the Door Structure.

ESPIONAGE

13

ORIGINAL TEXT:

孫子曰：凡興師十萬，出征千里，
百姓之費，公家之奉，日費千金，
內外騷動，怠于道路，不得操事者，
七十萬家，相守數年，
以爭一日之勝，而愛爵祿百金，
不知敵之情者，不仁之至也，
非人之將也，非主之佐也，
非勝之主也。

TRANSLITERATION:

Sun Tzu said: When an army that consists of one thousand officers and soldiers goes out to fight a war a thousand li away from home, the common people and the state treasury combined have to spend a thousand pieces of gold every day in order to support that action. Many civilians will be involved in the war effort, working themselves to the bone running transportation services, and there will be continuous disruption at home as well as on the front line. Approximately seven thousand households will be forced to abandon the cultivation of their land in order support the soldiers as they fight. If a general engages his state in a long and drawn out battle, striving for many years to secure a victory that could be decided in a single day because, he is ignorant of the enemy's situation and begrudges the expenditure of the one hundred pieces of gold that it would take to employ spies, then he has no humanity. Such a man will never be a good general, will offer no meaningful support to his sovereign and will never be the author of a victory.

COMMENTARY:

Here, Sun Tzu describes the great costs of competition for all sides. Although many of the ongoing expenses in a prolonged enterprise are not immediately obvious, they do exist and they have to be covered. The longer it takes to meet your objectives, the greater they will eventually cost you.

Often, a little more information can make the difference between pursuing the right course of action and the wrong one. Intelligent leaders know that good intelligence can save them from pursuing dead ends and shorten their route to victory. One mechanism for gathering such intelligence is espionage, which produces tactical competitive insight and leads to better assumptions and results (provided that the information retrieved using espionage is processed correctly).

There is usually a cost for acquiring intelligence via espionage and there are certainly risks involved. However, such costs and risks are always outweighed by the potential profit that can be made.

Leaders must make use of espionage to compete at a high level and they must create systems that filter, incorporate and utilize the information gathered via espionage. In other words, they must both seek out intelligence and act upon what they learn correctly. Doing this effectively will give them a huge advantage over the competition.

ORIGINAL TEXT:

故明君賢將，所以動而勝人，
成功出于眾者，先知也；
先知者，不可取于鬼神，
不可象于事，不可驗于度；
必取于人，知敵之情者也。

TRANSLITERATION:

An enlightened sovereign and an able general will achieve extraordinary things and will secure a rapid victory because they will be able to foresee events before they unfold. This foreknowledge is not gained from ghosts and spirits and it cannot be gleaned from past experiences. This foreknowledge can only be obtained from those who already know about the enemy's deployment and strategy.

COMMENTARY:

When you can anticipate events, you can either position yourself to benefit from them (e.g: investing in a stock that is about to sky rocket) or move to avoid unwanted fallout (e.g: end production of a service or product that is about to become obsolete). In both of these examples, the failure to anticipate the events described is harmful. Anticipating them instead creates victory.

You must make information gathering a priority. Use all available sources of information at your disposal. Information reduces risk. Information creates results.

One of the best types of information is information about your competitor's plans, schemes and methods. Understanding these will allow you to predict what they will do next and when. With this knowledge, you can adjust your own plans so that you get ahead of their efforts, nullify any first-mover advantages they may have and prepare to defend against attack. Even a partial picture, formed from tidbits of information, is superior to none – so even if espionage cannot give you a complete map of the future, it can still improve your odds in competition drastically.

ORIGINAL TEXT:

故用間有五：有鄉間、有內間、
有反間、有死間、有生間。
五間俱起，莫知其道，是謂神紀，
人君之寶也。鄉間者，
因其鄉人而用之。內間者，
因其官人而用之。反間者，
因其敵間而用之。死間者，
為誑事于外，令吾間知之，
而傳于敵。生間者，反報也。

TRANSLITERATION:

There are five kinds of spy that may be used: the native, the insider, the convert, the double agent or expendable spy, and the survivor.

Using these five kinds of spies simultaneously develops an intricate and complex web of intrigue, it is the greatest weapon that any sovereign has in orchestrating the defeat of the opposing forces and the enemy cannot and will not ever know of their operations.

Native or local spies are individuals employed from among the common people. Insiders are spies that are recruited from among the enemy's own officials. Converts are enemy agents that choose to defect to your side. Double agents are our own spies who befriend the enemy and seek to feed them false information, such agents take incredible risks and are often caught and put to death. Survivors are those spies who are able to travel safely between the enemy and ourselves continually passing on information.

COMMENTARY:

There are five possible sources of secret information and insight; use them and make sure you leave a complicated, elongated trail to conceal your involvement in espionage. By using many sources, you will receive the greatest variety and depth of information. Native spies are people with no affiliation to any side that you recruit to gather information on your behalf. Insiders are people within your rival organization or team who assist you. Converts are those who were formally loyal to your competitor but are now loyal to you and your goals. Double agents approach your competitor with false information on your behalf and return with genuine information on your rival's plans. Survivors are people who, for whatever reason, are in a position that allows them to freely associate with both sides and so easily obtain information that can help you.

Different people in different positions will be able to acquire different information at different speeds. Insiders will have more access to competitor secrets but may not be willing to take the same risks as a convert. However, a convert's information – by definition – may be out of date. Take advantage of all of them if the opportunity arises to do so.

ORIGINAL TEXT:

故三軍之事，親莫親于間，
賞莫厚于間，事莫密于間，
非聖智不能用間，非仁義不能使間，
非微妙不能得間之實。微哉，微哉，
無所不用間也。間事未發而先聞者，
間與所告者皆死。

TRANSLITERATION:

Of all trusted allies and members of the armed forces no relationship should be more closely bound that that of the spies and the commander to whom they report; of all the rewards gifted to any member of the armed forces, none should be more generous than that given to the spies who risk their lives; of all military secrets, none should be more closely guarded than those connected with espionage.

A commander who lacks in intelligence and wisdom will not be able to make use of spies, a commander who is not humane and just will not be able to command spies and a commander who is not careful and discrete in the use of information will not be able to gain the truth from spies. This above all must be remembered, it is of paramount importance to exercise care and discretion, for there is no situation in which espionage is not possible but if it is discovered that secret information has been divulged, the spy, and any other who may be suspected of spying, will be put to death.

COMMENTARY:

Secrecy and discretion are the glue which can hold a fragile operation together and minimize the risk of catastrophe. This is especially true when considering delicate espionage strategies. In order to cultivate loyalty and prevent betrayal from your informants - who by definition have proven themselves to be deceitful - you must reward them generously and keep your working relationship with them out of sight to create plausible deniability. Conceal the sources of your intelligence closely or you risk exposing them and losing their support. In most competitive situations there is an opportunity for espionage but just remember that the greater the value of the potential information that can be acquired, the greater the risks involved for everyone involved in acquiring it. Tread lightly.

Knowing how to handle the information you acquire via espionage is just as critical as seeking it out in the first place. It is important that you create institutional mechanisms that allow you to handle the intelligence you gather with your reconnaissance efforts. What good is information, after all, if you don't act upon it?

As you gather information, you must filter it through predefined systems within your organization so that you can ascertain what is and what isn't useful. Since espionage is an ongoing, dynamic process, you can then incorporate the feedback into your espionage efforts and seek out further detail so that your intelligence gathering is highly relevant and useful. Too much information can be overwhelming – seek and disseminate it selectively within your organization so it has the most profitable impact. As a leader, this is your job.

Intelligence can often reveal unwanted facts. The tendency for people to disregard contrary information is well documented; intelligence is only useful however when it is heard with an open mind. Recognize and respect intelligence data at all levels, especially if it indicates that your existing plans are misguided and out of touch.

Adopt a healthy degree of skepticism in regard to the validity of the information you are given. Filter it. Question everything, double check the facts, insure yourself against loss. Remember that there is always a possibility that you yourself are being deceived by the enemy.

ORIGINAL TEXT:

凡軍之所欲擊，城之所欲攻，
人之所欲殺；必先知其守將，
左右，謁者，門者，
舍人之姓名，令吾間必索知之。

TRANSLITERATION:

Whether you hope to attack the enemy camp, lay siege to an enemy city or assassinate their commanding officer you must first ascertain the names of the garrison commander, his aides-de-camp, trusted followers, ushers, gatekeepers and bodyguards and you must instruct your spies to investigate each of these individuals in detail.

COMMENTARY:

Before you can launch any strike against the opposition you must know who they are and where they come from. Employ covert surveillance, obtain insider information and research their past in order to determine their true strength, allies, reputation and learn about past transgressions and failures. Find out what their vulnerabilities are and determine if they have any liabilities. A thorough understanding of all of these things will help you find ways to undermine them and bring them down. In some cases it can even help show you that someone else is pulling the strings so that your efforts can be better directed.

13

ORIGINAL TEXT:

必索敵人之間來間我者，
因而利之，導而舍之，
故反間可得而用也。
因是而知之，
故鄉間、內間可得而使也；
因是而知之，
故死間爲誑事可使告敵；
因是而知之，
故生間可使如期。
五間之事，君必知之，
知之必在于反間，
故反間不可不厚也。

TRANSLITERATION:

It is important for you to identify the enemy spies in your midst and, once you have captured them, do everything within your power to convert them to your cause, exhort them, bribe them and convince them to work for you.

Through these converted spies you will not only be able to obtain important information about the enemy but you will also be able to recruit native spies and inside spies. Once this network is in operation, you may then be able to use your expendable spies or double agents to mislead the enemy with false information. These networks will also be able to support your survivor spies in their mission to travel back and forth between yourself and the enemy with greater and greater information.

A sovereign must know how to use these five types of spy and he will, by necessity, rely very heavily on the converted spies for information and guidance in order to develop his knowledge. For this reason converted spies should be rewarded very generously.

COMMENTARY:

Your competitors have a lot to gain by mounting reconnaissance of your plans and strategies and you must expect them to do so. You must always protect your intellectual property and your secrets at both a legal and organizational level. Follow up on your suspicions, expect betrayal and constantly question loyalties in order to identify leaks and untrustworthy people in your own team and organization.

When you identify a spy then you are in a good position, knowing that you have new access to your competitor's internal ranks. Offer great rewards or incentives to such spies so they will rearrange their loyalties and spy on your competitor, instead, while giving them wrong information. With this approach, you can turn the tables entirely – turning an intruder into an asset.

A good leader must know how to get the most out of the five types of 'spy' described and they will use them, wisely, while doing everything they can to ensure genuine loyalty and shield themselves from being deceived as they seek to learn about others.

In real world application, this is all about gathering useful data. Actual spies are not necessary as in many cases, much of the information about your competitor or the industry is already freely available on the internet or on the media (if they are famous). The question is, are you able to synthesize the enormous amount of data? More importantly, are you able to extract the information that is useful for you to outsmart and beat your competitors?

13

用間

Successful entrepreneurs will perform research and intelligence homework. They will study their target market and study their competitor's products and services thoroughly. With accurate and reliable intelligence, they are able to better use their resources, give better service, produce better products and perform better sales campaigns.

The gist of this chapter is mainly about the importance of having valuable information and preferably insider knowledge of the industry you are in.

ORIGINAL TEXT:

昔殷之興也，伊摯在夏。

周之興也，呂牙在殷。

故明君賢將，能以上智爲間者，

必成大功，此兵之要，

三軍之所恃而動也。

TRANSLITERATION:

In ancient history the rise of the **Yin** may be attributed to **Yi Zhi**, who had previously been the minister of **Xia** and the rise of the Zhou Dynasty was due to the actions of **Jiang Ziya**, who had formerly been a minister for Shang.

An enlightened sovereign and an able general will be able to locate and recruit intelligent men as spies and, with their assistance, achieve very great victories. The use of spies is absolutely essential in war for the army depends upon intelligence in order to plan their actions.

COMMENTARY:

Gather intelligence on the people in the opposition. Employ covert surveillance, obtain insider information and research their past in order to determine their true strength, allies, reputation and learn about past transgressions and failures. You must understand their strengths and weakness and better yet, be able to call their thoughts and moves. Find out what their vulnerabilities are and determine if they have any liabilities.

Protect your own intellectual property and secrets. You must take deliberate steps to prevent industrial espionage taking place against you. These can be both pre-emptive and ongoing action and include background checks, data protection policies and legal action against those who leak your organizations data. Put the same resources into protecting your own information as you put into acquiring the secrets of your competitors.

QI MEN DUN JIA :

In this chapter Sun Tzu discusses the importance of gathering information about the enemy (or industrial competitors), through espionage. In warfare, the kind of insight that can be provided only by an insider is an invaluable resource that can make or break a conflict. There are ancient tales of war where one Kingdom deploys a 'political marriage' strategy, by marrying female relations into the enemy camp in order to keep their enemies close while keeping a close eye on their operations. It could be argued that such women were the first femme fatales and master spies of their time.

We mentioned in Chapter 5 and also in Chapter 12, that there are *Three Nobles* in Qi Men Dun Jia known as - the *Yi* 乙, *Bing* 丙 *and Ding* 丁. All these are the allies of Jia 甲 (Yang Wood), the Grand Marshall in Qi Men Dun Jia . The Geng 庚 (Yang Metal) is Jia's natural enemy. If we look at the relationships between Jia and the *Three Nobles*, they could be characterized in the following way: Yi represents Yin Wood and as the feminine version of Jia (Yang Wood) this can be perceived as a sister, while Bing and Ding (Yang Fire and Yin Fire respectively) can be perceived as the children of Jia (Yang Wood). In the study of the Five Elements, Wood produces Fire. Hence Bing and Ding are regarded as the children of Jia – metaphorically speaking.

Jia may, as we have already discussed in the previous chapter, use the power of Bing and Ding as a kind of fire attack against his arch enemy Geng. Having already touched on the first two of the Three Nobles, the progression of Sun Tzu's 'Art of War' has led us to the third component of the Three Nobles. In this chapter we will look at the possibility of using Yi (the sister of Jia) to form a kind of 'political marriage' to subdue the enemy Geng (Yang Metal). As the sister, Yi may be married to Geng in order to pacify or control him, indeed to turn him into an ally through the marriage vow.

In Chinese Metaphysics the Yi Stem and the Geng Stem form a very natural relationship called The *Yi Geng* combination 乙庚合. It is believed, in Qi Men Dun Jia, that only the Yi Stem is strong enough to be able to bring the powerful Geng to heel without resorting to fighting.

In practice, we are looking for a very special formation to appear in order for the Yi Stem to gain the right kind of leverage over Geng. Such formations include the *Yi Noble Receives Envoy* 乙奇得使 formation and the *Yi Noble Rising Palace* 乙奇昇殿 formation.

The *Yi Noble Receives Envoy* combination is formed when the following conditions are met:

Yi Noble Receives Envoy 乙奇得使					
地 Earth		人 Man	天 Heaven	神 Universe	宮 Palace
天干 Heavenly Stem	地支 Earthly Stem	八門 8 Doors	九星 9 Stars	八神 8 Deities	
乙 *Yi* Yin Wood					離 Li (South)
乙 *Yi* Yin Wood	己 *Ji* Yin Earth				

Description

Suitable for collecting the necessary data, information and knowledge to proceed with plans and strategy. This formation enables privileged access to exclusive connections, including introductions to very important people, key personnel and decision makers. Channels will open and communications will be unobstructed.

It is favourable to ask for favors, pacifying someone angry, assuming a new job, getting married, operating a new business, negotiations and closing business deals.

Generally speaking, this formation is also an indication that the right talents are being put to the right uses. This person will be given the right platform to harness his or her true potential.

The following is an example Chart plotted on 30 April, 2011 at 1.30pm which shows the structure for *Yi Noble Receives Envoy*:

The Heavenly Yi Stem resides in the Li (South) Palace, forming the *Yi Noble Receives Envoy Structure*. Pursuing in this direction for your meeting or negotiation will help you garner the desired results.

Yi Noble Rising Palace 乙奇昇殿

地 Earth		人 Man	天 Heaven	神 Universe	宮 Palace
天干 Heavenly Stem	地支 Earthly Stem	八門 8 Doors	九星 9 Stars	八神 8 Deities	
乙 Yi Yin Wood					震 Zhen (East)

Description

This formation denotes positive outcomes in regard to obtaining privileged information, knowledge and data. It is also helpful in fighting against illegal acts and suppressing criminals.

Suitable for research and probing and seeking employment in the rival camp. As this formation enables vital information and data to be found or to present itself to the user, this means that it would favor trading, industrial research, marketing, sales campaigns, business expansion and opening up new markets.

The Yi Noble Rising Palace is also known as The Sun Rises From Misty Sea.

The following is an example Chart plotted on 6 March, 2011 at 1.30pm structure for Yi Noble Rising Palace:

Forecast Date	6 March, 2011 at 1.30pm	
局 STRUCTURE:	日 DAY:	時 HOUR:
陽三局 YANG THREE	庚申 Geng Shen **Metal Monkey**	丙子 Bing Zi **Fire Rat** (11pm - 12.59am)

SE 巽		S 離		SW 坤
壬 Ren / 柱 Zhu Pillar / 合 He Harmony 壬刑 Ren Xing 己 Ji / 開 Kai Open **2**		辛 Xin / 心 Heart / 陳 Chen Hook 辛刑 Xin Xing 丁 Ding / 休 Xiu Rest **7**		丙 Bing / 蓬 Peng Grass / 雀 Que Phoenix 月使 Yue Shi 癸白 Ying Bai 庚 Geng 乙 Yi / 生 Sheng Life **9**
乙 Yi 庚 Geng / 芮 Rui Grain / 陰 Yin Moon 日昇 Ri Sheng 伏宮 Fu Gong 戊 Wu / 驚 Jing Fear **1**		庚 Geng 庚 Geng		癸 Gui / 任 Ren Ambassador / 地 Di Earth 神㑥 Shen Jia 壬 Ren / 傷 Shang Harm **5**
丁 Ding / 英 Ying Hero / 蛇 She Snake 星使 Xing Shi 星甚 Xing Mu 朱投 Zhu Tou 癸 Gui / 死 Si Death **6**		己 Ji / 輔 Fu Assistant / 符 Fu Chief 龍返 Long Fan 相佐 Xiang Zuo 丙 Bing / 景 Jing Scenery **8**		戊 Wu / 沖 Chong Destructor / 天 Tian Heaven 辛 Xin / 杜 Du Delusion **4**
NE 艮		N 坎		NW 乾

符首 Lead Stem	己 Ji	馬 馬星 Horse Star	空 空亡 Death & Emptiness
直使 Envoy	杜門 Delusion Door	寅 Yin **Tiger**	申 Shen **Monkey**
直符 Lead Star	天輔星 Heavenly Assistant		酉 You **Rooster**

The Heavenly Stem Yi resides in the Zhen (East) Palace, forming the *Yi Noble Rising Palace* Structure. Sitting in this sector during an important negotiation at the determined Qi Men Forecast hour will enable you to obtain the desired information and knowledge you seek.

EPILOGUE

Epilogue

You might say that I have been working towards this book throughout the whole of my adult life. It has taken, not just study and the mastery of the metaphysical arts for me to reach the point where this was possible, but also working my way through the highs and lows of starting my own business and becoming a successful entrepreneur. It has been through the trial and error of working my way to the top that I have gained the acumen to bring Qi Men Dun Jia and 'The Art of War' together in a format that is both accessible and informative. It has been my great pleasure and privilege to put this piece of work together for you and it is my great hope that you will have gained as much from reading it as I have from writing it.

This book brings together the age old wisdom and practical insight of Sun Tzu and the keen precision of the Qi Men Dun Jia system of forecasting. Both of these ancient resources were designed to give the able General, or in this case, the able Entrepreneur and Business Professional, all the guidance they should need to make themselves truly unstoppable. While Sun Tzu, like a wise master, guides us in the right ways of thinking and perceiving in order for us to understand how to build an effective strategy, so Qi Men Dun Jia, that remarkable tool for reading the natural energies present in our lives, gives us the information we need to implement our strategies in order to achieve the best possible results. Both Qi Men Dun Jia and Sun Tzu's Art of War are profound subjects. This book in my humble opinion, as hard as I have tried, perhaps only at best managed to scratch the surface of a very deep, multifaceted study.

If you are new to the practice of Qi Men Dun Jia and this book has lit a spark of interest within you, then it has achieved all that I have set out to do. Chinese metaphysics and Qi Men Dun Jia are my passion and it has been my life's work to share that passion with the world and to create a comprehensive collection of works designed to inspire and enthuse. I have worked hard to share my knowledge through my many books and I relish the prospect of another eager mind absorbing my words and giving thought to the study of Qi Men Dun Jia. All in all, there is a grand total of eighteen books in the series so far which cover every facet of Qi Men from the basic principles to more complex systems and every possible angle of application.

Of course, for many of us, words on a page are no substitute for a face to face meeting and the opportunity to get to grips with learning in person. I do have regular workshops, seminars and learning programmes, all with an emphasis on real life, practical results rather than stale academic studies that may be difficult or even impossible for some readers to apply outside of the classroom. If you are keen to take your interest further, you are quite welcome to join me in one of these sessions someday soon. I would love to meet you in person.

WANT TO KNOW MORE ABOUT QI MEN DUN JIA?

You are invited to watch some of Joey Yap's recorded Qi Men Dun Jia workshops:

Watch the videos at:

www.masteryacademy.com/QiMenSunTzu

Here is your unique pass code to access the video for free:

QMDJ807

JOEY YAP'S
QI MEN DUN JIA
Reference Series

Qi Men Dun Jia
Compendium
Second edition

Qi Men Dun Jia
540 Yang
Structure

Qi Men Dun Jia
540 Yin
Structure

Qi Men Dun Jia
Year Charts

Qi Men Dun Jia
Month Charts

Qi Men Dun Jia
Day Charts

Qi Men Dun Jia
Day Charts
(San Yuan Method)

Qi Men Dun Jia
Forecasting
Method
(Book 1)

Qi Men Dun Jia
Forecasting
Method
(Book 2)

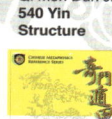
Qi Men Dun Jia
Evidential
Occurrences

Qi Men Dun Jia
Destiny
Analysis

Qi Men Dun Jia
Feng Shui

Qi Men Dun Jia
Date, Time &
Activity Selection

Qi Men Dun Jia
Annual Destiny
Analysis

Qi Men Dun Jia
Strategic
Executions

Qi Men Dun Jia
The 100
Formations

Qi Men Dun Jia
Sun Tzu
Warcraft

Qi Men Dun Jia
28 Constellations

Qi Men Dun Jia
The Deities

Qi Men Dun Jia
The Stars

Qi Men Dun Jia
The Doors

Qi Men Dun J.a
The Stems

This is the most comprehensive reference series to Qi Men Dun Jia in the Chinese Metaphysics world. Exhaustively written for the purpose of facilitating studies and further research, this collection of reference texts and educational books aims to bridge the gap for students who want to learn, and the teachers who want to teach Qi Men.

These essential references provide practical guidance for all branches under the Qi Men Dun Jia studies including Destiny Analysis, Feng Shui, Strategic Executions and Forecasting method.

These books are available exclusively at:
store.joeyyap.com

Email: order@masteryacademy.com | +6(03) - 2284 8080

JOEY YAP CONSULTING GROUP

Pioneering Metaphysics-Centric Personal and Corporate Consultations

Founded in 2002, the Joey Yap Consulting Group is the pioneer in the provision of metaphysics-driven coaching and consultation services for professionals and individuals alike. Under the leadership of the renowned international Chinese Metaphysics consultant, author and trainer, Dato' Joey Yap, it has become a world-class specialised metaphysics consulting firm with a strong presence in four continents, meeting the metaphysics-centric needs of its A-list clientele, ranging from celebrities to multinational corporations.

The Group's core consultation practice areas include Feng Shui, BaZi and Qi Men Dun Jia, which are complemented by ancillary services such as Date Selection, Face Reading and Yi Jing. Its team of highly trained professional consultants, led by its Chief Consultant, Dato' Joey Yap, is well-equipped with unparalleled knowledge and experience to help clients achieve their ultimate potentials in various fields and specialisations. Given its credentials, the Group is certainly the firm of choice across the globe for metaphysics-related consultations.

The Peerless Industry Expert

Benchmarked against the standards of top international consulting firms, our consultants work closely with our clients to achieve the best possible outcomes. The possibilities are infinite as our expertise extends from consultations related to the forces of nature under the subject of Feng Shui, to those related to Destiny Analysis and effective strategising under BaZi and Qi Men Dun Jia respectively.

To date, we have consulted a great diversity of clients, ranging from corporate clients – from various industries such as real estate, finance and telecommunication, amongst others – to the hundreds of thousands of individuals in their key life aspects. Adopting up-to-date and pragmatic approaches, we provide comprehensive services while upholding the importance of clients' priorities and effective outcomes. Recognised as the epitome of Chinese Metaphysics, we possess significant testimonies from worldwide clients as a trusted Brand.

www.joeyyap.com | +6(03) - 2284 8080

Feng Shui Consultation

Residential Properties
- Initial Land/Property Assessment
- Residential Feng Shui Consultation
- Residential Land Selection
- End-to-End Residential Consultation

Commercial Properties
- Initial Land/Property Assessment
- Commercial Feng Shui Consultation
- Commercial Land Selection
- End-to-End Commercial Consultation

Property Developers
- End-to-End Consultation
- Post-Consultation Advisory Services
- Panel Feng Shui Consultant

Property Investors
- Your Personal Feng Shui Consultant
- Tailor-Made Packages

Memorial Parks & Burial Sites
- Yin House Feng Shui

BaZi Consultation

Personal Destiny Analysis
- Individual BaZi Analysis
- BaZi Analysis for Families

Strategic Analysis for Corporate Organizations
- BaZi Consultations for Corporations
- BaZi Analysis for Human Resource Management

Entrepreneurs and Business Owners
- BaZi Analysis for Entrepreneurs

Career Pursuits
- BaZi Career Analysis

Relationships
- Marriage and Compatibility Analysis
- Partnership Analysis

General Public
- Annual BaZi Forecast
- Your Personal BaZi Coach

Date Selection Consultation

- Marriage Date Selection
- Caesarean Birth Date Selection
- House-Moving Date Selection
- Renovation and Groundbreaking Dates
- Signing of Contracts
- Official Openings
- Product Launches

Qi Men Dun Jia Consultation

Strategic Execution
- Business and Investment Prospects

Forecasting
- Wealth and Life Pursuits
- People and Environmental Matters

Feng Shui
- Residential Properties
- Commercial Properties

Speaking Engagement

Many reputable organisations and institutions have worked closely with Joey Yap Consulting Group to build a synergistic business relationship by engaging our team of consultants, which are led by Joey Yap, as speakers at their corporate events.

We tailor our seminars and talks to suit the anticipated or pertinent group of audience. Be it department subsidiary, your clients or even the entire corporation, we aim to fit your requirements in delivering the intended message(s) across.

www.joeyyap.com | +6(03) - 2284 8080

CHINESE METAPHYSICS REFERENCE SERIES

The Chinese Metaphysics Reference Series is a collection of reference texts, source material, and educational textbooks to be used as supplementary guides by scholars, students, researchers, teachers and practitioners of Chinese Metaphysics.

These comprehensive and structured books provide fast, easy reference to aid in the study and practice of various Chinese Metaphysics subjects including Feng Shui, BaZi, Yi Jing, Zi Wei, Liu Ren, Ze Ri, Ta Yi, Qi Men Dun Jia and Mian Xiang.

The Chinese Metaphysics Compendium

At over 1,000 pages, the Chinese Metaphysics Compendium is a unique one-volume reference book that compiles ALL the formulas relating to Feng Shui, BaZi (Four Pillars of Destiny), Zi Wei (Purple Star Astrology), Yi Jing (I-Ching), Qi Men (Mystical Doorways), Ze Ri (Date Selection), Mian Xiang (Face Reading) and other sources of Chinese Metaphysics.

It is presented in the form of easy-to-read tables, diagrams and reference charts, all of which are compiled into one handy book. This first-of-its-kind compendium is presented in both English and its original Chinese language, so that none of the meanings and contexts of the technical terminologies are lost.

The only essential and comprehensive reference on Chinese Metaphysics, and an absolute must-have for all students, scholars, and practitioners of Chinese Metaphysics.

The Ten Thousand Year Calendar (Pocket Edition)

The Ten Thousand Year Calendar

Dong Gong Date Selection

The Date Selection Compendium

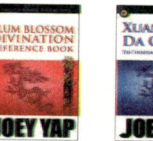
Plum Blossoms Divination Reference Book

Xuan Kong Da Gua Ten Thousand Year Calendar

San Yuan Dragon Gate Eight Formations Water Method

BaZi Hour Pillar Useful Gods - Wood

BaZi Hour Pillar Useful Gods - Fire

BaZi Hour Pillar Useful Gods - Earth

BaZi Hour Pillar Useful Gods - Metal

BaZi Hour Pillar Useful Gods - Water

Xuan Kong Da Gua Structures Reference Book

Xuan Kong Da Gua 64 Gua Transformation Analysis

BaZi Structures and Structural Useful Gods - Wood

BaZi Structures and Structural Useful Gods - Fire

BaZi Structures and Structural Useful Gods - Earth

BaZi Structures and Structural Useful Gods - Metal

BaZi Structures and Structural Useful Gods - Water

Earth Study Discern Truth Second Edition

Eight Mansions Bright Mirror

Secret of Xuan Kong

Ode to Flying Stars

Xuan Kong Purple White Script

Ode to Mysticism

The Yin House Handbook

Water Water Everywhere

Xuan Kong Da Gua Not Exactly For Dummies

www.masteryacademy.com | +6(03) - 2284 8080

SAN YUAN QI MEN XUAN KONG DA GUA
Reference Series

San Yuan Qi Men Xuan Kong Da Gua **Compendium**

San Yuan Qi Men Xuan Kong Da Gua **540 Yang Structure**

San Yuan Qi Men Xuan Kong Da Gua **540 Yin Structure**

Xuan Kong Flying Star **Secrets Of The 81 Combinations**

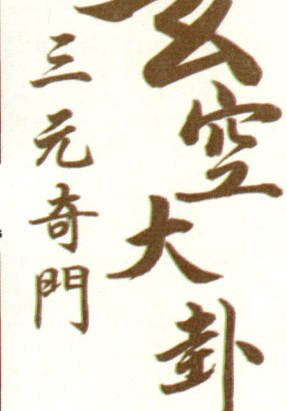

Xuan Kong Da Gua **Fixed Yao Method**

Xuan Kong Da Gua **Flying Yao Method**

Xuan Kong Da Gua **6 Relationships Method**

Xuan Kong Flying Star **Purple White Script's Advanced Star Charts**

The **San Yuan Qi Men Xuan Kong Da Gua Series** is written for the advanced learners in mind. Unlock the secrets to this highly exclusive art and seamlessly integrate both Qi Men Dun Jia and the Xuan Kong Da Gua 64 Hexagrams into one unified practice for effective applications.

This collection is an excellent companion for genuine enthusiasts, students and professional practitioners of the San Yuan Qi Men Xuan Kong Da Gua studies.

Xuan Kong Collection

Xuan Kong Flying Stars

This book is an essential introductory book to the subject of Xuan Kong Fei Xing, a well-known and popular system of Feng Shui. Learn 'tricks of the trade' and 'trade secrets' to enhance and maximise Qi in your home or office.

Xuan Kong Nine Life Star Series (Available in English & Chinese versions)

Joey Yap's Feng Shui Essentials - The Xuan Kong Nine Life Star Series of books comprises of nine individual titles that provide detailed information about each individual Life Star.

Based on the complex and highly-evolved Xuan Kong Feng Shui system, each book focuses on a particular Life Star and provides you with a detailed Feng Shui guide.

Joey Yap's BaZi Profiling System

Three Levels of BaZi Profiling (English & Chinese versions)

In BaZi Profiling, there are three levels that reflect three different stages of a person's personal nature and character structure.

Level 1 – The Day Master

The Day Master in a nutshell is the basic you. The inborn personality. It is your essential character. It answers the basic question "who am I". There are ten basic personality profiles – the ten Day Masters – each with its unique set of personality traits, likes and dislikes.

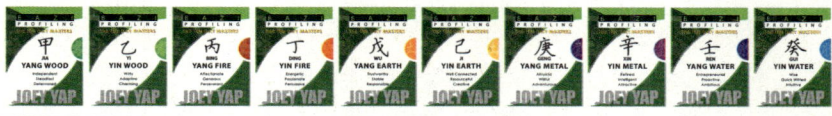

Level 2 – The Structure

The Structure is your behavior and attitude – in other words, it is about how you use your personality. It expands on the Day Master (Level 1). The structure reveals your natural tendencies in life – are you a controller, creator, supporter, thinker or connector? Each of the Ten Day Masters express themselves differently through the five Structures. Why do we do the things we do? Why do we like the things we like? The answers are in our BaZi Structure.

Level 3 – The Profile

The Profile depicts your role in your life. There are ten roles (Ten BaZi Profiles) related to us. As to each to his or her own - the roles we play are different from one another and it is unique to each Profile.

What success means to you, for instance, differs from your friends – this is similar to your sense of achievement or whatever you think of your purpose in life is.

Through the BaZi Profile, you will learn the deeper level of your personality. It helps you become aware of your personal strengths and works as a trigger for you to make all the positive changes to be a better version of you.

Keep in mind, only through awareness that you will be able to maximise your natural talents, abilities and skills. Only then, ultimately, you will get to enter into what we refer as 'flow' of life – a state where you have the powerful force to naturally succeed in life.

www.BaZiprofiling.com

THE BaZi 60 PILLARS SERIES

The BaZi 60 Pillars Series is a collection of ten volumes focusing on each of the Pillars or Jia Zi in BaZi Astrology. Learn how to see BaZi Chart in a new light through the Pictorial Method of BaZi analysis and elevate your proficiency in BaZi studies through this new understanding. Joey Yap's 60 Pillars Life Analysis Method is a refined and enhanced technique that is based on the fundamentals set by the true masters of olden times, and modified to fit to the sophistication of current times.

BaZi Collection

With these books, leading Chinese Astrology Master Trainer Joey Yap makes it easy to learn how to unlock your Destiny through your BaZi. BaZi or Four Pillars of Destiny is an ancient Chinese science which enables individuals to understand their personality, hidden talents and abilities, as well as their luck cycle - by examining the information contained within their birth data.

Understand and learn more about this accurate ancient science with this BaZi Collection.

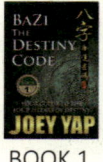 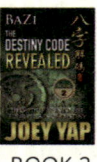 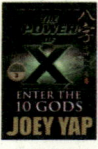  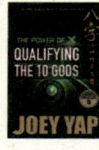 

BOOK 1   BOOK 2   BOOK 3   BOOK 4   BOOK 5   The 10 Gods

(Available in English & Chinese)

www.masteryacademy.com | +6(03) - 2284 8080

Feng Shui Collection

Design Your Legacy

Design Your Legacy is Joey Yap's first book on the profound subject of Yin House Feng Shui, which is the study Feng Shui for burials and tombs. Although it is still pretty much a hidden practice that is largely unexplored by modern literature, the significance of Yin House Feng Shui has permeated through the centuries – from the creation of the imperial lineage of emperors in ancient times to the iconic leaders who founded modern China.

This book unveils the true essence of Yin House Feng Shui with its significant applications that are unlike the myths and superstition which have for years, overshadowed the genuine practice itself. Discover how Yin House Feng Shui – the true precursor to all modern Feng Shui practice, can be used to safeguard the future of your descendants and create a lasting legacy.

Must-Haves for Property Analysis!

For homeowners, those looking to build their own home or even investors who are looking to apply Feng Shui to their homes, these series of books provides valuable information from the classical Feng Shui therioes and applications.

In his trademark straight-to-the-point manner, Joey shares with you the Feng Shui do's and dont's when it comes to finding a property with favorable Feng Shui, which is condusive for home living.

Stories and Lessons on Feng Shui Series

All in all, this series is a delightful chronicle of Joey's articles, thoughts and vast experience - as a professional Feng Shui consultant and instructor - that have been purposely refined, edited and expanded upon to make for a light-hearted, interesting yet educational read. And with Feng Shui, BaZi, Mian Xiang and Yi Jing all thrown into this one dish, there's something for everyone.

(Available in English & Chinese)

More Titles under Joey Yap Books

Pure Feng Shui

Pure Feng Shui is Joey Yap's debut with an international publisher, CICO Books. It is a refreshing and elegant look at the intricacies of Classical Feng Shui - now compiled in a useful manner for modern day readers. This book is a comprehensive introduction to all the important precepts and techniques of Feng Shui practices.

Your Aquarium Here

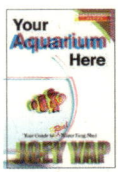

This book is the first in Fengshuilogy Series, which is a series of matter-of-fact and useful Feng Shui books designed for the person who wants to do a fuss-free Feng Shui.

More Titles under Joey Yap Books

Walking the Dragons

Compiled in one book for the first time from Joey Yap's Feng Shui Mastery Excursion Series, the book highlights China's extensive, vibrant history with astute observations on the Feng Shui of important sites and places. Learn the landform formations of Yin Houses (tombs and burial places), as well as mountains, temples, castles and villages.

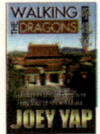

Walking the Dragons : Taiwan Excursion

A Guide to Classical Landform Feng Shui of Taiwan

From China to Tibet, Joey Yap turns his analytical eye towards Taiwan in this extensive Walking the Dragons series. Combined with beautiful images and detailed information about an island once known as Formosa, or "Beautiful Island" in Portuguese, this compelling series of essays highlights the colourful history and wonders of Taiwan. It also provides readers with fascinating insights into the living science of Feng Shui.

The Art of Date Selection: Personal Date Selection (Available in English & Chinese)

With the Art of Date Selection: Personal Date Selection, you can learn simple, practical methods to select not just good dates, but personalised good dates as well. Whether it is a personal activity such as a marriage or professional endeavour, such as launching a business - signing a contract or even acquiring assets, this book will show you how to pick the good dates and tailor them to suit the activity in question, and to avoid the negative ones too!

Your Head Here

Your Head Here is the first book by Sherwin Ng. She is an accomplished student of Joey Yap, and an experienced Feng Shui consultant and instructor with Joey Yap Consulting Group and Mastery Academy respectively. It is the second book under the Fengshuilogy series, which focuses on Bedroom Feng Shui, a specific topic dedicated to optimum bed location and placement.

If the Shoe Fits

This book is for those who want to make the effort to enhance their relationship.

In her debut release, Jessie Lee humbly shares with you the classical BaZi method of the Ten Day Masters and the combination of a new profiling system developed by Joey Yap, to understand and deal with the people around you.

Being Happy and Successful at Work and in your Career

Have you ever wondered why some of us are so successful in our careers while others are dragging their feet to work or switching from one job to another? Janet Yung hopes to answer this question by helping others through the knowledge and application of BaZi and Chinese Astrology. In her debut release, she shares with the readers the right way of using BaZi to understand themselves: their inborn talents, motivations, skills, and passions, to find their own place in the path of professional development.

Being Happy & Successful - Managing Yourself & Others

Manage Your Talent & Have Effective Relationships at the Workplace

While many strive for efficiency in the workplace, it is vital to know how to utilize your talents. In this book, Janet Yung will take you further on how to use the BaZi profiling system as a tool to assess your personality and understanding your approach to the job. From ways in communicating with your colleagues to understanding your boss, you will be astounded by what this ancient system can reveal about you and the people in your life. Tips and guidance will also be given in this book so that you will make better decisions for your next step in advancing in your career.

Face Reading Collection

The Chinese Art of Face Reading: The Book of Moles

The Book of Moles by Joey Yap delves into the inner meanings of moles and what they reveal about the personality and destiny of an individual. Complemented by fascinating illustrations and Joey Yap's easy-to-understand commentaries and guides, this book takes a deeper focus into a Face Reading subject, which can be used for everyday decisions – from personal relationships to professional dealings and many others.

Discover Face Reading (Available in English & Chinese)

This is a comprehensive book on all areas of Face Reading, covering some of the most important facial features, including the forehead, mouth, ears and even philtrum above your lips. This book will help you analyse not just your Destiny but also help you achieve your full potential and achieve life fulfillment.

Joey Yap's Art of Face Reading

The Art of Face Reading is Joey Yap's second effort with CICO Books, and it takes a lighter, more practical approach to Face Reading. This book does not focus on the individual features as it does on reading the entire face. It is about identifying common personality types and characters.

Faces of Fortune: The 20 Tycoons to bet on over the next 10 years

Faces of Fortune is Tee Lin Say's first book on the subject of Mian Xiang or Chinese Face Reading. As an accomplished Face Reading student of Joey Yap and an experienced business journalist, Lin Say merged both her knowledge into this volume, profiling twenty prominent tycoons in Asia based on the Art of Face Reading.

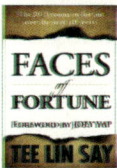

Easy Guide on Face Reading (Available in English & Chinese)

The Face Reading Essentials series of books comprises of five individual books on the key features of the face – the Eyes, the Eyebrows, the Ears, the Nose, and the Mouth. Each book provides a detailed illustration and a simple yet descriptive explanation on the individual types of the features.

The books are equally useful and effective for beginners, enthusiasts and those who are curious. The series is designed to enable people who are new to Face Reading to make the most out of first impressions and learn to apply Face Reading skills to understand the personality and character of their friends, family, co-workers and business associates.

2018 Annual Releases

| Chinese Astrology for 2018 | Feng Shui for 2018 | Tong Shu Desktop Calendar 2018 | Qi Men Desktop Calendar 2018 | Professional Tong Shu Diary 2018 | Tong Shu Monthly Planner 2018 | Weekly Tong Shu Diary 2018 |

Cultural Series

Discover the True Significance of the Ancient Art of Lion Dance

The Lion has long been a symbol of power and strength. That powerful symbol has evolved into an incredible display of a mixture of martial arts and ritualism that is the Lion Dance. Throughout ancient and modern times, the Lion Dance has stamped itself as a popular part of culture, but is there a meaning lost behind this magnificent spectacle?

The Art of Lion Dance written by the world's number one man in Chinese Metaphysics, Dato' Joey Yap, explains the history and origins of the art and its connection to Qi Men Dun Jia. By creating that bridge with Qi Men, the Lion Dance is able to ritualise any type of ceremony, celebrations and mourning alike.

The book is the perfect companion to the modern interpretation of the art as it reveals the significance behind each part of the Lion costume, as well as rituals that are put in place to bring the costume and its spectacle to life.

Educational Tools and Software

Joey Yap's Feng Shui Template Set

Directions are the cornerstone of any successful Feng Shui audit or application. The Joey Yap Feng Shui Template Set is a set of three templates to simplify the process of taking directions and determining locations and positions, whether it is for a building, a house, or an open area such as a plot of land - all of it done with just a floor plan or area map.

The Set comprises three basic templates: The Basic Feng Shui Template, Eight Mansions Feng Shui Template, and the Flying Stars Feng Shui Template.

Mini Feng Shui Compass

The Mini Feng Shui Compass is a self-aligning compass that is not only light at 100gms but also built sturdily to ensure it will be convenient to use anywhere. The rings on the Mini Feng Shui Compass are bilingual and incorporate the 24 Mountain Rings that is used in your traditional Luo Pan.

The comprehensive booklet included with this, will guide you in applying the 24 Mountain Directions on your Mini Feng Shui Compass effectively and the Eight Mansions Feng Shui to locate the most auspicious locations within your home, office and surroundings. You can also use the Mini Feng Shui Compass when measuring the direction of your property for the purpose of applying Flying Stars Feng Shui.

MASTERY ACADEMY
OF CHINESE METAPHYSICS

Your **Preferred** Choice to the Art & Science of
Classical Chinese Metaphysics Studies

Bringing **innovative** techniques and **creative** teaching methods to an ancient study.

Mastery Academy of Chinese Metaphysics was established by Joey Yap to play the role of disseminating this Eastern knowledge to the modern world with the belief that this valuable knowledge should be accessible to everyone and everywhere.

Its goal is to enrich people's lives through accurate, professional teaching and practice of Chinese Metaphysics knowledge globally. It is the first academic institution of its kind in the world to adopt the tradition of Western institutions of higher learning - where students are encouraged to explore, question and challenge themselves, as well as to respect different fields and branches of studies. This is done together with the appreciation and respect of classical ideas and applications that have stood the test of time.

The Art and Science of Chinese Metaphysics — be it Feng Shui, BaZi (Astrology), Qi Men Dun Jia, Mian Xiang (Face Reading), ZeRi (Date Selection) or Yi Jing — is no longer a field shrouded with mystery and superstition. In light of new technology, fresher interpretations and innovative methods, as well as modern teaching tools like the Internet, interactive learning, e-learning and distance learning, anyone from virtually any corner of the globe, who is keen to master these disciplines can do so with ease and confidence under the guidance and support of the Academy.

It has indeed proven to be a centre of educational excellence for thousands of students from over thirty countries across the world; many of whom have moved on to practice classical Chinese Metaphysics professionally in their home countries.

At the Academy, we believe in enriching people's lives by empowering their destinies through the disciplines of Chinese Metaphysics. Learning is not an option - it is a way of life!

MALAYSIA
19-3, The Boulevard, Mid Valley City, 59200 Kuala Lumpur, Malaysia
Tel : +6(03)-2284 8080 | Fax : +6(03)-2284 1218
Email   : info@masteryacademy.com
Website : www.masteryacademy.com

Australia, Austria, Canada, China, Croatia, Cyprus, Czech Republic, Denmark, France, Germany, Greece, Hungary, India, Italy, Kazakhstan, Malaysia, Netherlands (Holland), New Zealand, Philippines, Poland, Russian Federation, Singapore, Slovenia, South Africa, Switzerland, Turkey, United States of America, Ukraine, United Kingdom

www.masteryacademy.com | +6(03) - 2284 8080

The Mastery Academy around the world!

www.masteryacademy.com | +6(03) - 2284 8080

Feng Shui Mastery™
LIVE COURSES (MODULES ONE TO FOUR)

This an ideal program for those who wants to achieve mastery in Feng Shui from the comfort of their homes. This comprehensive program covers the foundation up to the advanced practitioner levels, touching upon the important theories from various classical Feng Shui systems including Ba Zhai, San Yuan, San He and Xuan Kong.

Module One: Beginners Course
Module Two: Practitioners Course
Module Three: Advanced Practitioners Course
Module Four: Master Course

BaZi Mastery™
LIVE COURSES (MODULES ONE TO FOUR)

This lesson-based program brings a thorough introduction to BaZi and guides the student step-by-step, all the way to the professional practitioner level. From the theories to the practical, BaZi students along with serious Feng Shui practitioners, can master its application with accuracy and confidence.

Module One: Intensive Foundation Course
Module Two: Practitioners Course
Module Three: Advanced Practitioners Course
Module Four: Master Course in BaZi

Xuan Kong Mastery™
LIVE COURSES (MODULES ONE TO THREE)
* Advanced Courses For Master Practitioners

Xuan Kong is a sophisticated branch of Feng Shui, replete with many techniques and formulae, which encompass numerology, symbology and the science of the Ba Gua, along with the mathematics of time. This program is ideal for practitioners looking to bring their practice to a more in-depth level.

  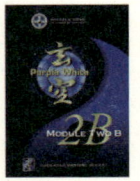 

Module One: Advanced Foundation Course
Module Two A: Advanced Xuan Kong Methodologies
Module Two B: Purple White
Module Three: Advanced Xuan Kong Da Gua

www.masteryacademy.com | +6(03) - 2284 8080

Mian Xiang Mastery™
LIVE COURSES (MODULES ONE AND TWO)

This program comprises of two modules, each carefully developed to allow students to familiarise with the fundamentals of Mian Xiang or Face Reading and the intricacies of its theories and principles. With lessons guided by video lectures, presentations and notes, students are able to understand and practice Mian Xiang with greater depth.

Module One:
Basic Face Reading

Module Two:
Practical Face Reading

Yi Jing Mastery™
LIVE COURSES (MODULES ONE AND TWO)

Whether you are a casual or serious Yi Jing enthusiast, this lesson-based program contains two modules that brings students deeper into the Chinese science of divination. The lessons will guide students on the mastery of its sophisticated formulas and calculations to derive answers to questions we pose.

Module One:
Traditional Yi Jing

Module Two:
Plum Blossom Numerology

Ze Ri Mastery™
LIVE COURSES (MODULES ONE AND TWO)

In two modules, students will undergo a thorough instruction on the fundamentals of ZeRi or Date Selection. The comprehensive program covers Date Selection for both Personal and Feng Shui purposes to Xuan Kong Da Gua Date Selection.

Module One:
Personal and Feng Shui Date Selection

Module Two:
Xuan Kong Da Gua Date Selection

Joey Yap's
San Yuan Qi Men Xuan Kong Da Gua™

This is an advanced level program which can be summed up as the Integral Vision of San Yuan studies – an integration of the ancient potent discipline of Qi Men Dun Jia and the highly popular Xuan Kong 64 Hexagrams. Often regarded as two independent systems, San Yuan Qi Men and San Yuan Xuan Kong Da Gua can trace their origins to the same source and were actually used together in ancient times by great Chinese sages.

This method enables practitioners to harness the Qi of time and space, and precict the outcomes through a highly-detailed analysis of landforms, places and sites.

BaZi 10X

Emphasising on the practical aspects of BaZi, this programme is rich with numerous applications and techniques pertaining to the pursuit of wealth, health, relationship and career, all of which constitute the formula of success. This programme is designed for all levels of practitioners and is supplemented with innovative learning materials to enable easy learning. Discover the different layers of BaZi from a brand new perspective with BaZi 10X.

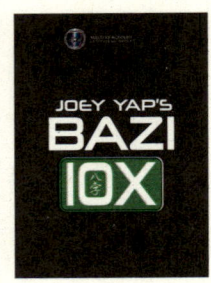

Feng Shui for Life

This is an entry-level five-day course designed for the Feng Shui beginner to learn the application of practical Feng Shui in day-to-day living. Lessons include quick tips on analysing the BaZi chart, simple Feng Shui solutions for the home, basic Date Selection, useful Face Reading techniques and practical Water formulas. A great introduction course on Chinese Metaphysics studies for beginners.

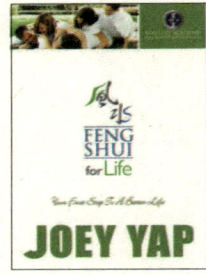

Joey Yap's Design Your Destiny

This is a three-day life transformation program designed to inspire awareness and action for you to create a better quality of life. It introduces the DRT™ (Decision Referential Technology) method, which utilises the BaZi Personality Profiling system to determine the right version of you, and serves as a tool to help you make better decisions and achieve a better life in the least resistant way possible, based on your Personality Profile Type.

Millionaire Feng Shui Secrets Programme

This program is geared towards maximising your financial goals and dreams through the use of Feng Shui. Focusing mainly on the execution of Wealth Feng Shui techniques such as Luo Shu sectors and more, it is perfect for boosting careers, businesses and investment opportunities.

Grow Rich With BaZi Programme

This comprehensive programme covers the foundation of BaZi studies and presents information from the career, wealth and business standpoint. This course is ideal for those who want to maximise their wealth potential and live the life they deserve. Knowledge gained in this course will be used as driving factors to encourage personal development towards a better future.

Walk the Mountains!
Learn Feng Shui in a Practical and Hands-on Program

 ## Feng Shui Mastery Excursion™

Learn landform (Luan Tou) Feng Shui by walking the mountains and chasing the Dragon's vein in China. This program takes the students in a study tour to examine notable Feng Shui landmarks, mountains, hills, valleys, ancient palaces, famous mansions, houses and tombs in China. The excursion is a practical hands-on course where students are shown to perform readings using the formulas they have learnt and to recognise and read Feng Shui Landform (Luan Tou) formations.

Read about the China Excursion here:
http://www.fengshuiexcursion.com

Mastery Academy courses are conducted around the world. Find out when will Joey Yap be in your area by visiting
www.masteryacademy.com
or call our offices at **+6(03)-2284 8080**.

Online Home Study Courses

Gain Valuable Knowledge from the Comfort of Your Home

Now, armed with your trusty computer or laptop and Internet access, the knowledge of Chinese Metaphysics is just a click away!

3 Easy Steps to Activate Your Home Study Course:

Step 1:
Go to the URL as indicated on the Activation Card and key in your Activation Code

Step 2:
At the Registration page, fill in the details accordingly to enable us to generate your Student Identification (Student ID).

Step 3:
Upon successful registration, you may begin your lessons immediately.

Joey Yap's Feng Shui Mastery HomeStudy Course

Module 1: **Empowering Your Home**
Module 2: **Master Practitioner Program**
Learn how easy it is to harness the power of the environment to promote health, wealth and prosperity in your life. The knowledge and applications of Feng Shui will not be a mystery but a valuable tool you can master on your own.

Joey Yap's BaZi Mastery HomeStudy Course

Module 1: **Mapping Your Life**
Module 2: **Mastering Your Future**
Discover your path of least resistance to success with insights about your personality and capabilities, and what strengths you can tap on to maximise your potential for success and happiness by mastering BaZi (Chinese Astrology). This course will teach you all the essentials you need to interpret a BaZi chart and more.

Joey Yap's Mian Xiang Mastery HomeStudy Course

Module 1: **Face Reading**
Module 2: **Advanced Face Reading**
A face can reveal so much about a person. Now, you can learn the Art and Science of Mian Xiang (Chinese Face Reading) to understand a person's character based on his or her facial features, with ease and confidence.